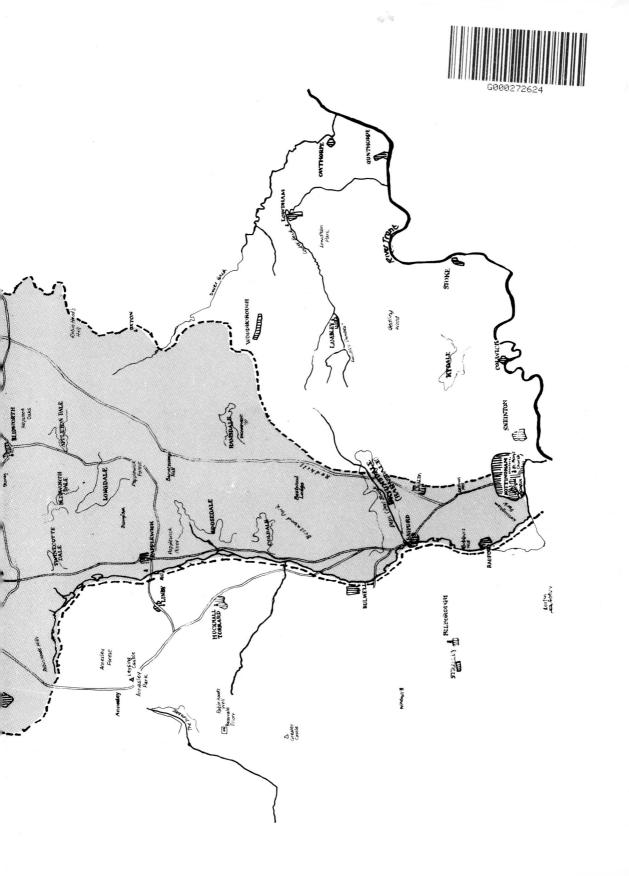

THE QUEST FOR
ROBIN HOOD

*Published in 1987 in a Subscribers'
Limited Edition*

THE QUEST FOR
ROBIN HOOD

ROBIN HOOD IN SHERWOOD FOREST. From a woodcut by Gilbert.

Robyn Hod in Scherewod stod,
Hodud and Hathud,
Hosut and Schod,
ffour and thuynti arowus he bar in his hondus.''
The earliest known ballad verse naming Robin Hood. (Early 15th century.)

Detail from the mural in the dome of the Exchange Arcade in the Council House, Nottingham. The painting was the work of two local artists, Denholm Davis and Hammersley Ball, and was completed in 1929. The figures were based on local personalities and it is known that Little John (top left) was based on Albert Iremonger, the giant goalkeeper of Notts. County Football Club. *(Photograph by DAN HYNDMAN, reproduced by courtesy of the Nottingham City Council.)*

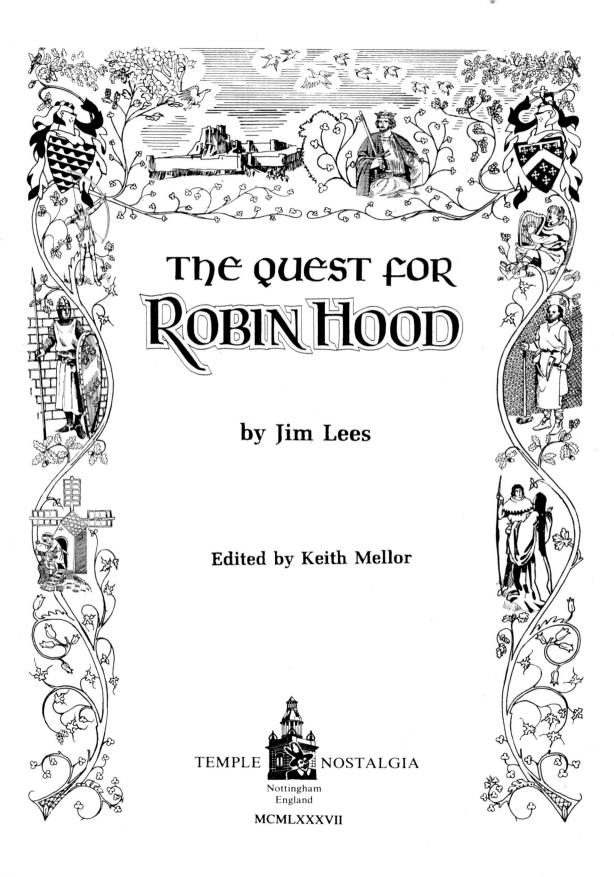

THE QUEST FOR
ROBIN HOOD

by Jim Lees

Edited by Keith Mellor

TEMPLE NOSTALGIA

Nottingham
England

MCMLXXXVII

PUBLISHED AND PRINTED BY
TEMPLE NOSTALGIA PRESS LTD.,
TRENT WORKS, WILFORD CRESCENT EAST,
NOTTINGHAM, ENGLAND

LAYOUT AND ARTWORK BY
ROGER HEATON

TYPESETTING BY
GEMINI TYPESETTING

COVER JACKET AND BOOK DESIGN BY
KEITH MELLOR

Copyright © 1987 Temple Nostalgia Press Ltd.

ISBN 1 8700 10 02 7

EDITOR'S NOTE

When, on the recommendation of Nottingham Libraries, author Jim Lees approached me with his manuscript which had a working title of *The Spirit of Sherwood*, there appeared few indications then that I was about to embark on a fascinating study into a subject that has intrigued historians for centuries. Armed only with a layman's knowledge, enhanced by the embellishments to the legends as perpetuated by the media and popular literature, I was to be transported on a journey back in time to Medieval England, and absorbed into this examination of existing claims and research into the reality behind the saga — hence the title of this resultant volume — *The Quest for Robin Hood*.

The conclusions are especially pleasing to me, and I should think also to my fellow Nottinghamians; most of us want to believe in the reality of Robin Hood, and now I hope we have presented at least some justification to do so. The volume itself is all the more gratifying for being, most appropriately I feel, produced by its exclusively Nottingham connections. As well as the author and myself, the other local contributors included artist Roger Heaton, typesetters Gemini, photographer Dan Hyndman, and of course, the printers and publishers. We all believe this volume to be the definitive work on Robin Hood and Nottingham — we hope that the reader thinks so too.

Keith Mellor.

CONTENTS

SHERIFFS OF NOTTINGHAM 8
FOREWORD by Emrys Bryson 9
INTRODUCTION by Jim Lees 11
THE UNIVERSAL POPULARITY OF ROBIN HOOD.
    Societies and Museums — Theatre — Sport — Humour and Fiction — Restaurants and Inns
    — Television and Films—Commerce — Advertising 13
CHAPTER 1. *Fact or Fiction* 23
CHAPTER 2. *The First Mentions of Robin Hood in Literature — Early Chroniclers — The Early Ballads*
    and Their Internal Evidence 29
CHAPTER 3. *The May Games — Source of Some of the Ballads — How They Corrupt the Facts and Create*
    Several Robin Hoods, Relics and Place Names 41
CHAPTER 4. *Barnsdale of Sherwood — Ballad Evidence — Watling Street — Basford — The Kings Great*
    Way — Breakdown of Place Names in Ballads 51
CHAPTER 5. *Sherwood Forest — And Outlaws* 59
CHAPTER 6. *The Named Outlaws and others — Sir Richard At The Lee, Kings, Sheriffs, etc. — Some*
    Identified From Records — How Nicknames Make Identification Impossible 73
CHAPTER 7. *Maid Marian — Her True Identity — Matilda Not a Ballad Name — How Marian Became*
    Matilda — Marian and 'Waltzing Matilda' 81
CHAPTER 8. *Friar Tuck — His First Mention — A Character Only* 91
CHAPTER 9. *Little John — His Reputed Birthplace and Graves — Fallacy of a Thirty-Inch Thighbone —*
    His Physical Stature, Character and Identity 97
CHAPTER 10. *The Robin Hood Relics — And Landmarks* 107
CHAPTER 11. *Existing Claims to the Identity of Robin Hood Examined* 117
CHAPTER 12. *Robin Hood — Yeoman or Nobleman — Middle English Word Meanings Give Clues — Chaucer*
    On Tragedies — Oral Tradition Supports Noble Birth 125
CHAPTER 13. *The Real Robin Hood and His Story — His Family — Earldom — Cause of Outlawry — And*
    Pardon 133
CHAPTER 14. *The Death of Robin Hood — His Grave and Epitaph — Elizabeth Staynton* 147
CHAPTER 15. *Conclusions* 155
BIBLIOGRAPHY 164
SUBSCRIBERS 166
ACKNOWLEDGEMENTS 168

A SCENE FROM SHERWOOD FOREST by Liz Wood. Oil on canvas depicting Robin Hood and his Merry Men portrayed by the artist's colleagues, craftspeople at the Longdale Rural Craft Centre, Notts. Councillor Frank Dennett, Sheriff of Nottingham 1984/85 plays his medieval counterpart. *(Reproduced by courtesy of The Corn Exchange, Nottingham and Mr Edgar Pownall.)*

SHERIFFS OF THE CITY OF NOTTINGHAM

Those relevant to the times discussed in the book.

1235	Robert de Vavasour, Lord of Bilborough
1236	Hugh FitzRalph
1240	Robert de Vavasour
1260	Simon de Asselacton (Aslockton)
1264	John de Grey
1266	William de Grey
1278	Reginald de Grey
1290	Sir Gevase Clifton

1927/28	Arthur Pollard	1947/48/49 William Sharp	1967/68 Henry James Hughes Bryan
1928/29	William Green	1949 Joseph Littlefair	1968/69 Bernard William Goddard
1929/30	William Hooley	1949/50 Leon Harold Willson	1969/70 Leonard Whitehouse
1930/31	Richard Ernest Ashworth	1950/51 Walter Murby	1970/71 Charles William Judge
1931/32	Mrs. Caroline Margaret Harper	1951/52 Sidney Hobson	1971/72 Edwin Bernard Bateman
1932/33	William Walter Weldon	1952/53 John William Kenyon	1972/73 Norman Hemmington
1933/34	Ernest Purser	1953/54 William John Cox	1973/74 Arthur George Wright
1934/35	Wallis Binch	1954/55 Leonard Mitson	1974/75 Leonard Francis Squires
1935/36	Frederick Mitchell	1955/56 William Ernest Maltby	1975/76 Gerald Henson Elliott
1936/37	Arthur Edward Savage	1956/57 Roland Elson Green	1976/77 Grace Roberts
1937/38	Walter Halls	1957/58 John Llewellyn Davies	1977/78 Rex Rolling
1938/39	Louis Pilsworth	1958/59 Frank William Wootton	1978/79 Percy Holland
1939/40	Ernest Archibald Braddock	1959/60 Sidney Pearson Hill	1979/80 George Howe
1940/41	Lazarus Judah Levin	1960/61 Cornelius Cameron	1980/81 Frank Dennett
1941/42	Augustine Herman Billingham	1961/62 Albert Edward Greenaway	1981/82 Thomas Harby
1942/43	John Edwin Mitchell	1962/63 Arthur William Norwebb	1982/83 John Kenneth Pennington
1943/45	Francis Carney	1963/64 Percy Holland	1983/84 Dennis Cecil Birkinshaw
1944/45	Wilfred Boothby Blandy	1964/65 William George Ernest Dyer	1984/85 Frank Dennett
1945/46	Thomas Reginald Scott	1965/66 Cornelius McNeil Reed	1985/86 Thomas Harby
1946/47	Harry Oliver Emmony	1966/67 Elliott Manery Durham	1986/87 Barrie Parker

SHERIFF'S ROOM
COUNCIL HOUSE
NOTTINGHAM
NG1 2DT
TEL. NO. 474331

CONGRATULATIONS TO MR JIM LEES ON THE
PUBLICATION OF HIS BOOK "THE QUEST FOR
ROBIN HOOD"

I WISH THE BOOK EVERY SUCCESS AND I AM
SURE IT WILL BE WIDELY READ AND CREATE
MUCH INTEREST IN THIS FASCINATING SUBJECT.

THE SHERIFF OF NOTTINGHAM
COUNCILLOR ROYCE YOUNG

Foreword

by *Emrys Bryson*

(Nottingham Evening Post; Author of ''Portrait of Nottingham'')

In Nottingham and less fortunate places throughout the world, Jim Lees is known as ''Mr. Robin Hood''. It is the biggest compliment he could be paid for his constant interest, researching, publicising and banging the drum on behalf of the most famous outlaw who ever was.

For some reason which I can never fathom, Nottingham has somewhat neglected Robin Hood. It's a bit like having Switzerland without William Tell or Hamelin minus the Pied Piper. The city does have Robin's statue ouside the Castle walls and if you peer up to the murals in the Council House dome you can spot him in action as one of the highlights of Nottingham's history.

But it is only lately that a more tourist-orientated Nottingham has cottoned on to the fact that it has a publicity man's wildest dream on its hands. At the time of writing, it still lacks anything on the scale of York's Jorvik Centre, somewhere visitors might steep themselves in the legend and the spirit of the men of Sherwood.

It is belatedly being realised that people want to visit Nottingham not simply for the shops, which these days can be found in any big city. They come basically through some deep, romantic vision they have. Of tough, daring outlaws flitting round the greenwood. Outwitting the Sheriff's men, rescuing the oppressed, springing to the defence of the poor, awesome in dealing with baddies. Admitted, it's a bit of a shock when they come across a squat, Palladian mansion, instead of a battlemented Castle awash with wimples, the clash of steel and the swish of arrows.

Nevertheless, the inner memory is still there. People to whom the name Nottingham produces a puzzled look will spark into life when you mention Robin Hood.

For there is something embedded in all of us about a figure facing up to evil authority. Small wonder that all those countless Robin Hood legends and stories have sprung up. If Robin Hood didn't exist we would have to invent him.

Did we invent him? You will have to make up your own mind about that. Even after reading this work by Jim Lees — and it is as good as any I have read so far — I am not solidly convinced. But I also find it difficult to accept that such a mass of material attached to Robin Hood's name could all stem from mere wishful thinking.

One thing is certain. Like the man who has consumed his thoughts and energies for so long, Jim Lees is as romantic as they come. ''Mr. Robin Hood'' answering letters re-directed by the Post Office addressed to our hero . . . sorting out queries that range from making a longbow to Robin Hood decorations on a cake . . . explaining why there isn't one of the outlaw's old suits of Lincoln Green on view in the Castle . . . or trailing the latest wide-eyed group round Sherwood Forest . . .

More than anyone else, Jim Lees has striven to make Robin Hood's arrows point towards Nottingham where they belong. Robin would have had no hesitation in putting him on the roll-call of the Merry Men. With free venison.

Emrys Bryson
Nottingham 1987

THE AUTHOR: JIM LEES (Left) began a serious study of the Robin Hood legends in the early 1950's. As a square dance caller, he made the acquaintances of many U.S. servicemen and their families, and discovered their interest in the outlaws and the associations with Nottingham. His services were increasingly sought as a guide for visitors around Sherwood Forest and, to enable him to relate the stories, he started to research the legends, becoming the accepted authority on the subject and dedicated to putting his work on record — establishing Robin in Nottingham. A regular contributor to T.V., Radio and Press, Jim is Life President and founder of the *Robin Hood Society,* and has been a proud member of the Scouting movement since 1922.

THE EDITOR: KEITH MELLOR (Right). An author of sporting and local histories whose works include *The Garibaldi Reds* and *Forest Road,* co-author of *The Story of Nottingham Football, The Avenue* and other books. Keith edited and produced Jim Lees' other work *The Legendary Exploits of Robin Hood,* and he is working on further manuscripts for the author for publication.

— *Photography by Dan Hyndman.*

Introduction

"For many, they say, speak of Robin Hood that shot never in his bow,
And many talk of Little John who never did him know."

By addressing his congregation thus in the early fifteenth century, a worthy monk of St. Alban's Abbey by the name of Hugh Legat, no doubt intended to warn them against talking about things of which they knew little or nothing. But for individual personal circumstances, and also the fact that the saga of Robin Hood is much in need of a fresh appraisal, I too would follow his advice and never put pen to paper, the moreso since his text may have been prompted by the ninth commandment — "Thou shalt not bear false witness", which ordinance I shall not knowingly transgress.

For many more years than the author cares to remember, he has been called, somewhat facetiously (but hopefully never unkindly) "Robin Hood", a man still sought after by successive Sheriffs of Nottingham.

The incoming officer, only too well aware that visiting dignitaries will expect him to know at least something of Nottingham's celebrated outlaw, normally invites me to take refreshment with him at an early opportunity, to talk about Robin of Sherwood, well knowing that I am always ready and willing to provide the necessary information.

Furthermore, letters addressed to "Robin Hood" are not "returned to sender" by Nottingham's Post Office, nor are they designated "dead letters". They are forwarded on to me, and have been for many, many years. Today, as the Founder and Life Member of the *Robin Hood Society,* I am able to pass some of this correspondence to our official Robin Hood for answering, thus easing my burden. Those that contain something that is new to me, no matter how unlikely or seemingly improbable their content at first appears, will receive my personal attention. Inevitably after so many years it is rare for me to get such a letter, and when I do the information is usually derived from works of fiction or media misrepresentation. Like the one stimulated by a television programme which the author had not seen, and enquiring after Robin Hood's connection with a certain Barnsdale, near Melton Mowbray. The place in question was in fact at Oakham, which since it had once been held by the Earls of Huntingdon had been consequently naively nominated in the television programme as the dale of the ballads.

In the early stages of my long association with Robin Hood, my own personal knowledge of him was slight, indeed, was very little more than that of the average person. Just enough actually to take some American visitors on a tour of Sherwood Forest, and to relate the legendary stories at places with which they are popularly associated. It was one of these American friends, Cal Golden, who first gave me the name "Robin Hood", and before long journalists from the United States were amongst those who sought interviews on the subject. It was only then that I began to realise just how little I really knew about history's most famous outlaw. I began to read serious works hitherto unknown to me, and to visit locations associated with the legend of Robin Hood in other counties, collecting stories from the local people as I went, and examining the alleged relics ascribed to him. When my researches indicated just one inescapable conclusion — that the legend of Robin Hood rested securely on a solid historical foundation, for me, the search for the real Robin Hood began.

One of the questions I am asked most frequently is why Robin Hood has remained so popular for so many years. This is a real poser. Some argue that it is because he personifies the *true* Englishman, possessing all of the qualities and ideals which we hold so dear. But can *foreigners* really idolise the English *that* much? Robin Hood is popular not just in English-speaking nations, but worldwide, and paradoxically, with both the Russians and Japanese, and for this to be possible it has to be accepted that he is nowhere seen as representative of any specific political or religious ideology. His appeal is truly universal, J. Goldman, in *Robin and Marian* records a poll conducted to determine the most famous figures in history, whether real or fictional, Robin Hood's name came second only to that of Jesus the Christ.

Whatever the answer may be, it contradicts the claim that Robin Hood is merely a product of the ballad muse, and that his story belongs to another man, or even to several Robin Hoods. This is the story of a historical figure, a real man, whose fame would live on even if no more than an oral tradition existed to perpetuate it.

In a survey carried out in Nottingham some years ago among adults of several different nationalities, many of those questioned could not say where they had heard their first stories about Robin Hood. Most had never read a serious book on the subject, and few could accurately place the period in which he lived, even though the original television series was then being screened. But despite all this, only a handful doubted his true existence. The majority "just knew" that he was real! You can count the author amongst them, and in my years of research I have heard all the arguments against. Nevertheless, I freely admit that apart from the bare bones of the saga, I cannot truthfully point to any one ballad story and state categorically — "this one is true." Some, certainly, bear a ring of truth, but so much has been lost, and so much has been added over the centuries that it is impossible today to unreservedly accept any as historically accurate.

Nevertheless, the contents of this work are by necessity drawn in part from the ballads — from the sublime *Robin Hood and the Monk* of 1450 (our oldest manusript source, where Robin defended himself bravely against the Sheriff's men, killing twelve and submitting only after he had broken his sword on the Sheriff's head) to the ridiculous *Robin Hood and Maid Marian.* The latter was a 17th Century ballad in which — "the blood ran apace from Robin's face, and Marian was wounded sore", following a fight between them which reputedly lasted an hour or more before they recognised one another! Other ballads set down during the intervening two centuries recount how Robin is beaten in turn by a potter, a tinker, a beggar, a friar and others, so he was clearly not looked upon as a medieval Superman.

Although I shall show a good reason for this, it is clear there was nothing superhuman about him as there was with other ballad heroes, and strangely enough even the stories of his remarkable feats of archery owe more to popular legend, and in particular to Sir Walter Scott's *Ivanhoe,* than to the ballads.

Though the main aim of this volume is to investigate Robin Hood's identity and to establish that the author of the epic poem *The Little Geste of Robin Hood and His Meyne, and the Proud Sheriff of Nottingham* was indeed writing about a historical person, I shall also establish for the first time the real, but surprising, identity of Maid Marian. I shall also identify Friar Tuck, and show why Matilda could not have been Marian's name before she entered the greenwood as claimed by other writers; I shall prove the reverse — *Marian* became *Matilda.* I shall explain why the Maid Marian could not have been Robin's spouse. I hope to present evidence to the reader's satisfaction that place names hitherto claimed to be in Yorkshire are, in truth, those of like or similar spelling in Sherwood Forest itself, and also how the legend of various *Robin Hood's Wells* and other relics grew out of the May Day Games (revels) and Midsummer revels. In fact, to offer a fresh look at the great saga that has mystified and intrigued mankind for centuries. Finally, as a Nottingham boy and man, in my head I have a sentimental spot that tells me — "The legend is true". All the more satisfying that in my appreciations of the assistance received on this volume the Nottingham associations prevail. These are all duly noted in the appropriate Acknowledgements section, but I really must particularly thank the following. Emrys Bryson, eminent journalist in the *Evening Post,* and the author of the finest book on the city — *Portrait of Nottingham* — who has generously written the Foreword. Fellow Nottinghamian and author, Keith Mellor, editor of the manuscript, whose sympathetic treatment of the text ensured that my own study of such a complex and controversial subject has been presented expressive to the layman whilst retaining the substance. The publishers, Temple Nostalgia Press, for their faith in the project, and of course all those former Sheriffs of Nottingham, and the present official, for their encouragement, along with the City and County Councils for their invaluable support.

Jim Lees
Nottingham
1987

ROBIN HOOD'S WORLDWIDE APPEAL

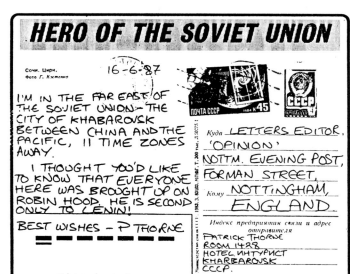

Right: RUSSIA. This letter appeared in the Nottingham Evening Post on Thursday, 25 June 1987.

HERO OF THE SOVIET UNION

16-6-87

I'M IN THE FAR EAST OF THE SOVIET UNION — THE CITY OF KHABAROVSK BETWEEN CHINA AND THE PACIFIC, 11 TIME ZONES AWAY.

I THOUGHT YOU'D LIKE TO KNOW THAT EVERYONE HERE WAS BROUGHT UP ON ROBIN HOOD. HE IS SECOND ONLY TO LENIN.

BEST WISHES — P. THORNE

Куда LETTERS EDITOR, 'OPINION' NOTTM. EVENING POST, FORMAN STREET, Кому NOTTINGHAM, ENGLAND

PATRICK THORNE ROOM 1428 HOTEL ИНТУРИСТ KHABAROVSK CCCP.

● Patrick Thorne's postcard was received yesterday. Look at the date: from Siberia to Nottingham in eight days!

Above: ON THE RECORD. This recording by Dick James was the signature tune to the ATV series Robin Hood, and entered the best-selling charts.

Below: JAPAN. How this publication was announced in the Japanese press.

Below: GRENADA. The first postage stamp to feature Robin Hood was issued in 1972 to commemorate UNICEF.

れている。(Oxford Univ. Press, £45.00)

● *The Quest for Robin Hood* 刊行予告　ロビン・フッドの歴史的実在性については、確証が得られていないこともあり、その発生の地でも依然として古文書、地名、発掘などの調査が熱心に続けられているようだ。The Robin Hood Society の会長 Jim Lees 氏は永年にわたりロビン・フッドの実像と Barnsdale の実在地を探求し続けてきたが、その成果を世に問うため *The Quest for Robin Hood* と題して近く（6月頃の予定）Limited Edition を出版するとのこと。予約者には、名前・ナンバー入り本 £9.95、刊行後は £12.50. 問合先：272 市川市大野町 2-1136-3　市川グリーンハイツ B 512 影山泰彦（電話：0473-37-0661）。

SOCIETIES AND MUSEUMS

ROBIN HOOD SOCIETY. Members of the Nottingham-based group, in period costume, leave the Castle Gates on their way to the City's Annual Medieval Market in the Square.

MUSEUM OF DOLLS AND BYGONE CHILDHOOD, Cromwell, near Newark, Notts. This group of figures are on display in the Museum and are based on characters in the ATV series *Robin Hood*. *(Reproduced by courtesy of Vina Cooke, Curator.)*

THEATRE

PANTOMIME 1987. *(Poster reproduced by courtesy of the Nottingham Playhouse.)*

Right: MISS EVELYN MILLARD, in her role as Robin Hood, at the Lyric Theatre, London, production in 1907.

Left: "SIT DOWN IN FRONT". A sketch during a children's performance of *Robin Hood and the Babes in the Wood* at the Royal Victoria Coffee Music Hall (The Old Vic, London). *(Reproduced from the graphic, 1882.)*

SPORT

ARCHERY: Above and right: Robin Hood is the sport's patron saint. It is practiced both competitively (above) and for pleasure (right). *(These photographs are reproduced by courtesy of Tom Foy.)*

ATHLETICS:
Right: *The Robin Hood Marathon* is held every autumn in Nottingham.

SOCCER: Above and below: The *Robin Hood* recording by Dick James is played prior to Nottingham Forest Football Club's home matches at the City Ground.

POPULAR FICTION

Above, above right, right: Examples of popular literature available between the Wars and immediate post-war years. Robin Hood and the merry men are presented in the classic schoolboy hero fashion.

Below: SEASIDE POSTCARD. Robin Hood and Maid Marian are portrayed in a humorous way in this modern "comic series" postcard produced by Bamforth & Co.

RESTAURANTS AND INNS

ROBIN HOOD RESTAURANT, Farnsfield

ROBIN HOOD & LITTLE JOHN, Arnold

ROBIN HOOD TAVERN, Market Street, Nottingham, with Loxley Hall and medieval banquets.

THE GRANARY, Edwinstowe. Proprietor, Ladislav Tvrdik produced this cake for a celebration party by the cast of the Nottingham Playhouse production of *Robin Hood and the Babes in the Wood.* (*Photograph by the Newark Advertiser*).

ROBIN HOOD INN, Rainworth

TELEVISION AND FILMS

Above: ERROL FLYNN as Robin Hood.

Left: "THE YOUNG ROBIN". John Derek as the son of Robin Hood in the Columbia Pictures film *Rogues of Sherwood Forest.*

THE RAUNCHY ROBIN. An article from *The Star* newspaper showing actors playing Robin Hood from the 1920s to the present day.

COMMERCE

Robin Hood is identified with commerce, industry and local government in various forms. Reading from top left: *Nottingham Time Recorders Ltd.*, Keyworth, *Nottingham Evening Post, Nottingham City Council, Nottingham Building Society, Mansfield Chronicle Advertisers, Nottinghamshire County Council, Fireworks Galore Ltd.*, Bulwell, *Nottingham Arrow, Barton Transport plc.*, Chilwell.

Examples of Advertising : Eayrs's Boot Shop is Pre-Great War Period, Whiteheads's c1960, Trent Jetfloor, Home Ales, Nofotec Group and Arrow Estates are Modern.

In his final desperate struggle the sea-earl slipped on the edge of the rock, and dragging Robin Hood with him they both plunged downward.

ROBIN HOOD IN FICTION: *The Sea-Earl's Secret*, No. 68 in the *Aldine Robin Hood Library* Series, typical of the pulp-press literature that was popular between the wars.

Chapter 1

There are few Nottingham people who have mentioned their place of origin without encountering the response, "Oh, Robin Hood country".

HERE has never been any doubt, none whatsoever, to the identity of the one to whom the above refers. *Robin Hood of Nottingham;* outlaw; bane of the Sheriff; enemy of the rich; benefactor of the poor; and eternal hero of the English people, at home and abroad. We are indebted to many well-meaning people who have been responsible for the popularity of our great saga. By collecting manuscripts and black letter copies of the Robin Hood ballads, to be published by others in Garlands (anthologies) from the year 1663 onwards; writing learned theories as to his identity, or denying his existence; creating books, sometimes for children, in which the popular stories from the ballads are used as a base for their own imagination, characters and localities; enacting plays of Robin Hood, some of which have become part of the great tradition; writing letters to the press; articles in intellectual magazines, and in my boyhood days, cartoon stories for the pulp press; producing films for the screen, large, wide and small; and passing anecdotes by word of mouth. To this must be added the remarks by early chroniclers, who are not at one in their dates for Robin's life period; folklorists, historians, mythologists and antiquarians who rode their own hobby horses, and folk who added their opinions. I could go on and on to the tedium of the reader, who no doubt can guess that the outcome of all this effort by so many over so many years is — confusion! As one gentleman said when I was relating the absurdity of some of the saga — "Anything goes for Robin Hood." *Anything? Everything?* Nobleman, yeoman, knight, thief, elf, fairy, witch, Norse god, Germanic god, saint, French peasant, patriot, rebel, hero, fact and fiction. Today he is on the telephone! Choose which you will, it is a fact that as far as I am aware only one man called him traitor, nor was he banished from the Kingdom as were many of the rebels. In examining whether or not the legend is fact or fiction, one thing at least is clear. To say that Robin Hood did not exist is to make a statement for which no evidence exists to substantiate it.

From various authorities we have been given periods in which our outlaw lived, varying from 1160 (birth) to 1347 (death), which would suggest that he lived for one hundred and eighty seven years, and were this so he would be famous enough for longevity alone. A close look at these claims is given in a later chapter to show that all the writers at least believed in the reality of Robin Hood.

When the great forest of Sherwood is mentioned it is not, with a few exceptions, its collieries, stately homes, the poet Lord Byron, or other people and places of interest to which the mind is moved, but to the exploits of the well-known outlaw and his merry men. If Barnsdale of Yorkshire, claimed by some as the locality of Robin, is mentioned it would mean very little to the majority of people, with the exception of those who have read the claims to our outlaw by the Yorkshire advocates.

In reality, Barnsdale of Yorkshire was never a Royal forest in the true sense of the word, which meant a place of recreation for the *monarchs* and their noblemen (including the clergy), certainly not merely a stretch of woodland as many imagine. As well as wooded areas for the deer and other game to take cover and browse, there had to be open areas where the huntsmen could give chase, loose an arrow, and throw a spear, or on occasions fly a falcon. This was in fact possible to an extent in Barnsdale of Yorkshire, but to be a *Royal* forest within which were the *Kings' deer,* it had to be so designated. Barnsdale was *not!* Sherwood *was!* and continued so for several centuries. Robin stole the *King's* deer — in Sherwood Forest. A dale in Yorkshire some thirty square miles in area cannot possibly fit the stories of the early ballads which specifically mention Barnsdale as a place located close to Nottingham town, and where it is clearly shown as part of the greenwood.

Barnsdale of the ballads was part of a forest and that forest was the Royal Forest of Sherwood in the county of Nottinghamshire.

Thus my first major discovery, and adequate enough reason for a more intensive search, if only because it set the whole thing on a new course from that which was generally accepted among the claimants to Robin Hood's identity. The Yorkshire claims, which will be examined in depth later, had first been put forward by the Reverend Joseph Hunter, in his contribution to a series of *Critical and Historial Tracts* in 1852, under the title, *The Ballad Hero, Robin Hood.* This theory was then taken up by P. Valentine Harris in his book, *The Truth about Robin Hood,* and also J.W. Walker in *The True History of Robin Hood.* Both of these later writers expanded on Hunter's claim by suggesting the identities of some of the other characters. The claims that Robin Hood was of Yorkshire were all based upon records in the *Wakefield Manor Court Rolls, The Household Accounts of King Edward II,* and *The Little Geste of Robin Hood and His Meyne, and the Proud Sheriff of Nottingham,* by Wynken de Worde (1500).

The theory was admittedly a good one, good enough to concern me that with a first class public relations officer, Yorkshire might have succeeded in claiming Robin Hood.

Here then was the author, Nottingham born and bred, taking American and other foreign visitors into Sherwood Forest ''in search of Robin Hood'', and forced to admit that on the interpretation of the available evidence, he might well have been a Yorkshire outlaw, who sometimes roamed into Sherwood Forest. However, many aspects were unclear and my curiosities were aroused when it was increasingly evident that so much of the existing material was conflicting and superficial. Added to this was my unashamedly parochial pride in Robin Hood's associations with my home town. It inspired me on to seek the *real* truth. The Quest for Robin Hood had begun.

The basis of all the serious claims to the identity and locations of Robin Hood is *The Little Geste of Robin Hood and his Meyne, and the proud Sheriff of Nottingham,* the first printed work on the saga, of which there are several editions published in the years (circa) 1508, 1548, and 1594. The poem is full of obsolete and middle English words and at the time of my early research I found no copy that contained Glossaries of these words which, as today, could have various different meanings, to take an example: *pay* = wages, punish, and settle a debt. To accurately interpret the message of the old English words was a task that I determined to undertake. I was not without errors, being driven more by enthusiasm than scholarship and it will help the reader appreciate the problems by relating one particular case.

In one of the ballads the phrase ''Marry gep with a wennion'' posed quite a problem. I was aware that ''marry'' was a shortened form of *''By St. Mary'',* so that was no obstacle. A further search established ''wennion'' as the Scottish *wanion,* as used by Shakespeare, so that I now had *''By St. Mary gep with a vengeance.''* But what was ''GEP''? My solution was to look for a mis-spelling, and the only words which might fit were GIP — gypo, gypsy — EGYPT! Mary, mother of Jesus was in Egypt. It appeared then to be: *''By St. Mary of/in Egypt with a vengeance.''*

A search of the *Oxford English Dictionary* and other works confirmed that I was right in my transcription, but wrong in my reasoning. This St. Mary was a martyr, in the time of Alexander the Great, who lived in Egypt for some years on a starvation diet; so I discovered later while on some other research. I had chosen the wrong saint but got the right answer. The operative word was OF.

That I was not alone in falling into error is shown in a remark of Francis James Child in his *The English and Scottish Popular Ballads (1858)* ''. . . or the whole poem *(Geste)* may have been put together as early as 1400, or before. There are *no firm grounds* on which to base an opinion.'' He was wrong. The sixth fytte (part) of the *Little Geste* relates that — ''The proud sheriff of Nottingham, and men of armys stronge, full fast came to the high sheriff, the country up to rout.'' This has been taken by some (a convenient interpretation) as indicating that the High Sheriff of Nottingham sought the aid of the High Sheriff of Yorkshire in seeking Robin Hood in Barnsdale, Yorkshire! On the contrary, the truth is, and this supports my assertion that Sherwood is the location of the ballads, that in a charter dated June 28 in the year 1448 King Henry VI ordered that ''The Mayor and Burgesses shall choose instead of two bailiffs on the 15th. September two burgesses as sheriffs, to take the powers hitherto held by the County (High) sheriff.'' *(Records of the Borough of Nottingham, Vol. 2).* By the same charter Henry made Nottingham a county of itself.

The Bailiffs of Nottingham town would have no jurisdiction in Sherwood, and to enter with armed forces they would need to ask permission and aid of the High Sheriff of Nottinghamshire. As the date of this change was 1448, and it is unlikely that the report would get abroad for some years, it may be that the compounder of this fytte (the *Little Geste* is made up from five ballads it is thought) was a local man. It most certainly dates the part as "after 1448." Nottingham still has its Sheriff and the county its High Sheriff but, alas, the City official has no powers these days.

By taking the *Little Geste* and the other earliest ballads, *Robin Hood and the Monk* from a manuscript of circa 1450, *Robin Hood and the Potter* ms.c.1500 and a fragmentary play *Robin Hood and the Sheriff* ms.c.1475, all of which are in the Cambridge University Library, and then interpreting the meaning of the texts at the time of writing (Middle English), I came up with some surprising answers which made more sense than if naively accepting word meanings in their modern usage. For example, in late Tudor times we get the merry men called *gay* — consider the meaning of the word today, and how some might relate it to a group of men living in the forest.

To understand the confusion surrounding the authenticity of the Robin Hood saga, it is helpful to examine conflicting statements that have been published. In the earliest mention of our hero, in William Langland's *Piers the Plowman* (of 1377), the author refers to rhymes of Robin Hood and Randolf, Earl of Chester. He is writing of two men of history, in a factual sense. Later chroniclers portray Robin Hood and Little John as subjects of ballads, comedies and tragedies which are the delight of the rustics, a matter I shall cover in depth before revealing their identities.

Everymans' Encyclopaedia describes Robin Hood as — "a legendary hero, regarded as a leader of a band of outlaws, who lived in Sherwood Forest. With his wife, Marian, and his companions, pre-eminent among whom were Little John, so called for his huge stature, and Friar Tuck, a jovial, pleasure loving priest. Robin Hood lived a life of careless freedom and good natured philanthropy, robbing the rich to give to the poor, and oppressing no righteous man." This version also refers to Langland's *Piers the Plowman,* and also Robin's popularity in the fifteenth century and onwards, and that he is variously mentioned by Shakespeare, Ben Johnson, Fuller and others. The Encyclopaedia goes on — "It is at least probable that there is some historical basis for Robin Hood, although he is regarded by some as simply a personification of the wind god or forest elf. Many of the customs and practices associated with his name were certainly added at a later date." They still are! *Brewer's Dictionary of Phrase and Fable* takes the other view — "It is doubtful whether he ever lived — the truth probably being the stories associated with his name crystallized gradually around the personality of some local hero of the 13th Century etc." If that local hero bore the name of Robin Hood, then he did exist — I cannot see the reasoning in the above quote. The writer goes on — "in the legends we have a late reminder of the old Scandinavian mythology of our ancestors. About the twelfth century, Woden — the old high German or Saxon term for the Norse deity Odin — was given the name of Robin! The tale of outlawry may be a later form of the legend of the wild huntsman, connected with Woden."

There are few who make the absolute denial that Robin Hood ever existed. Those who do seek to deny him, claim that he was either a composite figure stemming from several Robin Hoods, a small-time outlaw with an exaggerated legend, a character in the May Games and Morris dance or, as we have seen, a Northern-European deity. That Robin Hood is compounded from several characters is correct as far as the overall legend is concerned; there have been many Robin Hoods. These were characters in the May Games, and some of the stories come from the games — not the reverse.

We could not attempt to fill a single page with proveable acts by our hero — they are lost in the depths of time. However, the main features of his character are that of one man, and these endure from the oldest ballad to the latest book. Why has one man caught the imagination of so many people for such a long time? If he was a mere charade people would have seen through it long ago. There *was* such a man with the qualities of our hero, perhaps somewhat modified, although his emotions portrayed in the early ballads are very human.

That man was Robin Hood — self styled, not his given name, but one adopted to conceal his true identity as I shall show later.

It is a great tragedy that a piece of history has been lost that might well have provided the conclusive evidence. Richard Grafton, historian, in his *Chronicles* of 1562, claims to have seen an old and ancient document relating to our hero. After having told us that Robin Hood practised "robberyes" he adds — "the which being certified to the King, and he beyng greatly offended therewith, caused his proclomation to be made that whatsoever would bring him in quicke or dead, the King would geve him a great summe of money, as by the records of the exchequer is to be seene: but of this promise no man enjoyed any benefite." I have traced no such record in the Exchequer's accounts, but a similar statement does exist in a manuscript in the Harleian Collection (No. 1233), at the British Library — "a proclomation was published," and later — "The King att last sett forth a proclomation to have him apprehended."

Did the sources concerned see such a record, or did they concievably imagine the whole thing? It must be said that there are many records yet to be transcribed, and others quoted by historians appear to be lost.

Robin Hood's *fame* and reputation would be very local in the time of his outlawry. People did not travel very far from home, unless they were soldiers serving their King in his wars, or noblemen, churchmen or merchants, all of whom would have little interest in outlaws except in avoiding them. The minstrels would sing of the exploits of our hero to the common folk and in the homes and castles of the great. A visiting noble would have his own minstrel with him, who on hearing a worthwhile ballad story, would add it to his repertoire and thus it would spread, slowly but surely. But a mis-hearing of a word or place name could so easily set off a story on a new angle and to show how this *did* happen I shall later give examples of the effects of oral traditions on the Robin Hood ballads, showing how words and place names HAVE been changed.

Embellishment is not unique to Robin Hood — it can be said of most of the heroes — King Arthur is accepted as leader of a band of knights in full plate armour! We readily accept the image of these chivalrous men, and yet he, and they, lived several centuries before the invention of plate armour, and the advent of chivalry. Coming closer to our time, consider the legend of the Western cowboy; history does not support much of the legend, but does not deny the men.

Robin's rule of law and code of conduct appears to have been based on the Bible, and there is much in his way of life that is saintly. Joseph Ritson, in his classic *Robin Hood* (1823) states "he obtained the principal distinction of Sainthood, in having a festival allotted to him, and solemn games instituted in honour of his memory." His caring for the poor, the widow and virgin smack of Hebrew law — "to provide for the poor, the widow, and the stranger within your gates." His piety is never lost sight of in the early ballads, nor his devotion to the Blessed Virgin Mary who was his protector, and who he loved above all others, and because of this love for Her he honoured all women.

Could Robin Hood perhaps have been a reflection of a saint in the manner of Santa Claus? We can discount this, and I can find no saint, historical hero, or biblical character who we might identify with him. The nearest I could get was David, who also for a time lived an outlaw life and was sustained by his friend Jonathon. In spite of this, for myself I remain convinced that such a man lived, and with virtues fine enough to justify the great legend which exists attached to Robin Hood's name, absurd as some of it is. My research has not however confirmed all of the traditionally held belief's surrounding his contemporaries in the saga, some of which fail to survive the close scrutiny. As stated in the Introduction I shall show for the first time who Maid Marian really was. I have cut *Little John* down to *little John*; decided that Friar Tuck was a character representative of many people over the years and, unlike Robin, never existed as a real person. The Sheriff of Nottingham is not one man; he was several, and some would not have worried Robin too much. In fact the spirit of the early ballads is not that of real enmity between the two as men, but betwixt establishment and rebel. My happiest discovery was to find that Robin Hood's main camp existed within a mile or two of where I lived as a boy.

I have to say that I am amazed that earlier writers have missed so much, and why one of them had to distort two of the ballads to show that Maid Marian's true name was Matilda, just to enable him to support the name Matilda in the *Wakefield Manor Court Rolls*. Why has evidence been forced; why should one historian be called unreliable on the strength of a pedigree he produced from other historical sources (and which I have used in part). There are many more questions posed in the following pages. Some of the answers deny some of the beliefs and legends. Some substantiate some of them.

A section from the original manuscript of *Robin Hood and the Potter*, c.1500. Robin's name can be made out at the end of the 4th line and at the beginning of the 5th, with Hood spelt first *Hode* and then *Hood*.

A fight between Robin Hood and the Tanner after an engraving by Thomas Bewick, c.1795, from Ritson's *Robin Hood*.

THE LITERATURE OF **ROBIN HOOD.**

List compiled by
VIOLET W. WALKER, B.A.
(Central Reference Library).

Above: The literature of Robin Hood in the Nottingham Public Libraries was compiled by Violet W. Walker in 1933.

Right: *A Lytell geste of Robyn Hode*. Frontispiece illustration to the title page of Copland's edition, c.1550.

ROBIN HOOD'S GARLAND;

BEING A COMPLETE
HISTORY
OF ALL THE
NOTABLE AND MERRY EXPLOITS
PERFORMED BY
HIM AND HIS MEN,
ON DIVERS OCCASIONS.
IN SHERWOOD FOREST.
NEAR
NOTTINGHAM.

J. F. Freswell, Mond. Aug 15, 1859

IN THREE PARTS.

PART I.
CONTAINING

I. Robin Hood's Progress to Nottingham, in which he slew fifteen Foresters.

II. Shewing how the Jolly Pinder, of Wakefield, fought with Robin Hood Scarlet, and Little John, on a long summer's day.

III. Robin Hood and the Butcher; shewing how he robbed the Sheriff of Nottingham.

IV. Robin Hood's Golden Prize: shewing how he robbed two Priests of five hundred pounds.

V. Robin Hood rescuing the three Squires from Nottingham gallows.

VI. Robin Hood and the Shepherd: shewing how Robin Hood, Little John, and the Shepherd fought a severe combat.

VII. Robin Hood and Allen-a-Dale: or, the manner of Robin Hood's rescuing a young Lady from an old Knight, to whom she was going to be married, and restored her to Allen-a-Dale, her former lover.

NOTTINGHAM: Printed by C. SUTTON, at the New Printing-Office, in Bridlesmith-Gate,

MDCCXCIV.

ROBIN HOOD'S GARLAND. The title page of *Notable and Merry Exploits,* performed by Robin and his men, published in 1794 by C. Sutton in Nottingham. *(Reproduced by consent of Nottingham Local Studies Library).*

Chapter 2

"There is more historic truth in many of the old ballads than in many modern histories." — John Selden (1584-1654), Keeper of the records in the Tower of London.

MONG the transcripts made by Francis Peck in the early 18th century for a Register of the Order of Regular Canons, founded by St. Norman of Premonstre, France, there is a very curious Latin poem on folio 103 of *Registrum Premonstratense* (Add. M55. 4934-5) in the British Library, the heading to which reads as follows: "(This is a) Latin saying or rhyme by the Prior of Alnwick in the time of the Scots war at Dunbar in the time of Edward I about William Wallace, the *Scottish Robin Hood*. He sings (writes) many things, but scurrilously." In the margin is written the date "22 July 1304," along with a hand-written reference — "Regist., Prom., Folio 59". This, it may be observed, is the first known instance of our hero's name occuring in a written source and it provides clear evidence of his popularity even at this early date. Wallace was then still living, only being captured through treachery the following year (1305), and subsequently executed. It is not clear where Francis Peck found this reference, or the date he assigns to it; nor is it apparent whether he copied the poem itself from a manuscript in his possession and subsequently lost, or from a copy now in the Muniment Room at Belvoir Castle, Leicestershire. The latter differs from Peck's copy in having neither a date nor margin reference, and is headed (in Latin) "Rhyme, good, from the Scots war at Dunbar."

Maurice Keen, in his *Outlaws of Medieval Legend* writes "a note in a fifteenth-century hand beside the poem written by an English monk who was an actual contemporary of Wallace calls him the Scottish Robin Hood." Alas, he does not cite his source for this information. The next reference to Robin Hood, chronologically, occurs in *Piers the Plowman* by William Langland, its presumed author, who is supposed to have been born *c.*1322 at Cleobury Mortimer, Shropshire; he took minor orders, married and then removed to London. The greater part of his life was occupied with his great poem which presents a vivid picture of English life under King Edward III. In Part IV, concerning "The vision of the Seven Deadly Sins" (written not later than the year 1377) Langland portrays the seventh sin, Sloth, as an ignorant secular priest, who knew rhymes of Robin Hood better than he did his prayers:—
"I know not perfectly my Paternoster as the priest it sings, But I know rhymes of Robin Hood and Randolph, Earl of Chester."
Not surprisingly this reference is to be found in almost every book on the life of Robin Hood, with different transcriptions. I have modernised one of these transcripts for clarity. The fact that the passage couples our hero's name with that of a factual historical person, Randolph, Earl of Chester, is considered to be powerful testimony of Robin's reality. It also establishes beyond any reasonable doubt that he was the subject of ballads before 1377, which in turn gives credence to the heading accompanying the poem in Francis Peck's transcript; for it was a recognised convention for a minstrel to precis the content of his rhyme in prelude. This is to be seen in some printed black letter copies of the ballads still in existence — for example from *Robin Hood and the Bishop* (*c.*1663), "Showing how Robin Hood went to an old woman's house and changed clothes with her, to escape from the Bishop; and how he robbed the Bishop of all his gold, and made him sing a mass." (From Child's *English and Scottish Popular Ballads* and elsewhere.) Such preludes contained the bare bones of the story which the minstrel subsequently filled out from his own imagination.

By the end of the fifteenth century, Robin's name had appeared in literature, poetry, and perhaps even sermons, for one writer admonishes — "those who would rather go hear a tale or a song of Robin Hood or some other ribaldry then to hear Mass or Matins." In the same period we read of disorderly persons identifying themselves with the outlaw hero and his men. An example here given is from *Stow's Annals* (Folio 352b, edition of 1631) as quoted by James Francis Child in his ballad collection already mentioned (Vol. 111, folio 41) — ''In 1416 a commission was issued to Thomas Canoys, Thomas Poynynges and John Pelham to arrest a man using the alias Frere Tucke and other malefactors of his retinue who have committed divers murders, homicides, robberies, and depredations etc., in the Counties of Surrey and Sussex, and bring them before the council.''

They had no success, for in the following year another commission was given to William Lasyngley and Robert Hull,'' to enquire into the report that a certain person assuming the unusual name of Frere Tuck, and other evil doers, have entered parks, warrens, and chases of divers lieges of the King in the Counties of Surrey and Sussex and divers times; hunted therein and carried off deer, hares, rabbits, pheasants, and partridges; burned lodges and houses for the keeping of the parks, and threatened keepers.''

The man calling himself Frere Tucke was a Sussex chaplain, Robert Stafford, still at large in 1429 when he was pardoned for all offences past and present. It is somewhat strange that Robin Hood was not the name assumed by this man, for by this time, only Robin and Little John had appeared in any written material, and it was not until 1475 Friar Tuck was named as a member of the merry men. It is apparent that Robin Hood's fame had not by then reached the Southern counties and clearly the Frere (friend) was a different character from the Friar Tuck of the later play (1475) and ballad (1663), although in this, *Robin Hood and the Curtal Friar* the name, Tuck, is not given.

Similarly in a petition presented to parliament in the year 1439, one Piers Venables of Derbyshire is cited as having rescued a prisoner being taken to Tutbury, Staffordshire ''and after that time'', the petition continues, ''the same Piers Venables having no livelihood, nor sufficiency of goods, gathered unto himself many misdoers being of his clothing — and in a manner of insurrection, went into the woods of that county, like as it had been Robin Hood and his men.''

We now have then written evidence in an official State Record that Robin Hood existed, and also that he had a following. The closeness of the date to that of the chaplain who assumed the name Frere Tucke may be more than a coincidence, for even in such a casual reference it must be significant that Robin Hood and his men are treated as historical people. The one word that would have encouraged misgivings is notable by its absence; it is not *A* Robin Hood that is referred to; it is Robin Hood, the absolute definitive being in ellipsis.

That Robin Hood was also by then the subject of plays is shown by John Fordun, the Scottish chronicler; and by Sir John Paston, who is writing on a Good Friday of 1473 — where he complains that one of his servants, W. Woode, has left him after promising never to desert him. ''And thereupon I have kept him this three year to play St. George, and Robin Hood, and the Sheriff of Nottingham, and now when I would have a good horse he has gone into Bernysdale, and I without a keeper.'' It was the practice for the nobles and gentlemen of the time to keep their own minstrels and company of actors and records exist showing payments to the minstrel of Earls and others. Andrew Wyntoun, another Scottish Chronicler, in his metrical *Original Chronicle of Scotland*, written in that country in the year 1420, writes in the section under the year 1283:

> ''Little John and Robin Hood,
> Outlaws were commended good,
> In *Inglewood* and Barnysdale,   *(English wood)*
> They used all this time their travail.''

Wyntoun was an old man when he wrote this, and his memory would have taken him back to the middle of the 14th century. The verse is quoted by various authors with claims to Robin Hood's identity, with different spellings, and there are four separate manuscripts in the British Library. About the same time, or even earlier, four lines of doggerel were written on the back of a page in a collection of articles by John Garlandia. The writer was practising his alphabet and his handwriting, and these four lines in English and Latin is the oldest ballad verse naming our outlaw:

> ''Robyn Hod in Scherewod stod,
> Hodud and Hathud,
> Hosut and Schod,
> ffour and thuynti arowus he bar in his hondus.''

In the year 1341, John Fordun, then Canon of Aberdeen, and a man of the highest integrity who made excursions into England to collect material for his histories, included in his *Scottish Chronicles* under the year 1266 — "about this time arose from the dispossessed and banished that famous Robert (sic) Hood and Little John with their companions. They lived as outlaws among the woodlands and thickets, of whom the common people are so extravagantly fond of celebrating in *tragedy* and comedy; and the ballads concerning whom, sung by jesters and minstrels, delight them above all others; of whom certain commendable things are recited."

He then relates the first written story of our outlaw, from the *Harley Ms.* — "Once upon a time, in Barnsdale where he was avoiding the wrath of the King and the ire of the Prince, while engaged devoutly hearing Mass as he was wont to do, nor would he interrupt the service for any ocassion — one day, I say, while so at Mass, it happened that a certain viscount (sheriff) and other officers of the King, who had before molested him, were seeking him in that *retired woodland spot* wherein he was thus occupied. Those of his men who first discovered the pursuit came and entreated him to fly with all speed. But this, with reverence for the consecrated Host which he was then most devoutly adoring, he absolutely refused to do, *while* the rest of his people were trembling for fear of death. Robert alone, confiding with Him who he fearlessly worshipped, with the very few he had then with him, encountered his enemies, overcame them with ease, was enriched by their spoil and ransom, and was induced to hold ministers of the church, and masses, in greater veneration, as mindful of the common saying — God hears the man that often hears the Mass."

Fordun, who died about 1385, compiled the first five books and part of the sixth of his *Chronicles*. The remaining ten books are attributed to Walter Bower, Abbot of Incholm, who was apparently working on them about 1440 and 1447, and used material gathered by Fordun for the earlier sections; my source of information is the British Library in a letter.

"The reference to Robert Hood and Little John occurs in chapter ten of the seventh book and is clearly a portion of the text due to Bower, and the most likely to be based on Fordun's material." Bower again confirms the date, 1266 — "In this year obstinate hostilities carried on between dispossessed Barons and the Royalists; among whom where John Daynil (Deyville?) in the Isle of Ely (Hereward the Wake's old stamping ground) and Roger Mortimer occupied the Marches of Wales. Robert Hood now lived an outlaw among the woodlands, copses, and thickets." The source quoted is Goodhall's *Scotichronicon. Vol.II.*

The manuscript in the Cambridge University library under the title *Robin Hood and the Monk*, is in my opinion a classical ballad, and sets up the opening scene in a few words but gives a wonderful picture:

> 'In summer time when the woods are bright
> And leave be large and long,
> It is full merry in fair forest,
> To hear the bird(ies) song."

> "To see the deer draw to the dale,
> And leave the hills high,
> And shelter them mongst the leaves green,
> Under the greenwood tree."

It also gives a glimpse of Robin's character which is never lost sight of, and offers some evidence of time and place. These are not too evident in the early play (Malone Society Collection, 1st series, Vol. 2) but, once again, in the *Little Geste* there is plenty of material for the researcher.

It was during the 15th century, according to several writers that Wynken de Worde, probably Caxton's foreman, succeeded to the printer's shop and material upon the latter's death, and moved to Fleet Street from Westminster at the end of the year 1500. The earliest book from this address is dated 1501, and printing of the *Little Geste* was probably a year or two later. Nevertheless, according to E.G. Duff, in his *Fifteenth Century English Books* (1919) — "the poem may have been composed in the fifteenth-century, if not as one whole, then as four seperate ballads." The original is unversed and unpunctuated, which regretably has led researchers into error, primarily Hunter. Modern versions run to 456 four-line stanzas and are divided into eight parts making one story; the whole of which, as Duff implies, may have been compounded from at least four earlier ballads and ingeniously composed into an epic poem by one of some education. The ballads in question are *Robin Hood, the Knight and the monk, Robin Hood, Little John and the Sheriff, Robin Hood and the King,* and *Robin Hood's death.* Besides de Worde's printing, three other editions appeared in the 16th century. These were printed by Miller and Chapman, Edinburgh (c.1508); William Copland, to which is added — "a new play for to be played in May Games, very pleasant and full of pastime" (c.1547); and Edward White (c.1594). Several writers have produced the *Little Geste* in modern form and succeeded in making the story clearer, if less accurate.

In his 1847 edition of the *Little Geste* (preface P.V11) J.M. Gutch writes — 'It will elucidate more clearly than any other documents, his station in society, his character and actions." In fact, the early ballads contain much internal evidence on many aspects of the legend, some in clear terms and some by implication. This evidence is examined in the appropriate chapters that follow, but as a preamble it is useful to offer some preliminary examples of how the early ballad prose contains positive indicators towards identifying locations, periods and characters.

A study of the ballad of *Robin Hood and the Monk,* reveals a clear insight into the location of the stories. in this first story Robin is depressed because he has not been to Matin or Mass for a fortnight and, against the will of his men he decides to go to St. Mary's Church:

> S.7   "Today I will go to Nottingham", said Robin,
>   "With the *might* of mild Mary."   *(protection)*

He will take only Little John to carry his bow, but with this John does not agree and tells Robin that *he* can carry his own, but they will "shoot a penny" on the way. Shooting at declared objects as they progress they quarrel over the number of pennies that Robin owes John, who had proved the better shot. They part bad friends:

> S.16   "Then Robin goes to Nottingham,
>   Himself morning alone,
>   And Little John to *merry Sherwood,*
>   The paths he knew, each one."

Robin is recognised at Mass by a monk who warns the Sheriff; and after a fight the outlaw is captured. On learning of this, the outlaws in the greenwood elect Little John and Much, the miller's son, to go to Nottingham to secure Robin's freedom. They wait at Much's uncle's house until they see the Sheriff's messengers, the monk and his page, leave for London to get the King's writ on how to deal with the outlaw. The two are overpowered by John and Much, who then proceed onto London in their place, returning to Nottingham with the King's writ and seal. Robin is rescued, and while the Sheriff is still searching the town for him —

> S.76   "And Robin was in *merry Sherwood.*"

Nottingham is mentioned several times and the Sheriff is shown as "of Nottingham". The outlaws are shown, clearly, as living in a dale, in Sherwood Forest, *close to town.* Can it possibly realistically be read any other way —

> S.37   "And spare none of this venison,
>   That goes in this dale."

This is the warning that John gives to the outlaws before he and Much leave the camp to effect the rescue, and evidence enough that the outlaws lived in a dale in Sherwood. Nor need we seek further than the full title of the *Little Geste* for the true location of the outlaws camp and their escapades, for the "Proud Sheriff of Nottingham" had *NO* jurisdiction in Yorkshire. He was joint Sheriff of Nottinghamshire and Derbyshire, with some duties in Rutland. (Where in fact there is another Barnsdale). Not Barnsdale of Yorkshire as some would have it.

Child, in his *Popular Ballads* states "we have nothing to with Sherwood in the Geste." Admittedly perhaps, not directly Mr. Child! But with mentions of Nottingham and the "Greenwood," Sherwood is not only implied but *has* to be the forest of the epic.

> S.3   "Robin stood in Bernesdale."

Child failed to find this dale in Sherwood although, in a footnote dealing with the ballad of *Robin Hood and Guy of Gisborne* he admits: "The Sheriff flees from Barnsdale towards his house in Nottingham, in Stanza 57. In fact these places are *fifty miles* apart, the ballad treats them as adjacent." He should have been far more careful in his reading of this and other ballads which show *Barnsdale as part of a forest.* In the *Little Geste* the distance between the two places clearly must be much less than fifty miles, or every character was a supreme combination of sprinter and marathon champion.

In the third part of the *Little Geste,* Little John plays the part of servant to the Sheriff, and promises to be a bad one at that. On the Wednesday morning the Sheriff has gone hunting, and John wakes late in the morning. He has to fight both the butler and the cook to get his dinner, and then succeeds in winning the cook over to join the merry band. It was well passed noon before their fight:

> S.155 "Therefore he (John) was fasting,
> Till it was passed the noon."

and after a good meal together they decide to seek out Robin:

> S.173 "And when they had drunken well,
> Their troth together they plight,
> That they would be with Robin Hood,
> *That self same night.*"

and they arrive in time to trick the Sheriff, who is still hunting:

> S.182 "Then he met the proud Sheriff,
> Hunting with hounds and horn."

Fifty miles? A far lesser distance is suggested. The same conclusion has to be accepted from the story of rescue of the gentle Knight, who has been taken by the Sheriff whilst hawking by the river side. On receiving the news of the capture from the Knight's lady, who has ridden to the outlaw camp, and that the Sheriff's party is not yet *three miles* passed on its way, the merry men dash to the rescue:

> S.342 "Soon there were good bows bent,
> More than seven score,
> Hedge nor ditch they spared none,
> That was them before."

And they effected the rescue in Nottingham that same day. Over ditches, and through clumps of broom and hawthorne! As I have written, Robin Hood was no Superman so a much shorter distance is inferred.

When, ultimately, the King takes the matter in hand he seeks Robin Hood in Nottinghamshire, and makes the town his headquarters:

> S.345 "The King came to Nottingham,
> With Knights in great array,
> For to take that gentle Knight,
> And Robin Hood if he may."

In the guise of monks, the King and his party are stopped by the outlaws and taken to camp where Robin Hood states the case for he and his men, and the King grants them his pardon. They return to Nottingham with the King, playing at "pluck buffet" on the way. This is played by archers taking shots at random targets selected by one or the other. They receive a "buffet" (punch) every time they miss the chosen target. The King comes off worst. He and his men have dressed in Lincoln Green — Robin's livery:

> S.442 "When they were clothed in Lincoln Green,
> They cast away their *grey*,   (monk's habits)
> "Now we shall go to Nottingham",
> All thus our King did say."

By no means can we claim the *Little Geste* as history; but neither can we deny the fact that a King might have led an expedition into the forest, for we do have a factual historical precedent. Prince Edward led an attack on outlaws in the forest of Alton after the royalist victory at Evesham in 1265. He took a large military force to hunt them down, and their leader Adam de Gurdon was worsted in single combat by Prince Edward who, thereupon, pardoned Gurdon because of the valour he showed in the fight. There is no historical evidence to confirm Robin's pardon, but the *Little Geste* clearly illustrates that Robin was closer to Nottingham than any other town, that in fact, he was in Sherwood Forest. That attacks were made on the outlaws of Sherwood, if not by the King, then for certain, on his command, is the subject of a later chapter. The accepted period in which Robin and his men were active is that of Henry III's reign, with the probability of a short time in the reign of Edward I.

Bower and Wyntoun give respective dates 1266 (Henry III) and 1283 (Edward I). The former's remark that Robin was in the forest avoiding the wrath of the King and the ire of the Prince, under the year 1266, has support in the fact that both Henry III and Prince Edward were in Nottingham at the end of the year 1265; at a time when mopping up operations were taking place all over England, and particularly in the woodland areas. Henry III made another visit to Nottingham on the 23rd August 1268, and in the years 1279, 1280, and 1290 Edward I visited the town. As the *Little Geste* mentions "Edward as our *comely* King", and because Edward II was the only one of the three who was considered handsome, and also the only one who made a journey through Lancashire, Yorkshire and Nottinghamshire, is the reason for him being mistaken for the King Edward of that ballad. I suggest that the archaic meaning of "comely" was *proper*, or *seemly*, and that the correct interpretation should be, *Edward our rightful King*, and by implication he is King Edward I. The *Little Geste* does not show any King making the journey referred to above — he came to Nottingham to find Robin Hood (See Chapter Four comments on Lancashyre and also Plumpton, Yorkshire.) According to the *Calendar of Patent Rolls*, Public Records Office: "In 1272 by the King's writ of February 11th. at Westminster, Reginald de Grey was paid 100 marks to rid the counties of Nottinghamshire, Derbyshire, and Leicestershire of robbers on horse back and on foot who molested religious and other persons, and spoiled them of there good."

In the *Little Geste* story of Robin Hood and the gentle Knight, later identified as Sir Richard at the Lee, the Knight is asked the reason for his impoverishment and Robin puts the question to him:

> S.45 "Tell me one word," said Robin,
> "And secret shall it be;
> I trow thou were *made a Knight of force,*
> Or else of yeomanry."

In Stubb's *Constitutional History, Vol. II (1825-1901)*, we find: "Distraint of Knighthood, or the practice of requiring military tenants who had £20 per annum to receive Knighthood, or pay a composition, began under Henry III as early as 1224, and was contained under Edward I. This was regarded a very serious oppression under James I, and Charles I; and abolished 1641." And according to F.W. Maitland in *The Constitution of England* (1963): "We cannot say that a particular acreage of land or land of a particular value constitutes a Knight's fee; but it seems as if there was a vague theory that a Knight's fee should normally be worth £20 a year or thereabouts." The trouble was that by paying a composition in order not to be a Knight, or in accepting the "honour", either could place a man in dire straits. Robin's question suggests that being made a Knight of force was the reason for the Knight's impoverishment (a cause of bitterness at the time), putting him in the reign of Henry III. Robin makes the Knight a loan of £400 accepting only "Our Lady" as guarantor, and the Knight leaves with the money to repay a loan made

ST. MARY'S ABBEY, YORK, where, upon his arrival, the Knight, Sir Richard at the Lee, makes the pretence that he is unable to repay the Abbott's loan in the *Little Geste* story of Robin Hood and the Gentle Knight.

to him by the Abbott of St. Mary's Abbey in York. On arrival at the abbey the Knight makes the pretence that he is unable to pay and asks for a longer day; he asks for help:

> S.106 "Now good Sir Justice, be my friend
> And defend me from my foes."

To which the High Justice replies:

> S.107 "I am hold with the abbott," said the Justice,
> "Both by cloth and fee."

"In 1289 Edward I, because of the corruption by the Justices (in his father's time also) summoned a parliament, and brought the Justices to trial; where all of them except two who were clergymen (and could only be tried by an ecclesiastical court) were convicted of the flagrant iniquity, were fined and deposed. The King afterwards, made all the judges swear they would take no bribes," states Hume (1711-1746) in his *History of England,* and elsewhere in the same work: "The taking and giving of robes and fees is defined as conspiracy in a statute of Edward I 1305-06, although his (Edward's) expedient, of deposing and fining the old ones, was the more effectual. . ."

One further point can be made from *Robin Hood and the Monk.* When the King's writ is sought by the Sheriff of Nottingham to see what he must do with Robin Hood, outlaw:

> S.42 "Of a false outlaw, called Robin Hood,
> Was taken yesterday."

Somewhat strangely the King says of Robin Hood:

> S.56 "There was never a *yeoman* in merry England,
> I longed so sore to see."

Elsewhere also, when speaking of Robin Hood, the King makes no mention of him being an outlaw.

In the great roll of the Exchequer in the seventh year of the reign of King Richard the First, there is shown an allowance (of just two marks!) made to Thomas de Prestwude for bringing to Westminster the head of William de Elleford, outlaw. An outlaw's head or wolf's head, could be taken by any person, at least up to the time of Richard I. This fact is made use of in *Robin Hood and Guy of Gisborne,* where the tables are turned, and also in the 1475 play of *Robin Hood and the Sheriff,* but in the time of Henry III things were more lenient — an outlaw received special protection, so he could be tried at the first possible court.

A writ of November 1266 gave safe conduct for eight days for Robert de Remes, Nicholas de la Hus and Roger Godberd and three of their company coming to the king, to treat for peace for themselves and those of their company *(Calendar of Patent Rolls),* and again, in *Robin Hood and the Monk:*

> S.17 "When Robin came to Nottingham,
> Certainly without concealment."
> S.18 "All that ever were in the church within
> Beheld well Robin Hood."

He was arrested, imprisoned, and the King's writ sought, a situation to be seen many times in the *Calendar of Patent Rolls,* with other outlaws, rebels, robbers, and malefactors, as in the case of Richard Stafford (alias Frere Tucke), although this man does not appear to have attended court. Two stanzas in the *Little Geste* not only give a clue to the earliest date in which part of it could have been composed, but show that the writer may have been a Nottingham man — or at least one who knew something of the town's history:

> S.317 "Relax and listen gentlemen,
> And hearken to our song,
> How the proud sheriff of Nottingham,
> And men of armies strong."
> S.318 "Full fast came to the high sheriff,
> The country up to rout,
> And they beset the Knight's castle,
> The walls all about."

We have already seen that the bailiff(s) of the town of Nottingham had no jurisdiction over Sherwood Forest. This establishes a date after 1448 as the period when this was written, even though the *Little Geste* was printed after that year and we have no manuscript of an earlier date. There are many who seek to deny the existence of Robin Hood from the fact that the town did not have a Sheriff in his time, but the above stanzas do make the matter clear; the *HIGH Sheriff* of Nottingham. It is unfortunate that public records and Royal writs refer only to the Sheriff of Nottingham and that no ballad makes any reference to a *town* bailiff, but then I am citing references to our hero after his first mention by William Langland. The term bailiff could have been used in the lost ballads, but Robin Hood will still have been "a thorn in the sheriff's flesh," the Sheriff being the King's officer.

If there is one feature of Robin Hood's character that sets him apart from all other ballad heroes it is his extreme piety, and devotion to the Blessed Virgin Mary; he was fearless in the strength of Her protection. Because he so respected womanhood it was the law of the outlaw band that no harm be done to woman, or man in woman's company — a command he reminded Little John that had always been observed, and must be even at his death. A nun was the cause of his death, but before he died Robin would not grant the boon asked by John — to destroy the nunnery:

> S.15 *From Robin Hood's death*
> "Now nay, now nay," quoth Robin Hood,
> "That boon I'll not grant thee;
> I never hurt woman in all my life,
> Nor man in woman's company."

Robin was at all times courteous, just and generous. His leadership was never challenged, not even when he offered it to Little John out of contrition for striking him, as related in the ballad of *Robin Hood and the Monk:*

> S.79 "I make ye master," said Robin Hood
> "Of all my men and me."
> S.80 "Nay, by my troth," said Little John
> "So shall it never be."

He was human. Depressed, because he has not been to Matin or Mass for a fortnight; quick-tempered, because John has proved the better archer, then sorry, over his action. His humour is not stressed, but it is to be seen, somewhat subtly, but nevertheless it is there.

In spite of his devotion to the Blessed Virgin Mary, he has his doubts:

> S.206 *Little Geste*
> "For I dread Our Lady be wroth with me,
> For she sent me not my pay."

These qualities are all to be seen in the early ballads and we shall see that historians deal with him kindly; ballad writers never lose sight of some of his standing, although they do not show him as victorious in some of the fights. He is shown as the protector of virgins, widows, and the poor, be they nobility or commoners. Above all, he was a good archer. And in the telling of the stories the ballad writers show a very human trait in Robin Hood, something they saw for themselves or else they were good psychologists. On two occasions with the bow Robin Hood makes a bad score. In *Robin Hood and the Monk,* on the way to Nottingham with Little John, and on the King's visit to Sherwood in the *Little Geste.* In the former he is more mindful of his absence from the Mass for two weeks, and no doubt afraid of the consequences. In the latter, although the King is disguised as an abbott, Robin is aware that he bears the King's seal, and an invitation for him to "come to Nottingham to meet the King." Instinctively, the outlaw is uneasy in mind. Not surprisingly his aim is not good. Any archer or other sportsman, writer or artisan, no matter how expert, will know that it takes little to distract one's concentration. Either the ballad writers knew this from experience or perhaps, from an informant — one of the outlaws.

There is more than a ring of truth about these two ballads. Both are the work of educated men *for the educated,* the reader should be aware that the printed epic, or the written manuscript, would be of no use to most of the common man, who could neither read nor write. His history was the original sung ballad; stories told by older generations, and apart from those with good memories and the would-be balladeers, only the bare bones would be remembered.

One thing is certain. Only the wealthy could afford to buy the books of the early printers. That within 25 to 30 years of the moveable type press arriving in England, one of the earliest books published should be *A Little Geste of Robin Hood* proves the popularity of our outlaw hero to all classes in England and Scotland. In almost five hundred years that interest has not only remained undiminished, but become worldwide.

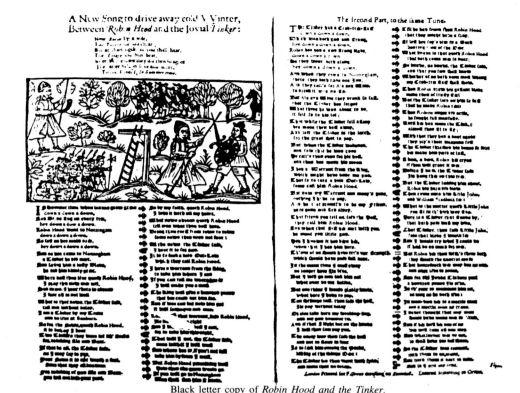

Black letter copy of *Robin Hood and the Tinker*.

ST. MARY'S CHURCH, NOTTINGHAM. In the ballad of *Robin Hood and the Monk,* Robin went here to Mass, and where he was recognised by a monk and betrayed to the Sheriff.

Scene in Robin Hood

THE

LIFE

OF

ROBIN HOOD,

OF

SHERWOOD FOREST.

EMBELLISHED WITH AN ELEGANT ENGRAVING.

London:

PRINTED BY HAMBLIN AND SEYFANG,
Queen-street, Cheapside,

And sold by PERKS, St. Martin's-lane, Charing Cross ; MAC-
DONALD, Crown Court, Princes-street ; PITTS,
Great St. Andrew's-street, Seven Dials ;
GRAY, Barbican, &c. &c.

Price Threepence.

THE

Robin Hood

Garlands and Ballads.

WITH THE TALE OF

The Lytell Geste:

A COLLECTION OF ALL THE POEMS, SONGS
AND BALLADS RELATING TO THIS
CELEBRATED YEOMAN;

TO WHICH IS PREFIXED HIS HISTORY AND CHARACTER,
DEDUCED FROM DOCUMENTS HITHERTO
UNREVISED.

EDITED BY

JOHN MATHEW GUTCH, F.S.A

WITH THE ILLUSTRATIONS ON WOOD, BY

F. W. FAIRHOLT, F.S.A

IN TWO VOLUMES—VOL. I.

LONDON:
JOHN RUSSELL SMITH, 4 OLD COMPTON ST., SOHO SQUARE;
JOSEPH LILLY, 19, KING STREET, COVENT GARDEN
MDCCCXLVII

Above: *THE LIFE OF ROBIN HOOD* by Hamblin and
Seyfang of Cheapside, London. *(Reproduced by courtesy
of Nottingham Local Studies Library).*

Left: Title page from John Matthew Gutch's *Garland and
Ballads* (1847).

Below: Woodcut printed on the cover of *Gest of Robyn
Hode and his meyne, and of the proud Sheryfe of
Nottingham,* published in 1508. It also appeared some years
earlier in an edition of Chaucer.

A True Tale of *ROBIN HOOD.*

Or, A Brief Touch of the Life and Death of that renowned Outlaw *Robert* Earl of *Huntington*, vulgar-
ly called *Robin Hood*, who lived and dyed in A. D.
1198. being the 9th. year of the Reign of King
Richard the Firſt, commonly called *Richard Cœur
de Lyon.*

Carefully collected out of the trueſt Writers of our
Engliſh Chronicles : And publiſhed for the ſatisfa-
ction of thoſe who deſire truth from falſhood.

By *Martin Parker.*

Printed for *J. Clark, W. Thackeray,* and
near *Weſt-Smitfi e u.* 1687.

A frontiſpiece borrowed from the *Tale of Adam Bell,* publiſhed in 1687 by W. Thackeray.

39

MORRIS DANCER AND MAID MARIAN.

FROM MR. TOLLET'S WINDOW.

In the celebrated ancient window at the house of George Tollet, esq., at Batley, in Staffordshire, there are twelve panes of glass representing the May-pole and eleven characters in the morris-dance; two of the latter are on this page, and two others, the fool and the taborer, are given subsequently: the May-pole has been already placed in this work, on May-day.

The morris dance, in which bells are gingled, or staves or swords clashed, was learned, says Dr. Johnson, by the Moors, and was probably a kind of Pyrrhick, or military dance. Blount says, " Morisco, a Moor; also a dance, so called, wherein there were usually five men, and a boy dressed in a girl's habit, whom they called the Maid Marrian, or, perhaps, Morian, from the Italian Morione, a head-piece, because her head was wont to be gaily trimmed up. Common people call it a morris-dance."

The morris-dance is presumed by Mr. Peck to have been first brought to England in the time of Edward III., when John of Gaunt returned from Spain, where he had been to assist Petro, king of Castile. He says, " This dance was usually performed abroad by an equal number of young men, who danced in their shirts, with ribands, and little bells about their legs. But here, in England, they have always an odd person besides, being a boy dressed in a girl's habit, whom they call Maid Marian, an old favorite character in the sport." The morris-dance became introduced into the May-games, in which there was formerly a king and queen of the May: subsequently, it appears, the king of the May was disused, and

VOL. I.—27.

2 E

A page from Horne's *Year Book. (Reproduced by courtesy of Nottingham Local Studies Library).*

40

Chapter 3

*"At Paske began our Morris, and ere Pentecost our May,
Tho' Robin Hood, Little John, Friar Tuck and Marian deftly play,
And Lord and Lady go to church with lads and lasses gay."*

OTH William Copland's and Edward White's editions of the *Little Geste* bear the sub-heading:
"A merry geste of Robin Hood and his life, with a new play for to be played in May
Games, very pleasant, and full of pastime." The play, in all probability, dates from the
preceding century and consists of only the two scenes. The first exhibits the story of the later
ballad, *Robin Hood and the Curtal Friar* (*c.*1663), and the second uses some variations of *Robin Hood
and the Potter* (*c.*1500). Both were "suitable for the May Games".

The May Games do not appear to have had any set pattern and were not peculiar to the month of May,
nor especially to May Day. John Stow, antiquary, in his *Survey of London,* published in 1598 writes,
"I find that in the month of May, the citizens of London, of all estates, lightly in every parish, or sometimes
two or three parishes joining together, had their several Mayings and did fetch Maypoles, with divers
warlike shows, with good Archers, Morris dancers, and other devices for pastime all the day long, and
towards evening had stage plays and bonfires in the street."

In a diary of Henry Machin is the entry: "That on the 26th. day of May 1555 there was a goodly
May Game at St. Martins in the Field, with giants and hobby horses, morris dancers, and other minstrels.
And the third day of *June* following a goodly May Game at Westminster with giants and devils and three
Morris dancers, and many disguised, and the lord and lady of the May rode gorgeously with divers minstrels
playing." In an entry for two years later, he states: "On the thirteenth day of May 1557 there was a
goodly May Game in Fenchurch Street in which the Nine Worthies rode and they had speeches, and
the Saladin and the lord and lady of May, and more besides. And, again on the twenty fourth of *June
1559* there was a May Game with giants, the nine worthies, with speeches and goodly pageant with a
queen, Saint George and the dragon, the Morris dance and afterwards Robin Hood and Little John, and
Friar Tuck and Maid Marian, and they all made speeches around the table." In the rural areas the games
were of a much simpler type. In some places they were known as Robin Hood's Day.

In the sixth sermon before King Edward VI, Bishop Latimer complained that "he could not preach
in a certain church upon a holy day, although he had given notice of his coming, because the church
door was set against him, and after waiting half an hour, the key was found by one of the parishioners
who told him it was a busy day for them, as it was Robin Hood's Day. The parish had gone abroad
to gather for Robin Hood and he was asked not to prevent them from doing so. He complained that
it was a sad day when Robin Hood was set before the offices of the Lord."

Various churchwardens' accounts show entries for Robin Hood and the May Games; the setting up
of Robin Hood's bower, and the providing of clothing for the actors (The horns used annually in the
Bromley Horn Dance, are kept in the church to this day). Protest against the use of Christian banners
and relics of knights, and other items, being allowed by the churchwardens was made by Gerald Leigh
in his *The Accidence of Armoury.*

"I say unto you, none can, by order of arms, tread under foot, or put to vile use any Christian banner
— therefore gentlemen should not suffer Little John, or Much the miller's son, to be arrayed in coats
of arms, as I have seen some wear at *Whitsuntide,* in day mirth, which have been pulled down and given
to them by the churchwardens at Gotham."

In his *Henry VIII* (1516), Hall tells us that some time after his coronation, King Henry VIII "came
to Westminster with the Queen and all their train; and on a time being there, his Grace, the Earls of
Essex, Wiltshire, and other noble men to the number of twelve, came suddenly in a morning into the
Queen's chamber all apparelled in short coats of Kentish kendall, with hoods on their heads and hosen
of the same, every one of them his bow and arrows, and sword and buckler, like outlaws, or Robin

Hood's men, whereof the Queen, the ladies, and all others there, were abashed, as well for the strange sight, as also for their sudden coming; and after certain dances and other pastimes made, they departed.''

The same author also gives the following curious account of a Maying in the seventh year of the same monarch, 1516: "The King and Queen, accompanied with many lords and ladies, rode to the high ground on Shooter's Hill to take the open air and as they passed by the way they espied a company of tall yeoman, clothed all in green, with green hoods, and bows and arrows, to the number of two hundred. Then one of them which called himself "Robin Hood" came to the King, desiring him to see his men shoot, and the King was content. Then he whistled, and all the two hundred archers shot and loosed at once; and then he whistled again, and they like wise shot again; their arrows whistled by craft of the head, so that the noise was strange and great, and much pleased the King and the Queen, and all the company." Hall continues . . .

"All these archers were of the King's guard, and had thus apparelled themselves to make solace to the King. Then Robin Hood desired the King and Queen to come into the greenwood, to see how the outlaws lived. The King demanded of the Queen and her ladies, if they durst venture into the wood with so many outlaws. Then the Queen said if it pleased him she was content. Then the horns blew till they came to the wood under Shooter's Hill, and there was an arbour made of boughs, with a great chamber, and an inner chamber, very well made and covered with flowers and sweet herbs, which the King much praised. Then said Robin Hood 'Sir outlaws breakfast is venison, and therefore you must content with fare as we use'. Then the King and Queen sat down, and were served with venison and wine by Robin Hood and his men, to their contentment. Then the King departed and his company and Robin Hood and his men then conducted them; and as they were returning, there met with them two ladies in a rich chariot drawn by five horses, and every horse had his name on his head, and on every horse sat a lady with her name written . . . and in the chair sat the Lady of May, accompanied by Flora, richly apparelled, and they saluted the King with divers goodly songs, and so brought them to Greenwich. At the Maying was a great number of people to behold, to their great solace and comfort."

In Scotland the Game of Robin Hood took place in May either on a Sunday or some other holy day. Although some respectable members of the corporation were chosen to play the characters of Robin Hood and Little John, and the revels mainly the enacting of the plays of Robin Hood and archery, they received far less favour with the magistrates than with the people. "The profanation of the Sabbath, by the making of Robin Hood plays" was considered unlawful by the bench but not by the corporation. The games were the peoples festivals celebrated at the great feasts, holy days, and saints days. The latter would be very special occasions for the trade guilds on the day of their patron and an excuse for merry making. Stubbes, in his *Anatomy of Abuses,* edited by Furnivall, gives:

"Myself remembereth of a childe, in contreye native mine,
A May Game was of Robyn Hood, and of his train, that time,
To train up young men striplings, and each other younger childe,
In shooting; yearly this with solemn feast was by the guylde,
Or brotherhood of townsmen etc . . .''

So an eye witness (c.1595) tells us the main purpose of the games at that time was for the practice of archery! In fact, the popularity of Robin Hood was by then being used to that purpose, and probably under a decreee by Henry VIII that all men should be trained in the use of the bow.

On the occasions mentioned with a precise date we have Ascension Day (Sunday) and Whit Monday in 1555, the feast of St. John the Baptist in 1559, and Thursday, 13th May 1557 (the old May Day prior to 1901 — *Whitakers Almanack)* which does not appear to have been a holy day — Easter being 18th April that year. As Mary I was then the monarch and had restored the Roman Church, the connection may lay there; or her birthday, coronation day, or of that nature. The May Games should not be confused with the Church Festivals, which were more suitably celebrated; "for there a moderate meal is taken at mid-day; soon thereafter, the people go to church to hear the Gospel of God; and such likewise is the custom observed at Easter, at Pentecost, and the rest of the solemn festivals." — reports John Major in *A History of Greater Britain,* of the celebrations on the continent, "But with these (the English) the festival is kept in a tavern, not a church, in such intemperance of eating and drinking as is the enemy of chastity, in dances and lewd songs that are, equally her foe." He was writing of the Feast of the Nativity, and after castigating King and Court for celebrating the occasion in such a manner that no respecting nobleman should take his wife out of fear for her chastity, makes the complaint that it was because of revels and lack of religious observations that Thomas a' Becket was murdered. If Henry II had been sober he would not have spoken the words he did, and the knights seeking his favour would have continued with their devotions.

The foremost feature of the festivals, religious or no, was the victory of good over evil; the giants, devils, and Saladin being overcome by the heroes among which were St. George, Robin Hood and Little John, Richard the Lionheart and other characters. Another feature was that of the death and resurrection. Both subjects came down from the religious plays, in which the leading actors took the part of Biblical characters, thence the moralities in which the themes remained, but the players represented the qualities, until they became a mere burlesque part of the May Games.

From these plays we have at least seven ballads which can be recognised. The play of *Robin Hood and the Sheriff* (1475) becomes an expanded version in *Robin Hood and Guy of Gisborne,* a ballad first printed in Percy's *Reliques of English Poetry* in 1765, but believed to have been much older. The locality is a dale in Sherwood Forest; Friar Tuck of the play has no part in it but more is added to the script. There are two heroes — Robin and John, and their two foe — the Sheriff and Guy of Gisborne. In Copland's play of *Robin Hood and Friar Tuck,* not so named by Copland, we have an earlier version of *Robin Hood and the Curtal Friar,* first printed in a garland of 1663 with somewhat changed circumstances, but the bare bones are there. This time it is Friar Tuck who is the ''baddie''.

The second play by Copland, in his edition of the *Little Geste* (*c*.1548) is pre-dated by a manuscript in the library of Cambridge University dated 1500, which suggests the ballad is older than the play. It is unfortunate that the former is incomplete, lacking a conclusion; Jack, the potter's assistant is not a character of the ballad, and it is not clear whether Robin, or John, or both, fight the potter. In the play the potter is a knave! In the ballad he is a good yeoman. The basis of both play and ballad may be a Mummer's play (story).

There is no doubt that the ballad of *Robin Hood and Queen Katherine* is from a play of the May Games. Our hero is shown as the Queen's champion and the foremost archer in the Kingdom. The King has made a wager that his own archers cannot be excelled, and the Queen may have her choice of all other bowmen in England. The action is to be on St. George's Day at Finsbury Fields in the presence of the King and Queen. With Scarlet and Little John, Robin wins the day and a pardon for his men. All good stuff for a merry May Game. That it is derived from a play is shown in the precis under the title *Renowned Robin Hood; or;* ''his famous archery truly related; with the worthy exploits hee acted before Queen Katherine, hee being an out-law man; and how shee for the same obtained of the king his own and his fellows pardon.'' London 1620-55.

In the ballad *Robin Hood and the Prince of Aragon,* printed 1650-1702, Robin is characterised as the champion of Christendom. The Prince, with two giants, has sworn to take the princess as his spouse or spoil the land, unless three champions can be found to fight against them. Maidens are sent to the four corners of the Kingdom to seek the champions, the prize of victory to be the hand of the princess in marriage.

Robin Hood, Little John, and Will Scarlet undertake the challenge and ride to London in the disguise of pilgrims so that they will not be molested on the way. They arrive to find the Prince getting anxious: ''The day is Midsummers Day, which is 24th June,'' shouted the Prince with his two giants striding about the lists, ''bring forth your champions or bring me forth my bride.'' ''Bring forth my bride or London burns, I swear by Acaron.'' (Alkoran, the Koran. As the Prince is now shown as a Mohammedan, Aragon is possibly Akko, or Acre, famous for sieges during the Crusades.) With that, Robin stepped forth and told the King it must not be so; such beauty as the fair princess is not for a tyrant's mouth, to which the Prince threatens to kill Robin, with a frown. Robin calls the prince, ''Thou tyrant, thou infidel.'' He likens the two giants to Goliaths, and Little John and Will Scarlet to ''two little Davids.'' The three outlaws are provided with armour, swords, and shields and the fight begins. Good overcomes evil in a very short space of time and, shades of David and Goliath, Robin cuts off the Prince's head! Among the great rejoicing Robin tells the King who he is and begs a pardon for himself and his men, which is freely given. ''There are three of thee, but one princess; she cannot marry all,'' the King tells the outlaws. The matter is solved by Robin suggesting she makes her own choice; she selects Will Scarlet, who later discovers his father at the court. All ends well, good has overcome evil. The plot is changed but it has echoes of *Robin Hood and Queen Katherine.*

Such was the manner of these plays at the May Games all over England and Scotland, and there is no doubt that the true story of Robin Hood has been distorted by them just as much as by childrens books, films, and other methods of portraying our hero.

The real truth does however survive in the legend in that he took from the rich and helped the poor, was of noble birth, and made his headquarters a dale in Sherwood Forest. It would be the wildest guess to state any of the stories we have as fact; they may be, they may not, but they do appear to be written around the character of one man.

In Staffordshire there exists some traditions of Robin Hood, and the Abbots Bromley Horn dance of that county, is the only one in which there is *the* Maid Marian which seems to have been introduced in Tudor times. The part is always played by a man and may have replaced the hobby horse. A young boy who carries a bow and arrows keeps snapping the bow (to no effect) and is known, locally, as Robin Hood. The county has the ballad with the longest title *Robin Hood's birth, breeding, valour, and marriage at Tutbury bull running; calculated for the Meridian of Staffordshire but may serve for Derbyshire or Kent,* printed in 1650-1702, and is an example which has been used by Staffordshire historians in making the claim that Robin, ''if not born at Loxley, spent some of his life there''. The second stanza was used by Joseph Ritson in his *Robin Hood* to prove that Loxley was in Nottinghamshire! Sherwood Forest and Tutbury are treated as adjacent, without any comment being made by F. J. Child.

The ''King of the fiddlers'' tells this story, and there is a bull running, singing (including an old ballad of Arthur A. Bradley), dancing, and feasting, and appears to start with a play of Robin Hood based on the ballad of *Robin Hood's Progress to Nottingham.* He meets Clorinda, Queen of the shepherds, in Sherwood and she agrees to marry him after a very short courtship if he will go with her to Tutbury fair. Taking a buck with them they start out, and after travelling five Staffordshire miles, eight yeomen are bold enough to stop them and demand the buck. Robin slays five, and at John's request spares the others. The fiddler saw the fighting, and fiddled away and so ''he knows that its true'', and Clorinda dances into Tutbury singing ''Fol de ray''. She and Robin are married and they return hand in hand to Robin Hood's bower in Sherwood.

By Staffordshire tradition the bower was at Loxley Hall near Uttoxeter. On my visit there I did see an old summer house which some still called the bower; my guide refuted the claim. The ''King of the fiddlers'' is fact; at one time they had become so numerous that by the King's order they had to establish a guild to keep out the riff-raff; he was the elected leader. Possibly from the same ballad source we get the traditional marriage of Robin Hood and Maid Marian under the old yew tree (the second largest in the Kingdom) in St. Cuthbert's churchyard, Dovebridge, Derbyshire. In the Staffordshire ballad we are told that the parson at *Dudbridge* sent for full fast to wed Robin to Clorinda; probable mishearing carried on by oral tradition.

In the ballad of *Robin Hood and Maid Marian,* printed 1632-95, and a very poor work, is contained a shorter version of the Staffordshire-cum-Nottinghamshire song. In this Robin and Marian meet in disguise and, failing to recognise each other, they try out their skills with the sword for an hour or more. After the blood is running fast, Robin calls a truce, and Marian recognises him. There is much kissing and squeezing and they return to Robin's bower where, after feasting and dancing, they retire for the night. There is no wedding ceremony, but they live happily ever after. By various traditions they were also married at Campsall Church and Harthill Church, both in Yorkshire, Edwinstowe Church, Nottinghamshire, and also under the greenwood tree by King Richard or Friar Tuck. Yet another tradition is that they received the rites of the church by Friar Tuck, and after Robin's pardon Marian insisted on a ''true'' wedding at Edwinstowe.

Although they are not paired by the antiquaries and historians, except as part of the Morris dance, it would appear the marriage was a favourite feature of the plays, and why not? Everybody loves a wedding. That they never could have been married will be observed in Chapter Seven.

Several of the authors of the works on Robin Hood have queried the number of ballads in which Robin is outfought, by a potter, a tinker, a tanner and a shepherd among others; eight in all in the Child collection. At first the idea of our hero being so manhandled is absurd, and Child makes the suggestion the personage may have been varied in broadside ballads to catch in turn the pence of tanners, tinkers, and the rest;

or, possibly, some member of the respective fraternities might do this for the glory of the craft. This suggestion is taken up by later writers as a satisfactory answer, but none of them show any knowledge of folklore.

We are told by Fordun and others that the tragedies and *comedies* of Robin Hood were loved by the people beyond all others. There is little comedy in the plays I have suggested as being the ballad source, so we should look elsewhere. A regular feature of the Mummers plays (stories) is the death of the hero! Usually, after a fight in which he receives a bad mauling. The term ''minstrel'' includes actors, singers, musicians, and also mummers, who acted off a stage, without scenery. Their plays were, and are, humourous, with one theme running through them; death and resurrection — sometimes the dead man will sit up and complain that he is not dead, only to be told that the doctor knows best. Among the heroes have been St. George, Father Christmas, Richard the Lionheart and Robin Hood. Beelzebub is the protagonist, the devil, the evil one; and the hero the good one.

The only thing missing in the ballads is the doctor who cures the hero to enable good to triumph. The cure *is* to be seen *Robin Hood and the Pedlars* but not by the doctor, it is by one of the pedlars who does carry a balsam in his pocket and administers it to Robin, making him vomit — an act always good for a joke. In the ballad involving the Tinker, he ''is a man of mettle'', ''a mettle man'', and of the Tanner, he ''has tanned Robin's hide'', and Little John will become a tanner and ''tan *his* hide''. All good fun.

In Nottinghamshire a group of mummers enact the ancient play of *Robin Hood and Arthur a Bland,* which roughly tells the story of the ballad of *Robin Hood and the Tanner* printed 1620-25, for the tanner is named Arthur a Bland, Little John's cousin! In the mummer's play Robin IS killed, and resurrected by the doctor. It is sheer burlesque and no spectator would take the Robin Hood for the ballad hero. Burlesque it may be but the serious message is there, good overcoming evil, and the resurrection. One can only conclude that previous researchers into the subject of Robin Hood were unaware of these latter plays, sometimes known as Ploughboys Plays, for no one could accept the ballad hero being so treated except in burlesque.

A good May Game Robin Hood would be retained for years; his home would be pointed out; the places where the games were celebrated would bear Robin's name, hence landmarks, wells, trees, caves, hills, crosses, stones, and other objects bearing the name ''Robin Hood'' must be regarded with some suspicion. On Robin Hood's Well, Hunter writes:

''It is manifest that there would be many Robin Hoods, that each vicinity would be likely to have one, and to this no doubt attributed that we hear of Robin Hood, having borne the name of Lockesley or any other name, and that we have places still pointed out, as those in which he was born. They were, doubtless persons who gained celebrity by their personation; year after year, of the character, and the places in which the personation was wont to be made.''

Wells have been the centre of festivals, gambols, and worship, both Christian and pagan, since ancient times. This tradition survives in the elaborate decorations in Derbyshire where the Well-Dressing themes are mainly religious. Both Robin Hood and Little John have been featured, but not as the main subject. In recent years Well-Dressing has spread to other counties.

In modern times, through plays, films, television and literature, the spirit of Robin Hood lives on, and for many generations to come stories will be added to the saga, and they can do little harm, for Robin is established as a great Englishman with everything that once meant. The question is how can plays and ballads enable us uncover his identity. The answer is given in both Copland's and White's sub-title to the *Little Geste* — ''A merry Gest of Robin Hood, and *his life,* with a new play to be played in the May Games etc.'' Both admit to fact and fancy. A careful study of the *Little Geste* gives Robin's true character, and the fact that his exploits were in the county of Nottinghamshire, and also that his camp was in a dale close to the town. ''The *Little Geste* will elucidate more clearly than any other documents, on his station in society, his character and actions'', so wrote J. M. Gutch in 1847. This is accepted by all who have attempted to identify our hero and it is used in a later chapter along with the addition of remarks by early chroniclers, to establish the ''true Robin Hood of Sherwood.''

Following in the tradition of the May Games, the spirit of Robin Hood was perpetuated through festivals, pageants, plays and pantomime. *(Reproduced by courtesy of Nottingham Local Studies Library).*

Above: An engraving by Thomas Bewick, c.1795, from Ritson's *Robin Hood*, showing Robin Hood slaying the foresters in *Robin Hood's Progress to Nottingham*.

Left: MORRIS DANCERS from Tollett's window designed for Betley Old Hall in 1621.

Below: WELL-DRESSING IN DERBYSHIRE. The Hall Well, Tissington.

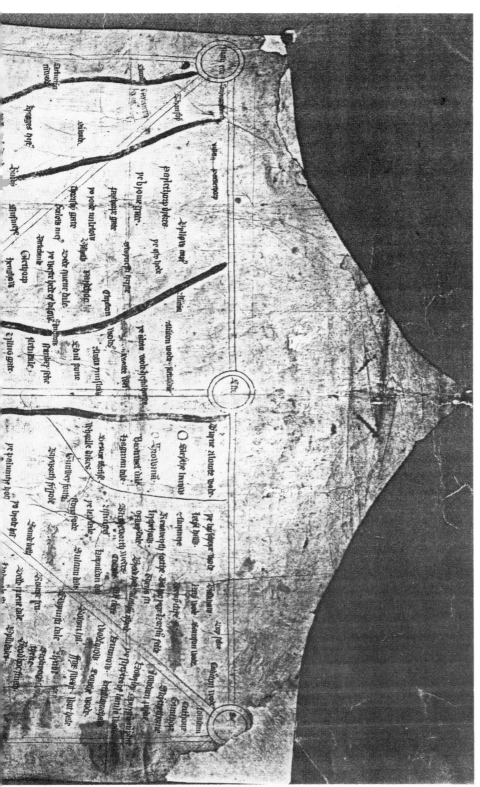

BARNSDALE
Sherwood
or
Yorkshire

In the next two chapters we examine the claims, and establish the *True Location of Barnsdale.*

14th Century map in Belvoir Castle Museum.
(Reproduced by courtesy of His Grace the Duke of Rutland).

An early medieval illustration depicting the King, with noblemen, hunting in the Royal Forest.

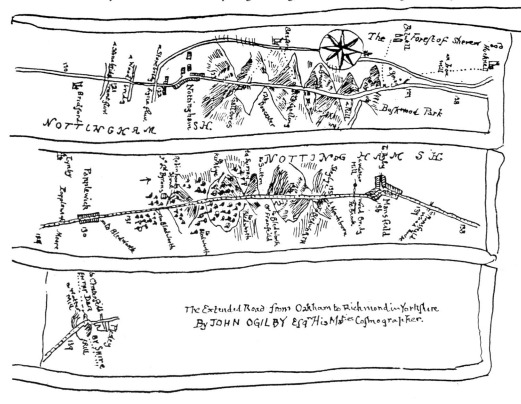

THE KING'S GREAT WAY (detail) by John Ogilby *c.* 1670.

Chapter 4

"Robyn Hod in *Sherewod* stod, Hodud and Hathud, Hosut and Schod,
ffour and thuynti arowus he bar in his hondus."
The oldest known verse of a lost ballad; early 15th century.

LTHOUGH it is easy to question the authenticity of many of Robin Hood relics and place
names, there can be no doubt that his principal haunt was a dale somewhere within Sherwood
Forest. The ballad evidence is clear on this matter, even though the forest is often referred
to as the "greenwood". The first manuscript ballad *Robin Hood and the Monk* (1450), tells
us in Stanza 16, "Then Robin goes to Nottingham, himself morning alone, and Little John to merry
Sherwood, the paths he knew each one". As we saw in Chapter Two, in this story Robin is captured
in St. Mary's church after betrayal by a monk, who is given the task of going to London to get the King's
will (writ) as to what action the Sheriff is to take. The outlaws are disturbed when they hear the news,
and Much the miller's son and Little John, leave to effect a rescue, telling the men:

S.37 "Look that you keep well our trysting tree,
Under the leaves small,
And spare non of the venison,
That goes in *this dale.*"

The monk and his page are subsequently killed. John and Much take their place and collect the King's
writ, returning to Nottingham to find the gates shut fast because Robin Hood, is held captive there. They
find the Sheriff in a drunken state and encourage him to drink more until he collapses in a stupor. They
then release Robin from gaol. The ballad continues:

S.76 "The Sheriff made to seek Nottingham,
Both by street and stye,
And Robin was in merry Sherwood,
As light as leaf on lime."

The King's writ commands the Sheriff of Nottingham to bring Robin Hood before his court, and grants
simple protection:

S.59 "He gave John the seal in hand,
The Sheriff for to bear,
To bring Robin Hood to him,
And no man do him *dare.*"   *(harm)*

The verse is compatible with normal procedure known to have been followed in such matters as witnessed
by the *Calendar of Patent Rolls,* however no such patent has been found relating to Robin Hood. That
Little John has "beguiled us all", and we will "speak no more on the matter", as the King says (Stanza
89), it is not surprising that the record was never entered in the Rolls.

Even in the earliest surviving manuscript ballad there is the clear, indisputable, evidence that the outlaws
were established in a dale in Sherwood Forest and, as we shall see, the ballads are unanimous in calling
it Barnsdale, to use the modern spelling. This name in medieval times was to be found spelt several
different ways, including the transposition of the letters AR thereby giving us "Bransdale" and other forms.

As already emphasised the full title of the *Little Geste* states "The proud sheriff of Nottingham". The
holder of this office had no jurisdiction outside of Nottinghamshire and Derbyshire. Admittedly Hugh
Fitz Baldric held the Sheriffdom of Nottinghamshire and Yorkshire in 1068 to 1080, but that is much
too early to be relevant to the Robin Hood story.

The *Geste* opens with Robin Hood, Little John, Will Scathelock and Much, the miller's son, standing
under a tree in "Bernesdale" and we discover something of Robin's character in his desire not to break
fast until he has some stranger to share with. He tells his men to go and find a guest and:

S.18 "Walk up the *saylis*   *(willows)*
And so to Watling Street."

51

Here the men meet up with an impoverished Knight who is invited, courteously, by them to dine with "our master", of whom the Knight has heard much good. He agrees with this:

> S.27 "I grant, he said, with you to wend,
> My brethren all in *fere*,   (company)
> My purpose was to have dined today,
> At Blyth or Doncaster."

He is on his way to York, it transpires, to seek extended credit on a loan from the Abbott of St. Mary's. He tells Little John:

> S.84 "Tomorrow I must be in York town,
> To Saint Mary Abbey."

So from these few details of his itinerary that he was on the way to York, and had planned to eat at Blyth or Doncaster, we know that Robin's men encountered the Knight *south* of Blyth in Nottinghamshire which places the event, indisputably in Sherwood Forest.

Elsewhere in this ballad, monks travelling to London from York are stopped by the outlaws in the same manner as the Knight, and are invited to dine with Robin. After Robin finds that the monks are from St. Mary's Abbey he believes them to be servants of Our Lady, and after the discovery of a far greater sum than the twenty marks that the monks declare as "their all", Robin is elated. He bids them drink with him and if Our Lady needs any more silver, to come again, but they will have none of it:

> S.259 "Nay for God," then said the monk,
> Me rueth I came so near,
> For better cheap I *might* have dined,
> In Blyth or in Doncaster."

Clearly, therefore, they had passed these two towns on the way to London to plead the Abbott's case against the Knight, and they were south of both — in *Barnsdale* of Sherwood Forest.

Following the betrayal of Robin and his men at the Sheriff's shooting match, and their subsequent escape, they are given shelter at the impoverished Knight's castle. For his part in the rescue the Knight is hounded by the Sheriff, and captured whilst hawking by the river. His wife dashes to Robin's camp and informs him, and he musters his men:

> S.342 "Soon there were good bows *bent*   (strung)
> More than seven score,
> Hedge nor ditch spared they none,
> That was them before."

The Knight is taken from the Sheriff in a Nottingham street, which again clearly indicates the town as adjacent to Barnsdale.

This is further emphasised in the story that tells of the King's visit to the greenwood, his pardon for the outlaws, and his return with Robin and his men to Nottingham, with Robin and the King playing "Pluck Buffet" on the way.

Even stronger evidence of Barnsdale being in Sherwood is to be found in three later ballads. In *Robin Hood and Guy of Gisborne* (written before 1765), Robin Hood and Little John enter the greenwood in search of an answer to Robin's dream of the previous night; they quarrel:

> S.11 "But often words they breeden bale,
> That parted Robin and John,
> John is gone to Barnsdale,
> The gates he knows each one."

Here, John finds two of Robin's men slain, and Will Scarlet running away with the Sheriff's men in pursuit. John is captured. Meanwhile Robin has met and defeated Guy of Gisborne in fair combat. He cuts off the head from Guy's body and puts on his opponent's "cappul hide" (horse skin) that covers him from head to toe, and carries the head to the Sheriff. He also takes Guy's horn and bow:

> S.45 "The bow, the arrows, and little horn,
> And with me now I'll bear.
> For now will I go to *Barnsdale*,
> To see how my men do fare."

Disguised as Sir Guy, Robin rescues Little John and hands him Sir Guy's bow which is used to good effect:

> S.57 "Towards his house in Nottingham,
> *He* fled full fast away,   (the Sheriff)
> And so did all his company,
> Not one behind did stay."

James Francis Child, in his *The English and Scottish Popular Ballads* (1889), states — "The Sheriff flees from Barnsdale towards his house in Nottingham (Stanza 59). In fact though these places are fifty miles apart, this ballad treats them as adjacent." He fails to note that, so does the *Little Geste.*

"Barnsdale (of Yorkshire), the name itself, although quite ancient and probably derived from the Old English Beorns Valley, scarcely occurs at all before the 15th century and owes nearly all its prominence to the Robin Hood legend." *(Place Names of the West Riding of Yorkshire,* by English Place Names Society, A.H. Smith). I have already shown that this prominence is misplaced in error.

Two other ballads will help prove that the Barnsdale of Yorkshire is neither stated nor inferred in any of them. In the second version of *Robin Hood and the Beggar,* first written down before 1795, the title adds "showing how Robin Hood in attempting to rob a beggar *near* Barnsdale, was shamefully defeated and left for dead etc."

> *S.2* "Robin Hood upon a day, he went forth alone,
> And as he came from Barnsdale, into a fair evening,
> He met a beggar on the way, that sturdily would go,
> He had a pike staff in his hand, that was both stark and strong."

The action is therefore in the greenwood, somewhere close to Barnsdale but clearly the fight takes place in another nearby dale. Our hero is in a very poor way and left for dead by the beggar. As we saw in Chapter Three, such ballads stem from the Mummer's plays. Nevertheless, I believe the places mentioned are fact.

> *S.30* "The beggar thought him dead *but fail,*   *(for sure)*
> And boldly bound away,
> I would you had been at the dale,
> And gotten part of the play."

Neither Sherwood nor Nottingham receive mention in this ballad but the reference to dales and woods, and the fact that Robin came out of Barnsdale shows that the writer had Sherwood in mind. For the writer to have written "near Sherwood Forest" would have been nonsense, but to be close to Goosedale, Coldale, Kings Wood, Samson Wood or any other place that was a smaller part of Sherwood would, and does, make sense.

In *Robin Hood and the Bishop of Hereford* (ballad, before 1741) Robin Hood is expecting the Bishop of Hereford to pass *near* Barnsdale. (Consider the difference if the word had been *through.*) He and six of his men dress as shepherds and prepare a sheep by the wayside:

> *S.2* "As it befell in merry Barnsdale,
> All under the greenwood tree,
> The Bishop of Hereford was come *by,*   *(near)*
> With all his company."

Upon encountering them the Bishop threatens to take them before the King and will not hear Robin's request to be pardoned. The tables are turned when our outlaw takes out his horn and blows on it till three score and ten of his men appear. The Bishop, in turn, begs a pardon, to which Robin replies:

> *S.16* "No pardon I owe thee,
> Therefore make haste and come along with me,
> For to merry Barnsdale we shall go."

Do we need further evidence that Barnsdale was *part* of the greenwood and that the greenwood was *Sherwood Forest?*

One other ballad includes the name *Barnsdale* and offers some evidence, although it is a paraphrase of the seventh and eighth fyttes of the *Little Geste* and popularly known as the *King's disguise and friendship with Robin Hood.* It is not older than 1753 and appears to have been written by some miserable retainer to the press; being in fact a most contemptible effort. In his ballad the King is riding from Fountain's Abbey to Barnsdale, although he is staying in Nottingham — a rather long way round.

The ballad of *Robin Hood and the Tanner* first appears in the Garland of 1663 where the two men of the title meet and fight. The Tanner gives his name as Arthur á Bland and he joins the band after the contest, which clearly took place in Sherwood Forest:

> *S.3* "And as he went forth in a Summer's morning,
> In to the forest of merry Sherwood,
> To view the red deer, that range here and there,
> There he met with bold Robin Hood."

W.J. Thoms, an early editor, observed that "this, perhaps, induced Arthur á Bland to think more of Barnsdale Wood and his cousin, Little John, than of toiling with rawhides in the unsavoury solution of oak and bark and ditch water." It would be interesting to know if Thoms was acquainted with such a place in Sherwood — certainly it seems likely that he was, because at the time that he was writing, in 1827, the vale might well have still been in existence.

In the thirty eight ballads collected by Child, we find that Nottingham is named in 21 of them; Nottingham*shire* in 2; Wakefield in 1; Plumpton Park in 1; and no town at all in the remaining 13, making 38 in all. In addition Sherwood Forest occurs in 9 of them; a King's park (Clipstone) in 1; Bernesdale or Barnsdale in 5; Yorkshire and Lancashire in 1; Fountain Dale (Notts.) in 1; and "the greenwood" in 21. Nottingham is associated with a King's park in 1; with Bernesdale as part of the forest in 1, and with Barnsdale as part of the forest in another. Nottinghamshire is associated with Sherwood Forest in 1; Nottingham with Sherwood Forest in 8; Nottingham with "the greenwood" in 9; and Yorkshire and Lancashire in 1. In addition, Yorkshire and Lancashire are mentioned in Martin Parker's *True Tale of Robin Hood* (1632), though he reports that the King came to Nottingham specifically to seek Robin Hood, and Parker borrows from several ballads; Wakefield occurs in the ballad which relates Robin Hood's visit to the pound (pinfold) to meet George ó Green. In fact there is no ballad evidence that puts Robin Hood anywhere other than a place close to Nottingham. This is a fact that is accepted by worldwide popular opinion.

THE EXACT LOCATION OF BARNSDALE

In the 14th century map of Sherwood Forest in the possession of the Duke of Rutland at Belvoir Castle (A copy of this is in the Nottinghamshire Records Office, Ref. XF IS), there is to be found adequate confirmation of Barnsdale being in Sherwood, when allowance is made for corrupt spellings.

Close to the town of Basford, and in the parish of that name, is *Bryunsdale,* or as some interpret, *Brimsdale,* for the first spelling, in Fordun's Scotichronicon 15.c., not only has an abbreviation which can be either AR or RA, ER/RE or IR/RI, etc. This is followed by three digits which can be either M, IN/NI, etc. Bryunsdale, my choice, stood five miles north of the old Nottingham town wall and, most significantly, in close enough proximity to give credibility to the stories of Robin, and the escapades of his band of outlaws, in the town.

In *The Sherwood Forest Book,* 13th century references to Bryunsdale, originally in Latin, contain similar place names that are set down according to the whims of the writers over various periods. In 1895, this place name had developed into Barnsdale, according to a lease of that year in the Nottinghamshire Records Office. Some of these references contain the following:

i) Ralph of Algathorpe (Bagthorpe, part of Basford) has assarted (enclosed) three acres and a half in Brunnesdal, and keeps it, but it is to the harm of the beasts." (Temp. Henry III).

ii) "That Richard Algathorp has made one ditch in Brounesdal to the harm of the forest of the King."

iii) "It is presented and he is convicted that the same Nicholas with his men took a mare from Manor Achard in the pasture of Basford and led it into Beskewood (Bestwood) and loaded it with venison and led it into Brinnesdal." (Temp., Edward I).

Some shades of Robin Hood himself here, since close to this period he was in Barnsdale and he did steal deer. Following the River Leen from north to south, The Duke of Rutland's map shows Basforde, Walton Gate (street?), Coldale Gate, Depe Broke, Basford Lingges, Brymmisdale (Bryunsdale), Basforde Wode, the How, Brymmisdale Knoll and Basforde Towne.

The *City of Nottingham Archives* lease of 1895 relates to the enclosure at Bagthorpe (Algathorpe) farm near Basford — "From the Duke of Newcastle to Elias Cockerham of Basford, farmer." The lands leased include *Barnsdale Close,* which the plan included in the deed shows was west of the water works reservoir on Haydn Road. Most of these lands comprise plot 122 in the Enclosure Award (1792) and unfortunately are simply described as "part of the forest", the place names are not detailed." (See Archive records No. M24, 515). However, from all this it is fair to assume that by 1500 when the *Little Geste* was first printed, the name had become *Bernesdale;* a similar evolution took place with Barnsdale in Rutland, originally "Briun's Dale."

As we have already seen earlier, Robin Hood sent his men *out of* Barnsdale, to seek a stranger to break fast with him:

"And walk up to the saylis,
             And so to Watling Street,
             And wait after some unketh guest
             Up chance you may them meet."

The various editions of the *Little Geste* render saylis, as *sayles, sayle,* or even *shore* (a small wood), which may be taken for a mill, e.g. as in "He wende (thought) that the sayles were mangoned" (mangoled, a war machine). This is from a stanza of *The Lament of Simon de Montfort* which tells how King Henry III's brother, Richard de Almaigne, took refuge in a mill.

The Reverend John Eagles, M.A., formerly of Wadham College, Oxford, volunteered to attempt to turn the *Little Geste* into somewhat more modern and popular language, whilst at the same time preserving as much as possible of the spirit and phraseology of the orginal. He transcribed sayles as sallies, sallows or willows, as do several writers as early as the 16th century; a reasonable supposition if we take shore as a small wood of willows, which would have been plentiful in Barnsdale, with the Day Brook running through it to the Leen. The first mention of "shore" was made by Edward White in his edition of the *Little Geste,* registered at the Stationers' books, on 13 May 1594.

The preposition used in the various editions is *under, up to, unto, into,* and *up unto,* any of which would fit a mill, with the possible exception of *under* unless it was a windmill (which is doubtful), while watermills on the Leen and Day Brook were plentiful. On the other hand a windmill standing on high ground would require one to go *up to* it. So for the word *saylis* we have a clear choice between *mill* and *willows.* The fact that one edition of the *Little Geste* as we have already seen gives *shore* (small wood), tends to support the case for the latter, which would therefore make it a reference to an osier bed, or willow wood, an interpretation which has widespread support. My own conclusion is that it was a copse of willow!

The *Little Geste* goes on to relate that after passing the willows, the outlaws came to Watling Street. *This is clearly a corruption.* The Roman road known as Watling Street ran from Dover to Central Wales; Ryknield Street ran North from the junction of the Fosse Way against Bourton, while Ermine Street ran from London to the Humber via Lincoln, and probably, on to York. Hence the Roman road from Doncaster was referred to as Ermine Street or Herman Street.

The ancient highway from London to York, shown on a map of 1670, is named the Kings' Great Way", for Nottingham was the seat of more provincial parliaments than any other town, and the castle was visited regularly by the monarchs of England. "From the beginning of this reign" (Henry II), says Thoroton, in his *Nottinghamshire* (1677), "the castle has for the most part, belonged to the Crown, neither is there any place so far distant from London that has so often given entertainment and residence to the Kings and Queens of England."

The Kings' Great Way ran through Papplewick, passed Newstead Abbey (seat of the Lord Byron) under an outcrop of rock called Robin Hood's Seat, from which by tradition he kept watch on the Great Way; on, then, to Mansfield, a Royal manor, and then forked through Pleasley, to Richmond on the one side, and through Mansfield Woodhouse and York to the other.

The *Sherwood Forest Book* contains the following entry: "These beare the marks and bounds of the haye of our lord the King and of the park of Bestwood. Bestwood beginning at the heade of Coldale and so to the hay of Bestwood is divided by a way that is called Walton Gate, unto the heath and so by the heath unto the ford of the Leen that is called Beskewood Ford and so by the waters of the Leen unto More Brook."

As Leman again observes: "We see therefore that Walton Gate is the older name of the highway running from Papplewick to Nottingham." *Gate* was the Danish term for a street, and would have been more widely used in Nottingham and its locale, once one of the five boroughs. It is interesting to note that *Place Names of West Riding,* published by the Place Names Society, states that, "in 1433 the whole of the road from Ferrybridge through Barnsdale to Worksop in Notts., was described as "the highway called Watlyngstreete." But it does not cite its source, and nor have I managed to discover it. A branch of this road runs from Wroxeter, Shropshire, via Manchester, Leeds and Tadcaster to York, but was un-named. "Crossing Ilkley Moor via Bramham Moor and Tadcaster to York is the remains of a Roman ridge named 'Watling Street." This is from *Some Historic Mansions of Yorkshire: Bramham Hall.*

However, this is still some 20/30 miles north of Barnsdale and, therefore, cannot be the Watling Street of the ballads. North of this point and onwards to Catterick the Great North Road is, and was, known as Derne Street. Apart from those of the Yorkshire advocates to Robin Hood, I have found no other reference to Watling Street in that county, and none to one in Barnsdale, and a close look at any of the claims will show that they are all based on the ballad; no other source is offered.

Hunter, in his *Robin Hood* (1852) gives ''The Great North Road, as heretofore it was called, crosses it (Barnsdale) between Doncaster and Ferrybridge.'' And again, ''Watling Street, as the ballad writer calls the ancient, doubtless the Roman highway.'' This route left the ancient road from Nottingham to York at Papplewick Hall Gates (Blidworth Way), and it is abundantly clear, therefore, that the Watling Street of the ballad is in reality, Walton Gate. For the sake of rhyme *gate* is made *street,* and by oral tradition or continued mishearing over several generations *Walton* became *Watling.* It is south of Blyth and within Sherwood Forest and was the road on which the gentle Knight and, later, the monks, were accosted by the outlaws:

> S.21   ''But as they looked in Bernysdale,
> By a derne strret,
> Then came a Knight riding,   (Later shown as Sir Richard at the Lee)
> Full soon they did him meet.''

The Knight was travelling from his home in Versydale which is shown as Uterysdale by Hunter, and Wrysdale in North Lancashire by Child. There is no more stupid nor naive thinking than that of those who suggest the Knight was of Lancashire because ''his son slew a Knight of Lancaster.''

There is, utterly, no suggestion that Sir Richard at the Lee was from Lancashire, so that Rydale and Wrydale in Sherwood have a good claim, as do the Derun (derne) Way and Walton Gate. I state emphatically that the Knight was not travelling from Lancashire. The confusion may have arisen from the mention of Inglewood and Barnysdale by Wyntoun in his chronicle, as he was a Scotsman, and at the time (1420) Yngle-wood was Sherwood, an English Wood. In the ballad *Adam Bell, Clim of the Clough and William Cloudesley* (William Copeland edition, 1548) *Inglis* and *Ingles* wood is used for Sherwood. Somewhat loosely *Englishwood* is used in the ballad of *Robin Hood and Queen Catherine* (*c.* 1663), Stanza 5; ''Search all those English Wood for Robin Hood — near to Nottingham.'' A further reference to Lancasshyre in the *Little Geste,* which is used by others to prove that it was Edward II who came to Nottingham, is here given with my profound repudiation of their claim:

> S.354 ''The King came to Nottingham,
> With Knights in great array,
> For to take that *Gentle Knight,*
> And Robin Hood if he may.''
> S.355 ''He asked men of that country,
> After Robin Hood,
> And after that gentle Knight,
> That was so bold and stout.''
> S.357 ''All the *passe of Lancasshyre,*
> He went both far and near,
> Till he came to Plumpton Park
> He failed many of his deer.''

The word *passe* means compass or bounds of an area. To the east of the north forest of Sherwood are Bothamsall, Holme, Gamston, Houghton, Crophull, West Retford and Ranby parishes as shown in old accounts of Nottinghamshire. *They were owned by the Dukes of Lancaster!* As a Royal inheritance it goes back to the year 1266, in the time of Robin Hood. In 1377 Lancashire was created a Palatine with John of Gaunt as Duke of Lancaster. The Duchy of Lancaster still belongs to the Crown and is known as Duchy holdings, not Crown lands. The King, Henry III, travelled around the ''lands of Lancaster'' which would bring him close to the Royal Hunting Park of Clipstone, where he did ''fail many of his deer.'' In a letter from the Duchy of Lancaster Office to the author, they state, ''I would think that your ingenious suggestion about how the *Passe of Lancasshyre* came by its name might well be correct.'' It is signed by the Clerk to the Council.

''The estates and jurisdiction known as the Duchy and County Palatine of Lancaster have been attached to the Crown since 1399, when John of Gaunt's son came to the throne as Henry IV. As the Lancaster inheritance it goes back to 1265. Edward III erected Lancashire into a County Palatine for his son, John of Gaunt, Duke of Lancaster.'' (Whittakers Almanac).

At, or near to, Clipstone Park, lands were held by a family known as Plumpton for the services of blowing a horn to scare wolves out of the forest. The ballad writer either confused the two names; or at some point was misheard, especially as it sometimes appears at Plympton.

Unless it can be shown that the Sheriff was of any other County than that of Nottinghamshire and Derbyshire — or evidence produced to show he lived elsewhere — or that the King went anywhere else to seek Robin Hood, then the matter must rest as stated above.

Barnsdale, in Basford, was a big area of woodland and waste in the Forest of Sherwood abutting on Bestwood Park and Walton Gate. In the reign of Edward III, ''Ralph Cromwell, Knight, and John Dinnoc, that be dead held twenty three acres of ground by estimation of old, assarted, which Oldham Palm of Nottingham held that is called Bryunsdale Wonge of the fee of Basforde, and it belongeth to the same town and it layeth waste'' (Leman). This part of Barnsdale, the boundaries of which are not known, but having the Depe Broke — (Day Brook) running through, it appears to be of some considerable size.

There is one claim made by Joseph Hunter in his *Robin Hood*, which has been accepted by advocates of the Yorkshire claim without careful examination, or thought. In the *Little Geste* we are told that the gentle Knight was returning to Barnsdale to repay Robin, but he was delayed by a wrestling match (Stanza 135), ''it happened,'' writes Hunter, that — ''As he *went* at a *bridge* there was a wrestling'' (where the name of *Wentbridge* appears to be enigmatically indicated). This is really concocting the evidence! *Went* is the past tense of *wend*, — to proceed on one's journey; to travel, make one's way. Punctuation was not used in the original *Little Geste,* and this line has survived as first written, but when the *Geste* was versed and punctuated this line should (does in fact) read ''as he went, at a bridge there was a wrestling,'' or, ''as he journeyed, at a bridge there was a wrestling (match)''. The preposition ''at'' means *on, in, near,* or *by.* Careful search would have shown that two copies of the *Little Geste* show ''by a bridge was'' (Copland) and ''as he went up a bridge'' (Edward White). This is a point which must be borne in mind when making an attempt to identify our outlaw and place names — the evidence has not always been thoroughly examined — only developed, mainly from Hunter's inaccurate claim.

The Barnsdale of the ballads and the Robin Hood legend was Bryunsdale, in the ancient Royal Forest of Sherwood, and situated where today the district of Basford stands — and just five miles north of the centre of the City of Nottingham.

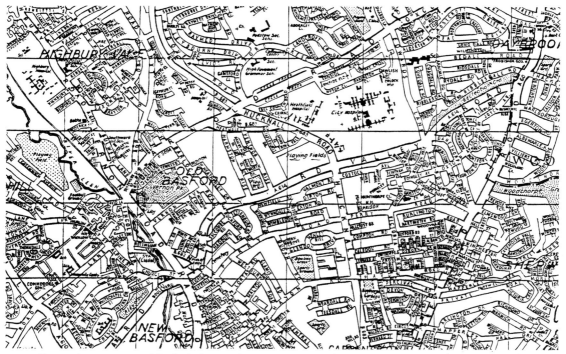

Present day street map of Basford: the area around Valley Road being the most likely location of Barnsdale.

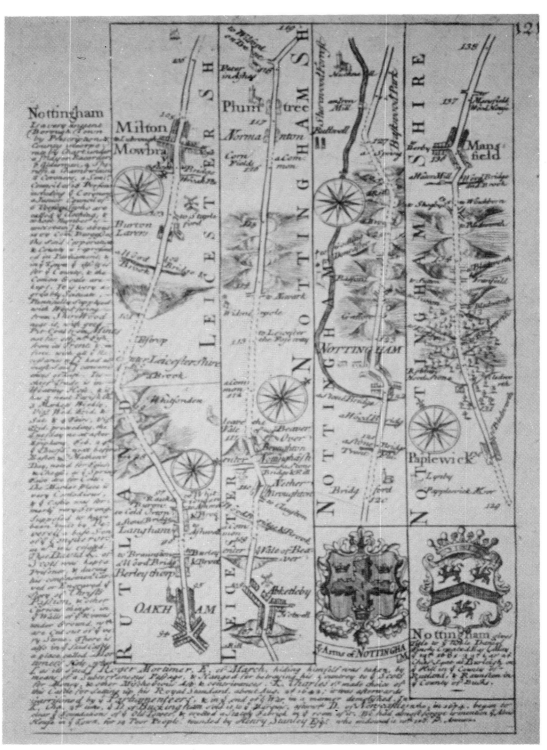

THE KING'S GREAT WAY by John Ogilby.

Chapter 5

HE first written mention of Sherwood Forest is in 1154 — "William Peverill in the first year of Henry I, answers to the Pleas of the Forest 3. Peverill seems to have had the whole profit and command of it in the reign of King Stephen (1135-1154). After him it devolved to the Crown and was managed by the sheriffs for the time being. This forest, it appears, was anciently divided (in two), or rather (had two parts) known by the names of Thorneywood and High Forest, the first which although the least, contained within its boundaries nineteen towns and villages, of which Nottingham was one. The High forest abounded with fine, stately oaks, and was free of underwood." *(Hayman Rook Ms., 1799)*.

In 1218, at the command of King Henry III, a jury of knights and free men set out to define the boundaries of the forest, and recorded in the perambulations of Sherwood Forest is the following: "leaving by Stoney Street in Nottingham they rode through Whiston, then a hamlet on the Nottingham to Mansfield road (and now is known by an old people's home so named) then to Blackstone Haugh (a meadow running by the Dover Beck, west of Oxton) to Rufford, and following the way to the village of Wellow and on to King's ford. They then struck west across the *north boundary* following the water to Perlethorpe on the Thoresby estate, and followed the same water to Pleasley, the water being the river Meden."

As some people would insist that Sherwood Forest ran north as far, and into, South Yorkshire I would ask any who believe this to be so to read the above again. By a Royal commission the northern boundary is stated to be the river Meden, which flowed west to east joining the river Maun at Gosling Carr and is at least 15 miles south of the Yorkshire border. I have read no perambulation of the Royal Forest of Sherwood which went beyond the river Meden.

To continue with our knights and free men: "Thence by Newboundhill to Windhill (now travelling south) — and thence by the hedges between the roads of Sutton and Kirkby to the middle of the pond at Newstead Priory, and so by the river Leen to the Trent."

The forest had three parks enclosed by pales; Nottingham, Bestwood, and Clipstone; these were the hunting grounds of the kings and their nobles when staying in Nottingham Castle, Bestwood Lodge, or Clipstone Palace. In a survey of Sherwood Forest made in the year 1609 these three parks contained respectively 129, 3672 and 1583 acres of woodland and waste (uncultivated land). Although many still today expect to see, and believe that Sherwood was, all woodland they are in error. A fourteenth century map of the area shows many dales, some of which exist only in name today. Larkdale, now recalled by a street name, and inn within the City of Nottingham; Maydendale, Goosedale, Coldale and others which can be traced, and many which are now built upon, and lost forever. Budby owte (oat?) fields, Papplewick Meadow, Bulwell Ground, Blidworth Fishpool, and the Hawfield, all tell of open spaces surrounded by woodland; Nottingham Wood, Bulwell Ground, Sutton Wood, Kirkby Wood, Gedling Wood, Mansfield Wood and others.

Ancient ways are shown; Brome Gate, Swyne Gate, Papplewick Way (traces of which may be seen) and more. There are signs of much older Roman ways which crossed the forest east to west, but they are not marked on the map; nor is The King's Great Way, of which I found traces close to Papplewick church. It is strange that whereas some of the local people tell of the "great way" from London to York, one hears nothing from official sources, although a map exists showing part of it (John Ogilby, His Majesties Cosmographer, *c.*1670, no other source on my copy but it is apparently from a book). There are two castles shown other than the famous Nottingham castle: Linby and Leysing, of which the earth works of one can be traced in Annesley Plantation, but the castle itself is not known.

Towns and villages in the north of the forest include Mansfield, Mansfield Woodhouse, Sutton, Kirkby, Edwinstowe, Blidworth, Warsop and several others. The rivers Poulter, Meden, Vicarswater, Maun, Rain, and the Beck run west to east; others are now shown. One mill is marked at Sutton; others are omitted. The map is laid with the north to the left and the east at the top and places are not always in their correct location. They are listed one above the other in close proximity, giving no idea as to distance; nor, strangely enough, as the map is the work of a monk, no churches or abbeys are listed.

The Royal Forest was about twenty miles from north to south and five miles east to west. The common man's idea of Sherwood Forest covered two thirds of the county of Nottinghamshire, and over-spilt into Derbyshire and Yorkshire, and also *Lincolnshire,* taking Robin Hood with it. Today, much is modern forestry, the oak giving way to birch and conifers. Around the village of Edwinstowe is the finest example of a Royal hunting forest anywhere in the world. Billaugh and Birklands are two areas where the oaks, dying out in recent years, are now coming back, self seeded.

This part of the forest with its Sherwood Forest Visitor Centre, manned by Rangers, is the mecca of all who come to the county, for here is the Major Oak. Over thirty feet in circumference at the trunk, once her boughs covered an area of two hundred square yards. Today these boughs are held by iron chains and heavy beams support them from underneath. She is hollow, and before being fenced in, as many as eight to twelve people could stand inside her at one time. Fencing-in became necessary to prohibit visitors treading down the ground around the base, thus allowing a more porous surface and letting leaf mould form and mulch her, and save roots from the damage of many feet; and hopefully adding many years to her life.

The oak tree takes her name from Major Hayman Rook, a Mansfield Historian, who wrote several works on Sherwood Forest. The original name was the Queen oak, and being fifteen hundred years old according to some, is said to have been named after Queen Boadicea (Robin Hood is not her only legend!). In recent years she has become famous as Robin Hood's tree and legendary tales are told of his exploits, mainly hiding from the Sheriff in the hollow bole, but these stories in fact are not much older than the turn of the century.

Just over the border in South Yorkshire in the village of Todwick, which some would have us believe was once part of Sherwood Forest, is an oak with a plaque containing this inscription — "On this site once stood Robin Hood's Trysting Tree, immortalised in Sir Walter Scott's *Ivanhoe.* " The original tree ultimately was replaced by a sapling of the Major Oak, planted by the Duke of Leeds. This plaque was erected to celebrate the planting of its successor by Gerald F. Young esq., the Lord Lieutenant of Yorkshire on the 18th May 1974. The inscription continues: "By the same tradition an oak standing within a few yards of this was known as Robin Hood's larder."

The original oak was felled in 1961 to make room for the old people's bungalows which now stand on the spot. There was an outcry against "this desecration" both public and civic, and for some time was a topic of readers letters and news items in the Sheffield newspapers. And yet folk would have passed by the original tree before publication of *Ivanhoe* without a second glance. So much for the powers of legend.

Another great oak, Robin Hood's Larder in Sherwood, was blown down in a gale in the 1960's. Originally known as Butchers Shambles or Shambles Oak, it was here that by tradition Robin Hood stored his venison in the manner of the Red Indian. Such is the power of the Nottinghamshire outlaw; for many other well known oaks have passed into oblivion without comment, such as Simon's Oak, Cludd's Oak, The Duke's Walking Stick and also the Greendale Oak which surely WAS unique. Being over 1560 years old it was so vast that a passage ten feet high and six feet wide was cut through her in the 18th century, sufficient for a coach and horses to be driven through; and, of course, there were the Seven Sisters of which I believe none are left. Hollow and decayed, many ancient oaks still stand and some of them bear leaf and fruit in their seasons, but none have captured the imagination like the Major Oak, and as did Robin Hood's Larder.

Nottingham, Sherwood Forest, and Robin Hood are synonymous! It would take more than a day to visit the locations in Nottingham that are associated with our hero, and at least a week to travel the forest and take in the places with tales of the greenwood outlaws. Mansfield is the largest town in Sherwood and a plaque can be seen in West Gate, marking the spot where the Centre Tree (oak) stood until quite recently. It is claimed that this was the dead centre of the forest.

Travelling north, from Nottingham on the Mansfield road, one is in old Sherwood once he has crossed Parliament Street, within the city boundary. At the Leapool junction, not only have several places associated with the legend already been passed, but one is now among the trees many of which are seeded from the trees of Old Sherwood. But there is none of our story to tell, for this was not the way of the knight and his squire, the yeoman that walked the greenwood shore, the husbandman, the merchant, nor villager of days long ago. We are on the turnpikes of modern times. Whichever way one takes at the junction — Mansfield to the left or Ollerton straight on, he will soon meet up with a green sign — SHERWOOD FOREST? Forestry commission. Indirectly, the Monarch still has control.

Following the Mansfield road, by the edge of Ravenshead, stands the entrance to Newstead Abbey with the guardian Pilgrim Oak still standing in majesty and pride. Once, the authorities did threaten to cut her down, but protest was so great that the matter was dropped. This great tree was probably a sapling when Robin was an old man. Most certainly it would have seen, and perhaps given shelter to, the Lord Byron, Nottinghamshire's soldier poet. At Larch Farm turn right to Blidworth. At the bottom of the hill stands an Inn, *The Little John,* and just by, a footpath to Fountain Dale. Tradition has it that the lane was once known as Blood and Guts Lane and it was here on a bridge over a stream now culverted (or dried up) that Robin Hood and Little John fought at their first meeting, and John then became a member of the band.

Continuing on to Blidworth, on the right hand side of the road stands the Church of Saint Mary of the Purification, and in the churchyard stands a stone, once part of the old tower and under which, according to old tales, lies the body of Will Scarlet, lieutenant of Robin Hood. Legend has it that he was buried against the old church but the exact spot is unknown. Local folk will tell you it was from a cottage in Blidworth that Robin Hood took Maid Marian for their marriage at Edwinstowe. (How these old cottages keep turning up, and it seems that the author was born *just* too late to see even one of them.) It appears they built cottages far stronger than castles, for of the castles and manor houses of the legend, they are either in ruin or long gone.

A cave on the hill on which the village stands was used by Robin Hood and his band for the storage of their food and goods. This is folk history, but written history does actually tell of two men being taken by the steward of Sherwood's servants (the steward at that time being a John de Lascelles) to be held for trial, for carrying bows and arrows in the forest, in the year 1276. A band of outlaws armed with bows and arrows, and swords effected a rescue and in their anger broke the windows of the steward's house and beat up the men. *The Victoria County History of Nottinghamshire* reports that sixteen names were mentioned at the inquest, one was dead and two or three had fled into Yorkshire. The ballads do not tell of this, nor is the story still part of the legend in the area.

North-west of the village stands Fountain Dale (not to be confused with the house of that name) with an old Saxon moat running north to south on the west side, and where, according to a notice board now long gone but in living memory, the King's officers collected taxes from the surrounding villages; i.e. one hundred head of deer. The board was ivy covered, and barely readable but alas is no more. It was interesting because I thought it strange that the King should be paid in his own *coin.* It is more likely that the villagers counted the deer and reported to the officers, for to get a herd of one hundred deer into the moat and keep them there would be a remarkable feat.

Tradition says that on the north side of Harlow Wood there was formerly a brass plate with an engraving (now renewed) on a stone pillar where the forest officers of the Crown assembled annually on Holyrood Day, early in the morning. There they received the charge of the Lord Chief Justice in Eyre to view fences and take account of the deer, in order make presentment, at the Swanimote Court, which was held on that day in Mansfield by a steward appointed by the Lord Chief Justice of Eyre (journey or circuit). The counting of deer in the various glades well known to the villagers (most of whom were good poachers) is a more likely probability than of herding them. They would then present their tally sticks to the King's officers at their meeting place.

In the same area is Friar Tuck's Well, now broken down and dry. At one time it was protected by an iron railing on a low wall, but a beech tree falling across it some years ago did it little good. In recent times there has been some investigation as the earth has been removed and the stone steps leading into a brick, shallow well can be seen, but of a much later period than the legendary Friar. Close by stood his cell in which tradition has it that he told his rosary in a falsetto voice, and the villagers complained

Above: KING JOHN'S PALACE. The remains.

Left: ROBIN HOOD'S SEAT, near Annesley.

Below: ROBIN HOOD'S STABLES.

that he had a woman with him. Until fairly recent times the cell, a cave with window and door, was still to be seen.

In the long undergrowth and through the interlaced branches of the rhodedendron, with fallen boughs to trip the unwary, nettles which show no mercy, trees that hide the sky, and flies which seemingly are just breaking a seven years fast on human perspiration, if one has the determination to cover the ground and the luck to find what he seeks, there is a chance of seeing the famous moat where Robin and the Friar carried each other backwards and forwards over the water. They fought a great fight, and ended up friends. And if one's luck is really at its zenith he may well see water in the moat which is oblong and at one time surrounded a shrine, signs of which exist in the many carved stones one comes across by stubbing his toes.

It is said that the monks of Newstead put a curse on the waters so that the moat is dry for six years and filled during the seventh. Coincidence or no, I can personally vouch for ONE seven year period. There are those who swear to it being fact. One phenomenon has been related to me by two families who lived in Fountain Dale House, that of the presence of the spirit or ghost of Sir Walter Scott. Clara Wilde, one time occupier claimed to have seen him, and the present family profess to feel his presence, and have had some strange things happen there.

West of the dale is Thieves Wood which was the home of robbers and footpads and it was here that Robin rescued many a maiden and loot, returning them to their rightful places. The Friar is said to have warned Robin of these robbers' escapades and kept him informed of events in the locality, and at one time legend says he nursed Robin back to health. It must be emphasised that there was a difference between outlaw and robber; the former need not be a rogue, and in many cases was not, as we shall see.

North of Blidworth is Rainworth and just south of the main road, behind the houses and shops, is Bishophill Plantation. On the 14th century map already mentioned it is shown as Bishop's Wood, and legend places it as where Robin played a trick on the Bishop of Hereford, and after taking one hundred pounds for the meal supplied, insisted on the Bishop saying a mass for him and his men. Another version increases the payment to three hundred pounds and has the Bishop made to dance barefoot, to the enjoyment of the outlaws.

Further north are the new and the old villages of Clipstone. In the old village at the rear of the "old tin chapel" one can see King John's Palace, the ruins thereof; once regarded as a heap of stones and now preserved as a National Monument. Although named after King John the original is much older and built by Edwin of Northumbria for a chapel. It was discovered by Henry I, who extended it, and used for many decades by the monarchs as a hunting lodge. Here Richard the Lionheart met William the Lion of Scotland. Here also, or close by, King John ordered the execution of his Welsh hostages in Nottingham Castle, mere teenagers. And it was here that Robin Hood and some of his men, disguised as minstrels, released prisoners whilst the King was leading his men to capture the outlaw at Cresswell Crags, where one of his caves is still to be seen, the biggest one of course.

Close by on the Mansfield to Edwinstowe road stand the Parliament Oak, where Edward I held Parliament with his nobles in 1290, and at one time on the same road at a place undefined, tradition is that there once stood a cottage where Little John, the son of a nail maker lived. Travelling towards Edwinstowe a glimpse can be seen of the Duke's Folly, or Archway House, as it is now called. On it are carvings of forest life, and statues of Robin Hood in Saxon dress, Little John and Maid Marian on the south side; and Friar Tuck, King Richard, and Alan-a-Dale on the north side. A magnificent edifice, erected in the year 1842, and was intended to be a gatehouse on a green ride from Welbeck Abbey to Nottingham, which never materialised, hence the term "folly".

Edwinstowe is the Mecca for Robin Hood enthusiasts and seekers of leisure in Sherwood Forest. It was here that the body of King Edwin, first Christian King of Northumbria, lay. Close by stands the remains of his shrine, now an iron cross surmounting a mound of stones, said to be the original stones of the shrine, where hermits received a fee to pray for the Kings and Queens and their families over many generations. The church in the village was built in unison with others all over the country as penance for the murder of Thomas-a-Becket, on the orders of King Henry II. A carving of a head on a pillar on the north side, is claimed to be that of Thomas-a-Becket. History is all around us, but that is not the reason why people flock in their many thousands to the village and forest. They come because of

Above: ST. JAMES'S CHURCH, Papplewick, known as "The Foresters' Church".
Right: EDWINSTOWE CHURCH, where legend has it that Robin Hood married Maid Marian.
Below: LINBY CROSS.

Robin Hood. He is said to have married Maid Marian in the church, and his tree, as already stated, stands within the forest.

From here to Worksop the Forest is known as the Dukeries, for in it were three great houses. Welbeck Abbey, seat of the Dukes of Portland, and now a military college; Clumber Hall, one time chief seat of the Dukes of Newcastle, now demolished, although the church still stands and the lands are kept by the National Trust; and Thoresby Hall, home of the late Earl Manvers; now owned by British Coal. It is a shame these fine homes are going, never to be rebuilt, nor anything again like them. But the legend of Robin Hood will never die and most certainly will keep the name of Thoresby alive, as many folk associate the two, the Major Oak being on Thoresby land.

Steetly Church, which lies north of the Dukeries just off the Worksop to Chesterfield road, is a gem of Norman architecture well worth a visit. Now restored and reconsecrated it is one of the finest examples of Norman building, either in Britain or in Normandy. For many years it was a ruin with holes in the side walls to let the cattle get in for shelter. Robin hood is said to have hidden in the false roof, now gone; and Friar Tuck reputedly preached many a sermon there. It is more probable that the legend stems from the Clerk of Copmanhurst (Friar Tuck) of *Ivanhoe*. It is claimed locally that Robin Hood is buried at the farm almost on the doorstep of the church.

In Worksop Priory Church, on the north wall just inside the west door, there is a small glass covered opening behind a door. In it is part of a skull with an arrowhead embedded, which at one time was featured as the skull of a Sherwood forester. Now the notice simply, and more honestly, states that it was found close to the West door.

Such is legend that a Mansfield story is told of an old house being demolished, and in a *secret place* was discovered a cap and clothing of Lincoln Green with other items (skeletons?). There are no official records to confirm the discovery, but connected with the town there are many stories of Robin Hood and his escapades with Will Scarlet and Maid Marian.

At Pleasley Mill on the Chesterfield Road from Mansfield, there once stood a cross named Robin Hood's Cross of which there is now no trace in fact or legend.

At Annesley Woodhouse between Mansfield and Nottingham, is a range of sandstone hills known as Robin Hood's Hills at the eastern end of which there is a stone slab, Robin Hood's Seat. It was on this that he sat watching the King's Great Way which ran beneath it and helped many wealthy abbotts to spend their money! Close by, the ordnance survey map shows a Robin Hood's Cave, no longer visible, being a mere hollow in the ground. The only story I could find was one of Irish labourers camping there whilst building the railway nearby, and their's was a more dangerous situation than that of passing abbotts in day's gone by, for the dynamite was stored in the same cave!

Further south at Papplewick stands the Church of St. James, the "Forester's Church", so called because one of the old grave stones in the church floor bears the carvings of bow and arrows, along with the belt and hunting horn of a forester. It was here that Robin Hood reputedly rescued a fair maid from a forced marriage to a Norman Knight and restored her to her true love, Alan-a-Dale. To ensure that the banns were called, Little John wore the bishop's cope and mitre and called them seven times. Another account of this story has an earlier date, and in this version the outlaw who was married was Will Scarlet.

Close by, on private land, can be found Robin Hood's Stables. The cave has been known as The Stables for many, many years. It was sixteen feet high and dug out of soft sandstone; an attempt had been made to carve the pillars with tracery. At the back are two mangers; one to feed a single horse and the other large enough for two. The roof, which collapsed under the weight of the heavy snows in 1940 has been restored but the arches and all signs of tracery are gone, although the pick marks are still in evidence. Legend has it that Robin Hood kept his horses here and used them when robbing the wealthy people travelling to Nottingham or Mansfield on the King's Great Way, which ran just west of the stables. Little credence can be placed on this as the road was only a stone's throw from the stables, and even less likely is the story that they were kept so secret by Robin that not even his men knew of them.

As well as countless other stories, there are many more caves, wells and stones that are associated with them, but no longer visible, as well as examples of Robin Hood lore all over the Sherwood area. In Warsop it is said that the local folk never bolted their doors as Robin Hood was always welcome. Today in the Mansfield area if one enters a room and fails to shut the door he will be greeted with "Do you come from Wass'up (Warsop) then?" The author knows! — he has been asked!

It is unfortunate that so much legend has overlaid the facts, and that Robin Hood and Sherwood are now more synonymous with the image created by the media and screen. In truth, Sherwood is a very BIG slice of England's real history and heritage, the playground of monarchs, the home of abbeys, stately dwellings, the source of oak for our naval fleets, timbers for church and cathedral, the home of the common man — the Sherwood Forester — and the resort of those who fought for England's right to be ruled by the English. Without Robin Hood she is famous; with him she is a household name world wide — Sherwood! Let us look at her through the eyes of history.

Not even a King could hunt outside Royal boundaries, and Manwood, in 1562 states: *"On the 29th day of March 1194 Richard, King of England, set out to see Clipstone and the Forest of Sherwood, out of which he did chase a hart into Barnsdale, Yorkshire, and because he could not there recover it, he made proclomation that no person should kill, hurt or chase the said hart, but that it might safely return into Sherwood Forest again, which hart was afterwards called a hart royal proclaimed."* In the year 1327 by Royal order to the Sheriff of Nottingham, the church of St. Mary Magdalene, Newark, was granted six oaks from the forest of Sherwood for repairs to the said church, a fact recorded by Cornelius Brown in his *History of Newark.* Vol.1.

In the first year of his reign, King John visited Nottingham and for a short time took up residence at Clipstone Palace in Sherwood. He loved the chase and was often in Nottingham and Clipstone. The palace was burned down during the disorders that followed John's death, and was restored in 1220 during the reign of Henry III.

There were numerous grants by various kings, of timber, deer, underwood, and such, to nobles and clergy. The rights to take fallen timber to burn charcoal was given to the monastries within the boundaries of the forest. As late as the 18th century the soil of the Portland lands was owned by the Duke but the trees were the property of the Crown. The *Calendar of Patent Rolls* show instances of Lords, clergy and others taking more than their *rights* from the forest — a crime of which Robin Hood was not the only culprit. Under William the Conqueror, the laws of the forest were very rigid, and cruel. A man could have his eyes put out for taking a boar or buck; for taking a hare there was a fine of twenty shillings, and for taking a rabbit, a fine of ten shillings — somewhat harsh when one could be purchased much cheaper. Fingers and thumb could be cut off for using a bow and arrow within the forest — or a heavy fine for carrying them with ''intent'' to take the King's game. At least one of William's successors laid down that there be no distinction between a man who killed a man — and a man who killed a buck. Although I take this report from an erudite work, I must confess at not seeing such punishment in any of the records I have examined.

A man in Sherwood was never an easy quarry to find, and we do have practical modern-day experience to illustrate this fact. Annually, the Robin Hood Society organise a ''Hunt the Outlaw'' competition, the object of which is for children, accompanied by adults for their safety, to seek out the ''outlaws'' who are dispersed over an area of roughly half a square mile. So difficult did it prove initially that the game had to be modified by having the outlaw show himself periodically. Sixteen quarry — and over two hundred searchers in a small area. In medieval times there were far fewer foresters to police over a hundred square miles and neither poacher, outlaw, or robber would be an easy catch. The outlaws in the Society's hunt had to show themselves, or it is doubtful that one would have been spotted. Again in medieval times, the law was lax — there was no police force. Village ''constables'' often reported to the magistrates ''All's well'' — especially at seed time and harvest for, after all, the job was unpaid. Some nobles paid handsomely to be *not* appointed Sheriff, or give military service, and the officers of the forest kept well away from outlaw country. Over the years the laws were relaxed, and we find occasions where complaint is made of noblemen taking from the forest without punishment; and of poachers being brought before the forest courts and merely fined, or held at the court's mercy. We do find men fined for taking timber from the forest without permission but my bet is that these men were found out after the event — not during. The first court of trespass in Sherwood Forest took place, it is believed, in 1154, Hugh, Bishop of Durham presiding. Another such court was held at Blidworth in the eighth year of the reign of Edward I which seems to point to business being somewhat slack.

Although we read of the sheriff being the keeper of the forest it was not always so, even though he was the Royal officer with jurisdiction over the whole counties of both Nottinghamshire and Derbyshire. The office of Head Forester was held by a nobleman at the King's command, and he was permitted a bow-bearer, who carried a bow as the wand of office. The point is taken up by Robin Hood who says in two ballads "Little John shall carry my bow!" (After all he was "keeper of the forest", and states so in the ballads.) The Head Forester was a Crown appointment, carrying the high remuneration of a shilling a day. other officers were, the *verderers,* who looked after and protected the timber; the *agisters,* who looked after the grazing rights; and the *foresters,* who took care of the game and enforced the law. These men were few in number and allotted their district, but once in the greenwood a man could stay hidden as long as he wished.

In the lifetime of Richard I the forest was held by his brother John, who by a Royal charter granted to Ralph FitStephen and Maud de Caux, his wife, all liberties and custody of the forest of Sherwood. This included permission to hunt hare, fox, cat, and squirrel with dogs, and hounds; collect all fallen wood; the valuable inner bark or bast of the lime trees; and claim a skip of every cartload of salt passing through the forest, and a half-skip from half a load. They were responsible for the pannage for pigs (being food picked up by pigs — beechmast being the most popular); fines or pleas of unlawfully owned dogs; together with goods and chattels recovered from thieves and 'brybours' (pick-pockets!). By upholding their rights and in many instances overstepping them, in a place where the forefathers of the common man had for years enjoyed the right to hunt, gather timber, and pasture his animals, much bad feeling would be engendered towards noblemen and clergy, and it is plain how any man who opposed these *rights* would become both a friend and hero of the people.

SHERWOOD'S OUTLAWS

The outlaws of Sherwood Forest are not fictitious. They were in the forest before the coming of the Normans, which is suggested by the derivation of the name Warsop, *a town in the forest.* Several writers share the opinion that the first part of the name comes from the Old English *Waer,* meaning cautious, or *waegr* meaning outlaw, the second part, *hop* meaning valley; thus we have *Waers-hop* meaning *the home of the outlaws.* They were real, but there is confusion in the accepted state of outlawry. An outlaw did not have to be a rogue. He could be outside the law for debt incurred by sheer bad luck, and alleged misdemeanours of which he was innocent, he was "one without benefit of the law." Sentence was pronounced by the Sheriff in the County Court. Restoration of the outlawed man to his original status could only be made by the King's act of Pardon addressed to the Sheriff, to be read in the County Court. A complaint, genuine or manufactured, could be made against a man by two Knights of the shire, and in the man's absence. Failure to appear before the court three times would lead to automatic outlawry, so that a person could return home from a Crusade to find his land and goods forfeited to the Crown, and himself an outlaw. Fortunately there was a right of appeal.

Though an outlaw would be a fugitive, it did not always mean that a fugitive would be an outlaw. He could be running away from his wife, or he could be living in a free town, where after a year and a day he would claim freedom from his master or lord. He could be running from danger, or an enemy. In any case his goods and chattels would be held by the King in custody, according to *The Medieval Sheriff to 1300* (Morris): "After each circuit the names of fugitives were placed upon a roll, one copy of which was left in the custody of the sheriff and coroners so that these people *might* be demanded at the first County Court thereafter, and so on until they appeared or were outlawed." Nor did an outlaw necessarily have to live out of the town, or in hiding. There are several records of names with the word "outlaw" bracketed after his name; sometimes as witness to a charter. Hume, in his *History of England* writes: "In later years we see outlaws in Parliament. In the 35th year of Elizabeth I, 1593, the Commons after great debate, expressly voted that a person outlawed might be elected." Then again:- "In a parliament of James I (1603-1625), who advised commons not to elect outlaws, in the case of Vaughan, who was questioned for outlawry, having proved all his debts to be contracted by surities, and MOST of them being honestly compounded, he was allowed to keep is seat." And later: "Outlaws whether by debt or *crimes* had been declared by the judges (in earlier times apparently) incapable of enjoying a seat in the house, where themselves be lawgivers but the opinion of the judges had frequently been set aside."

It would be interesting to know how long outlaws had been chosen from the Knights of the County to sit in the House against the opinion of the judges; in Simon de Montfort's Parliament there must have been many. Many men of noble birth led outlaw bands, supported outlaws and rebels, and periodically

Above: ALL SAINTS CHURCH, Steetley, near Worksop.

Right: ARCHWAY HOUSE with statury depicting Robin Hood, Little John and Clorinda. View of the south side.

Below: WILL SCARLET'S GRAVE, Blidworth.

returned to the King's peace. It is because of this that we do not read of Robin Hood being in the forest during the Winter — all the ballads are in Summer time. Did he and his men find refuge with a *maintainer*, of whom there were many, including some members of the clergy?

Magna Carta makes reference to the outlaw and does not appear to have treated him too badly. Indeed, several of the barons supporting the Charter were outlawed at some time! Article 39 reads: "No freeman shall be siezed, or imprisoned, or strippped of his rights or possessions, or *outlawed* or exiled, or deprived of his standing in any other way, nor will we proceed against him, or send others to do so, except by the lawful judgement of his equals or by the law of the land." On non-appearance at court for a third time the process of outlawry would be started by the Sheriff, a long and tedious job; and after all that there was the right to appeal. Then, as today, any person may have presented a bill to a grand jury, accusing any other person of any crime whatever. This is still the general rule to which as yet hardly any exception has been made. Thus anyone may prefer a bill even against one of the Monarch's ministers. "An indicted person will be tried — unless he cannot be found, in which case he may be (theoretically) outlawed. An outlawry, however, would be a tedious process conducted by the sheriff, the outlaw in the case of felony or treason, would be in the same position as if he had been tried, and even in a case of misdemeanour his goods would be forfeited. Outlawry is not now used — indeed it is not worth using." *Constitution of England* — Maitland).

Magna Carta has become the most important single document in the devlopment of constitutional and legal freedom, not only in Britain, but in many countries. Within recent years it has provided an example which has been followed in the *Universal Declaration of Human Rights and Fundamental Freedoms.* Article 38 of Magna Carta states: "In future no official shall place a man on trial upon his own unsupported statement, without producing credible witnesses to the truth of it." Article 39: "No freeman shall be siezed or imprisoned or stripped of his rights," and Article 40: "To NO ONE will we sell, to NO ONE deny or delay right or justice." The rule of law proclaimed. English law! NO ONE, neither King, archbishop, bishop, nobleman, nor slave, stands above the law — only GOD! Without such law there is no liberty. What a thrill it was for the author some years ago to look upon the American Constitution and Bill of Rights and reflect with pride that it came from the Magna Carta.

Yet ironically, many of the men whom we accept as being outlaws — the correct term being rebels, were set outside the law by *defending it*. Article 61 states: "If we, our chief justice, our officials, or any of our servants offend in any respect against any man, or transgress any of the articles of the peace of this security, and the offence is made known to four of the twenty five said barons, they shall come to us — or in our absence from the kingdom to the chief justice — to declare it and claim immediate redress. If we or in our absence abroad, the chief justice makes no redress within forty days, reckoning from the day on which the offence was declared to us or to him, the four barons shall make the matter known to the rest of the twenty five barons, who may distrain upon and assail us in every way possible, with the support of the whole community of the land, by siezing our castles, lands, possessions, or anything else, saving our persons and those of the queen and our children. Having secured their redress they shall resume their normal obedience to us." This is pretty strong stuff and, no doubt, although given under duress it was a majority decision. Unfortunately it does appear to open a way to make anarchy a political weapon.

Article 61 takes the matter further: "*Any man* who so desires may take an oath to obey the commands of the twenty five barons for the achievement of these ends, and to join with them in assailing us to the utmost of his power. We give public and free permission to take this oath to any man who so desires, and no time will we prohibit any man from taking it. Indeed, we will *compel* any of our subjects who are unwilling to take it to swear it at our command."

King John repudiated his charter under a Papal Bull from Pope Inoccent III. For a time tyranny returned to England, and good men fighting for the rights of her people — as commanded by the King in his charter — became outlaws, or more correctly, rebels. This continued on and off, for several reigns, the charter being confirmed by monarchs for two hundred years. King Henry III confirmed his father's charter, with some alterations, but at his coming of age followed the example of his father and filled the court with Frenchmen who despised the English law — and the barons revolted. After the Battle of Evesham in 1265 many would not accept the terms of the Dictum of Kenilworth and stayed in the woodlands and thickets. Sherwood Forest became a main refuge for them as history proves.

Above: SHERWOOD FOREST.

Above left: THE MAJOR OAK (Robin Hood's Tree) in Sherwood Forest.

Below left: PARLIAMENT OAK.

Below: ROBIN HOOD'S LARDER, in Sherwood Forest. Now destroyed.

Among those Frenchmen to be returned to their native land after the sealing of Magna Carta were Gerald de Athee and Philip Marc. What is interesting is the fact that both men had served as Sheriffs of Nottingham, Athee 1208-9, and Marc 1211-14, and in defiance of Magna Carta the latter was re-appointed in the year 1216. All of the succeeding Sheriffs appear to be of French origin. "Reginald de Gray, Sheriff of Nottingham, waged war on the rebels in Sherwood Forest in the years 1266-67." (Calendar of Patent Rolls.). There are no reports of him having any success. According to Keen in *The Outlaws of Medieval England:* "In 1267 the outlaws of Sherwood Forest had again become a serious menace. Roger de Leyburn, the lieutenant of Reginald de Grey, the King's constable at the castle, fought two large scale engagements with them, one in the heart of the forest itself . . . He does not seem to have achieved much, and the horses which his men lost in the two fights were valued at £63." This statement shows that outlaws were in Sherwood, and that they must have had a leader. Nowhere is that man named except in the ballads which Seldon claims have more truth than written histories and Gutch says will elucidate more clearly than any other documents and, in fact, were the peoples' history. Joseph Ritson in his *Robin Hood* (1823), explains why the ballads only refer to Robin by his nom-de-plume:

"Nay no more honour, I pray thee, Little John,
Henceforth I will be Robin Hood."

He is quoting a line, which is again repeated as the rule of the band, that Robin shall not be known as Earl, Lord, or any other title than that of a yeoman, from the Chettle and Munday play *The Downfall of Robert, Earl of Huntingdon, afterwards called Robin Hood of Merry Sherwood* (1601). The only named outlaws are known *after* being caught: "The Duke of York retained control of Nottingham and Derby with the castle in Nottingham, for until Roger Godberd had been caught and the Earl of Derby unwilling to accept his fate, this was the most turbulent part of England." This statement, from Powicke's *King Henry II and the Lord Edward,* appears to deny that outlaws were not named until after their capture, but the fact is that in 1265, as a rebel, Godberd surrendered and sought a pardon; he did not accept the terms of the Dictum of Kenilworth which was effective if he stood by the award with regard to his lands which the King had given to others. *"All his lands or nothing"* were *his* terms, so he relapsed into outlawry — a known man. No "Robin Hood" surrendered under the Dictum. He was still busy. Powicke again: "Nottingham Castle was in need of special protection, and local rebels were not crushed until Leyburn defeated them at Charnwood on September 14 1267." Had Leyburn succeeded in capturing Robin we would have evidence as with Godberd, but the outlaws of Sherwood remained at large.

That the outlaws were still busy in Nottinghamshire for some years is shown by a proclomation made at Westminster on 11th February, 1272. "Wereas on the showing of the magnates of the council and of the many complaints by others the King lately understood that in the counties of Nottingham, Leicester, and Derby, as well in the common ways as in the woods, numbers of robbers on horseback and on foot, were abroad so that no religious or other person could pass without being taken by them and spoiled of his goods, and perceiving that without extra force and stouter pursuit these could not be taken or driven from the counties he, after consultation with the council, paid to Reynold de Grey to attack them; and wereas the said Reynold had pursued them manfully and captured Roger Godberd, their leader and master, and delivered him to prison." Later we find the three counties enforcing a levy and collecting the sum of one hundred pounds to be paid by the Sheriffs to the Archbishop of York, who paid for the expedition. Note the absence of the county of Yorkshire.

The ballads are conclusive that Robin Hood was in Sherwood Forest, they tell of the Sheriff with Knights in great array trying to take the outlaws and failing, and place him in the period of 1265, before and after. The public records confirm this, but with the exception of Roger Godberd and his colleagues, no other outlaw is mentioned. Godberd has not come down in any Nottinghamshire legend; in no way is he connected with the "merry men of Sherwood". Most certainly *he* was not Robin Hood. So, who was? And who were the other outlaws of the legends?

ROBIN HOOD AND GUY OF GISBORNE, from an engraving by Thomas Bewick, *c.*1795, from Ritson's *Robin Hood.*

ALAN-A-DALE, as portrayed in *Robin Hood's Justice,* from *Thriller Comics Library.*

Chapter 6

OST of the characters associated with Robin Hood live only in the ballads and legend. There is insufficient evidence to go further than to accept the probability that they were real people. Others' existence can be proved, but their life spans have been taken out of their true periods and incorporated into the ballads by later writers. Queen Catherine is an obvious case in point, for in the ballad her husband is "King Henry". Henry V married Catherine, daughter of Charles VI of France, who reigned 1413-1422; much too late to be the King and Queen of the ballad. Henry VIII (1509-1547) married Catherine of Aragon, and both were present at a Maying where they saw "Robin Hood and his men" perform with bows and arrows. The seeming blunder in putting Queen Catherine in Robin's lifetime is seen to be the reverse — she was in fact linked with a May Games Robin Hood, of her own lifetime.

On of the first outlaws named is Will Scarlett, in *Robin Hood and the Monk:*

> S.63 "John, and Much, and Will *Scathlock*   *(Scarlet)*
> Forsooth as I you say,
> They slew our men upon the walls,
> And assault us every day."

In the *Little Geste of Robin Hood* he is one of the outlaws named and is with Robin Hood and Little John at the King's court after others of the band had gone away — returned to the forest.

> S.435 "By then the year was all agone,
> He had no men but twain,
> Little John and good Scathelock,
> With him all for to go."

Will Scarlet is not in the forest with Robin Hood and Little John when Robin decides he will go to Kirklees Nunnery for a bleeding. In *Robin Hood's Death* (1765) he is named as Scarlet, and counsels Robin not to go to Kirklees excepting he takes fifty men with him. In other ballads Will marries a princess, *Robin Hood and the Prince of Aragon* (S.54), where he is last seen running from the Sheriff's men, and *Robin Hood and Guy of Gisborne* (S.13), both already mentioned. Will claims to be Robin's nephew in *Robin Hood newly revived*, (1641-74): "In Maxfield was I bred and born, my name is young Gamwell," and "I am his (Robin's) own sister's son." In a variation of this ballad entitled *The Bold Pedlar and Robin Hood* (c.1846), he is given the name Gambol Gold by the ballad writer, and made out to be Robin's cousin, "You are my mother's own sister's son, what nearer cousins can we be?" says Robin. By oral tradition Scarlet is buried in Blidworth churchyard, but no report on the manner of his death has ever been found. Scathelocke is a nickname derived from "scathe" — to burn or harm, and "locke" meaning hair. Scarlet was a red head!

The name does not appear in the Household accounts of Edward II in which some claim to have found Robin Hood; it is somewhat strange that neither Scathelocke or Little John are included in these accounts although we are aware that Little John was another nickname. An outlaw who married a princess would be a well known story, or in written history, but we find no Scathelock or Gamwell among the nobles who were outlawed and restored to their former condition, sometimes more than once. We are left with the probability of Robin being a cousin or uncle to Will, both appelations being used for either case. The historian Camden reports of a family by the name of Gamwell (Gambol?) living in Yorkshire, one in particular who was a forester. Stukeley tried to fit this man into a pedigree of Robin Hood basing the claim on the ballad of *Robin's birth, breeding etc.* A family by the name of Gamlyn were seated in Lincolnshire; Gamelere held lands at Cuckney, Nottinghamshire for the purpose of shoeing the King's horses when he was in the area; this man died in 1160 without issue, but may have had relatives. These all point to the fact that Gamwell was not a name concocted for the ballad. In fact Gamston in Nottinghamshire was originally Gamelstune, and land was held by Gamel at the time of the Conquest. By Robin Hood's time it could have become Gamwell, and one married into the family. That Robin Hood did have a sister, Margaret, and possibly older than he, I shall show, along with a note on his brother Phillip who had a son William, born before 1282, and who married Johanna daughter of Adam, Lord Welle of Hellowe. William was summoned to Parliament in the seventeenth year of Edward II until the ninth year of Edward III, and died 1337 without issue. His family supported the Barons against Henry II, John, and Henry III but returned to the King's service. William would have been a boy when he met his uncle Robin — "a deft young man" as the ballad states.

Much, the miller's son, is considered to be the subject of a ballad *The King and the Miller*, in which Henry II and the Miller of Mansfield are the principal characters. Another dubious claim is that he was the Miller of Wakefield's son, who in answer to King Edward's question as to his identity, said, "Much is my father, and he is one of your tenants in the Kingsmill at Wakefield all on a green," whereupon the King replied, "Much be thou ever master of that mill, I will give it thee for thine inheritance." *Some outlaw!* Much was among the first outlaws named in (*Robin Hood and the Monk*), and a close companion of Robin. Robin's family, as shown later, held the manor of Bilborough from the time of Henry II to Edward II, including the mill on the Leen known as Boburmilne, now Bobbers Mill, close to Nottingham, and now within the City boundary. It is probable that Much was the son of the miller there. The name Much is derived from the Old English Mycel, Muchel and various spellings, meaning great; so we are faced with yet another nickname.

The Pindar of Wakefield who kept the pound on Wakefield Green was known as George o' Green, and is a character in ballads other than those of Robin Hood, and of the May Games:

> "The Pindar's valour, and how firm he stood,
> In the town's defence 'gainst the rebel *Robin Hood*
> How stoutly he behaved himself, and would
> In spite of Robin, bring his horse to fold
> His many May Games which were to be seen,
> Yearly presented upon Wakefield Green."
> (*A Stappado For The Devil*, 1615 — Richard Braithwaite.)

Samuel Butler, the author of "*Hudibras*" (1664), gives the following:

> "I am George o' Green, true leigeman to my King,
> King or Kaiser, none shall pass this way,
> Except King Edward."   (Edward II.)

George was known by the writer of the Sloane Manuscript, which includes a *Life of Robin Hood* and of the early 17th century, but has no place in the *Little Geste*. Although in the ballad *Jolly Pindar of Wakefield* (c.1663), George makes a promise after a fight with Robin, John, and Will.

> "At Michelmas next my cov'nant comes out,
> When everyone gather his fee,
> Then I'll take my blue blade in my hand
> And plod to the greenwood with thee."

We are left with the assumption that he joined the band. Nevertheless he is assumed to have been a real person, son of Geoffrey, a husbandman. Will Stutly, Alan-a-Dale, Right Hitting Brand, and David of Doncaster also are named in ballads, along with other outlaws, some in only one, but there are no clues by which identity can be attempted.

Gilbert with the White Hand is named as one of Robin's outlaws in the *Little Geste* (S.401) and is noted by Bishop Gawin Douglas in his *Palace of Honour* written before 1518:

> "There I saw Maitland upon old Beard Grey,
> Robin, and Gilbert with the White Hand,
> Whom Hay of Nauchton slew in Madin land."

In two editions of the *Little Geste* he is named Gilbert of the Lily White Hand — a symbol of purity. Perhaps a borrowing from Sir Galahad, "My strength is as the strength of ten because my heart is pure."

Little John, Maid Marian, and Friar Tuck are dealt with at length in later chapters, as their importance deserves.

Sir Roger of Doncaster, the favourite of the Prioress of Kirklees in the *Little Geste*, was a King's clerk who had business in religious houses all over the country, and was in Lenton Priory, near Nottingham, in the period of Robin Hood's outlawry. An entry in *The Calendar of Patent Rolls*, dated, at Westminster, 14 March 1270: "Mandate to Roger de Doncastre, King's clerk, Keeper of the Prior of Lenton to deliver the said priory to Matthew, late almoner at Lewes, appointed to be the prior thereafter by Ivor, Abbott of Cluny." That he should be termed "Sir" in the *Little Geste* is questioned by some writers who suggest that it was common for ballad singers to give titles where they did not exist. To omit the title in the *Calendar of Patent Rolls* as above was commonplace. Of the 60,255 Knights' fees in England during the reign of Henry III, almost half were held by the clergy!

Dodsworth (16th century) and Dugdale (17th century), in their *Monistcons* name the Prioress of Kirklees in the 13th century as Elizabeth de Staynton, whose gravestone is still to be seen, badly mutilated, with the words carved around a now vanished cross on a *three step calvary* — "Sweet Jesus of Nazareth have mercy upon the soul of one, Elizabeth Staynton late prioress of this house." She is not mentioned by name in any of the ballads. More of the Prioress in Chapter Fourteen.

Guy of Gisborne, styled in the ballad as *Sir*, may, according to some, have come from a market town in the West Riding of Yorkshire by the name of Gisburn. These, though, appear not to have knowledge of a man of the same name holding lands in Derbyshire and Staffordshire, who *was* named Guy of Gisborne, they state only that a family by the name of Gisburn "may have" lived in Yorkshire. The Knight of Derbyshire and Staffordshire is the most likely candidate, although with no more than the name I have only the proof that one bearing it did live. A Derbyshire family named Gisborne are said to claim a pedigree showing descent from Sir Guy, and there is a Gisborn Arms Inn in Derby. In the ballad *Robin Hood's Birth, Breeding, etc.*, Robin Hood's mother is Joan, niece to a Coventry Knight, whom people call Sir Guy. He is easily identified through the remark which follows — "For he slew the Blue Boar that hangs up at the gate, or mine host at the bull tells a lie." He was the legendary Sir Guy of Warwick. His story is that of a Saxon, sometimes Norman, who did brave deeds all for the love of Felice, the Earl of Warwick's daughter, whom he eventually won in marriage as a reward for his prowess. His most famous deed was the slaying of the dun cow on Dunsmore Heath between Rugby and Coventry, not a blue boar, so mine host did lie. Bones from the said beast were later exhibited in many places.

In the same ballad, Robin's mother is the sister of George Gamwell of Gamwell Hall, Nottinghamshire, of whom no record exists. On Gamwell himself: "A noble housekeeper was, ay, as ever broke bread in sweet Nottinghamshire, and a squire of famous degree." The ballad then relates how he held open house for any who called — food and wine was offered, and he had his own musicians and entertainers in residence. The ballad was printed in 1650 and George Camwell appears to have been a maintainer of outlaws, of whom there were many.

In 1590, Sir William Holles died at Haughton, Nottinghamshire, and is buried in the local church. He was known as the good Lord of Haughton for his display of hospitality. No one was ever turned away from his door, and during *Christmas* he held open house, providing food, shelter, and entertainment to all-comers without question.

> S.16   "But not a man here, shall taste my March beer,
>   Till a *Christmas* carol he sing;"

One is tempted to suggest that the ballad, based on a May Game, has material borrowed from both fact and fiction, and of the former is the good Lord of Haughton, portrayed as Robin's uncle. There is no suggestion of Robin or Little John being outlaws in the ballad, although Robin has a band of yeoman in Sherwood Forest.

Robin Hood's main protagonist in the legend is the Sheriff of Nottingham. Like the Pope and King, this rank was carried by successive noblemen for many centuries. The Sheriff lived at the Red Lodge, on what is now Angel Row in the market place of Nottingham; the ballad *Robin Hood and the Potter* relates this without actually naming the house. The known Sheriffs during Robin's time, according to the *Pipe Rolls* were as follows:

1235 - 54	Robert de Vavasour, Lord of Bilborough.
1236 - 40	High fitz Ralph.
1260	Simon de Asselacton (Aslockton).
1264 - 65	John de Grey.
1266	William de Grey.
1278	Reginald de Grey.
1290	Sir Gervasse Clifton.

Robert de Vavasour seems to be an error, and he appears to have been appointed twice, 1235 to 1236, and 1240 to 1254. Strangely enough we find in the Rolls: ''On the 31 (1247) Henry III the King committed to Robert de Vavasour, Sheriff of Nottingham, the manors of Clipstone, Retford, and several others to hold during his pleasure.'' Clearly, he must have served twice. John le Gray was appointed Sheriff of Nottingham and Derbyshire on 14 April 1264, and was re-appointed 8 August 1265. He was, clearly, a loyalist.

In 1278 Reginald de Gray was appointed Sheriff of Nottingham and Governor of Nottingham Castle. Between 1270 and 1272, whilst he was Justice of Chester he captured the outlaw Roger Godberd, and in 1266 and 1267, waged war on the rebels in Sherwood Forest. The dating of Godberd's capture varies but it would seem the earlier date is correct, and the later date that of the entry in the Rolls. This is frequently seen. In 1266 William de Gray was Sheriff of Nottingham. He was another Sheriff who was clearly a loyalist, and as one who waged war on the outlaws in Sherwood Forest, would be good enough reason for Robin Hood to tell his men to bear him in mind. Outlaws were active in Sherwood Forest and the Nottingham area but no leader is named except by tradition. What history has not supplied, tradition and legend has, for as already shown ''this was the most turbulent part of England.'' A rabble would be a mere nuisance, but a band of men who could fight off the Sheriff's well-equipped posse, and cause considerable losses, must have been well organised under a leader. We cannot write off one without the other; and the Sheriffs and their activity against the outlaws *is* written down, in Public Records.

Of the other characters named in the ballads, Sir Richard at the Lee, the impoverished Knight of the *Little Geste,* plays a big part, but I cannot agree with those who say that he was a Lancashire Knight. In the ballad, he is stopped by Little John, Much the miller's son, and Will Scarlet, whilst travelling through the forest, and invited to dine with their master. On asking who is their master and being told ''Robin Hood'', he remarks ''of him I have heard much good'' and well he may for he was holding lands at Leigh within three miles of Loxley, Staffordshire, where Robin lived for a period. Later, after he had dined, he is asked by Robin if he is a Knight of force or else of yeomanry, and replies: ''A hundred years my ancestors Knights have been.'' The *Staffordshire Rolls* reveal that — ''In the reign of Edward I, Richard de Lee, in court proved that his ancestors were granted the rights of food, ale, and gallows at Fulford. The manor of Fulford was granted to his ancestors in the reign of King John by the Prior of Great Malvern. Sir Richard held lands and manors at Forebridge, the town of Lees Billington, Berlaston, Aston, Swindon, and many other places.'' In 1236, during King Henry III's reign, William de la Lee held one Knight's fee in Beeston, near Nottingham, and lands in Gedling (within Sherwood Forest) of the honour of Chartley. Sir Richard, as his heir, inherited these lands and manors. William de la Lee, held Aston for one Knight's fee. Margaret, wife of William de la Lee, sued Richard her son, for dower lands in Hanyard in the reign of Edward I.

To continue the ballad story, Sir Richard is unable to pay for the meal Robin has set for him as ''he has only ten shillings on his person,'' and upon being asked why a Knight is so impoverished he makes the reply — ''I have a son forsooth Robin that should have been my heir, when he was twenty years old, in field would joust full fair. He slew a Knight of Lancaster and a squire bold, for to save him in his right my goods both *set* and sold'' (*mortgaged*). To save his son, he had borrowed £400 from the Abbott of St. Mary's Abbey, York, giving his lands as security. The day for repayment is nearly upon him and he is on the way to the abbey to ask for a *longer day* (more time to pay), or be allowed to work it off. The son's crime is established in the *Staffordshire Rolls* — ''Robert de la Lee, son of Richard de la Lee was outlawed (*before*) 1275 for felony; the prior of St. Thomas, Staffordshire, did bring a hue and cry after him and took possession of his lands.'' Details of the crime are given in a later entry and a further entry shows that John, son of Robert de la Lee, makes a plea for possession of his father's lands, the date being 1275, which explains my reason for placing the crime before that year.

Robert's crime as entered in the *Staffordshire Rolls,* is almost the same as that related in the *Little Geste* by Sir Richard at the Lee: ''Robert de la Lee, and his son, Roger, and thirteen others have taken Thomas de Wyshawe of the manor of Maddeleye, and Alexander, his groom, from Robert Staundon, the coroner. Thomas de Wyshawe had murdered Ralph de Frend and John, his groom, on the road from Newcastle under Lynne. Robert de la Lee, his son Roger, with William Frend and John Frend took *Thomas and his squire* from the King's bailiff, beheaded them and carried the heads into Cheshire. For this they were outlawed.''

After hearing the Knight's story, Robin and his men lend him £400 to be repaid twelvemonth hence, and equip him with clothing, horse, and spurs (Little John's personal gift) befitting a Knight. The guarantor named and accepted is 'Our Lady', who has helped the Knight before. This Robert, and Richard, his father, are the men of the ballad. The £400 may be an exaggeration, although history tells of a Jew *lending* King John 10,000 marks — £6,666.13.4d! Barons who supported insurrection against King John and then returned to the King's allegiance when Henry III took the throne, paid the sum of £100; the same sum was paid for the relief of inheritance, and less by a Knight.

That monastries acquired lands by the lending of money and distraining on non-payers is shown by Dr. Coulton in his *Scottish Abbeys and Social life:* "The monks seem to have largely engaged in money lending, and we constantly find them taking lands and tenements in satisfaction of loans which they had made to people in their necessity. Adam, a burgess of Glasgow, transferred his property, lying in the street of fishers below the bridge over the Clyde, for a sum of money to the Abbott of Paisley, to enable him to discharge his obligations." Thomas de Multon of St. Mary's Abbey, York, was a notorious moneylender. In 1338 he claimed against John Green, Thomas the parson of St. Edward's church, Walmgate, York, and Richard le Horner of York, a debt of £22. 13s. 4d.

The ballad story has a ring of truth as Sir Richard would travel through Sherwood on the way to York, but there is no evidence in the rolls of him losing all his lands.

Sir Richard, after paying the abbott his due, says "Had thou been courteous at my coming rewarded would'st thou have been" — the Abbott had kept the Knight kneeling too long for his dignity. His reference to reward was in the fact that usury was not practised in England except where the loan was made to a foreigner; the usual way of payment was to add a sum of money as a gift, to the loan. Nothing is more facetiously told than the *repayment* of the Knight's debt to Robin. The ballad relates how the Knight is delayed in bringing his payment plus 100 bows and sheaves of arrows as a gift whilst, in the meantime, Robin's men stop two monks of St. Mary's Abbey in the forest. Robin believes that they are "Our Lady's messengers", bringing the £400 he lent to the Knight "in Her name." Although the monks claim they have little money a search brings forth over £800. "Our Lady has overtold the loan by £400" says Robin. The monks are dined, and thanked for their service, and go on their way to London, somewhat disgruntled.

Upon the Knight's arrival he explains his delay to Robin, who will not take the money offered, because "Our Lady" has already sent it; and he bids Little John pay the Knight the "£400 Our Lady overtold to me", via her servants.

At a shooting match in Nottingham the Sheriff betrays Robin and his band. Making good their escape they are followed by the Sheriff's men, and Little John is injured in the knee. He is carried by Much, the miller's son, "and bears him well a mile" until they came unto "a fair castle a little within the wood", and the gates are thrown wide open by Sir Richard at the Lee, who will not give up his friends at the Sheriff's demand until he has the King's will in the matter. In England there were 1115 castles in the reign of Henry III, of which many would be fortified manors. The manor of Beeston was the castle of the ballad as we have already seen.

Such support for outlaws was common. "Richard Foliot of Fenwick was accused of harbouring the leaders of the band of outlaws of Sherwood. Richard had been active on the baronial side in the war 1264-5, and was an important person", from the district Close Rolls 1268-1272 *(Welsh Wars of Edward I,* J.E. Morris). Although the claim is made by some that Richard at the Lee came from Leigh in Lancashire, a look at any map will show that there was no way would he pass from there through Sherwood (or Barnsdale in Yorkshire) to get to York.

The Bishop of Hereford, another saga figure, is named in two ballads, *Robin Hood and the Bishop of Hereford* and *Robin Hood and Queen Catherine,* and in both instances he is a rotter. J.E. Morris, again in his *Welsh Wars of Edward I,* states that "The Bishop of Hereford, Peter Digue Blanche, was the first victim of the Barons war, 1263".

There are three kings involved in the ballads and legend. King Henry III, in whose reign the outlaws were active, and his brother Richard, King of the Germans, who sustained the rebels for a while, as did his nephew, Prince Edward. At the battle of Evesham they were both on the King's side. Henry was a weak King and for some time "King Richard" was regent of England. Neither of these Kings are named in the *Little Geste* but we do get references to "the King" and "Our comely King Edward". The word "comely" is interpreted by some in its modern form *handsome,* and used together with the *travels* made by the King prove that it was Edward II. In truth, King Edward's *travels* through Lancashire were not as some of these writers claim; see Chapter Four, and the supporting evidence. The word "comely", 1300 to 1420, meant *excellent, stately, befitting*. Up to the year 1500 it was applied in courtesy to those of noble station — especially Kings and Jesus Christ (sometimes God, to whom only the King came second). It also was used to mean proper and seemly, and would apply to ANY King, and there is no justifiable evidence to apply it *only* to Edward II. In fact, Edward IV was considered to be England's most handsome king in his time. Our Comely King Edward may have been a courtesy title or simply "our *rightful (proper, seemly)* King Edward", or any other. Although Edward was active as Prince in later years, these deeds would be attributed to *King Edward*.

Above: A 14th century miller and his windmill from the *Lutterell Psalter* (1335-40).

Above right: THE SHERIFF OF NOTTINGHAM of the period.

Right: *WILL SCARLET'S BLUFF. (Reproduced by courtesy of Nottingham Local Studies Library).*

KINGS — Fact and fiction

EDWARD I (1239-1307). The "comely King Edward" of the *Little Geste,* he was prince until 1272 but, as the ballad was written after his death, he was referred to as King. He has been described as "the best of our kings".

HENRY III. King of England from 1216 to 1272, he faced strong baronial opposition led by Simon de Montfort. A bronze effigy, made by William Torel is in Westminster Abbey. Henry was a weak king and for some time his brother Richard, King of Germany, was regent of England.

RICHARD I. Known as "Richard the Lionheart", he was associated in legend as the King who gave Robin Hood his pardon. The "King Richard" of the ballads was really the brother of Henry III.

JOHN, from Matthew Paris' *Chronicle.* In popular legend, together with Richard I, John is the King most usually associated with Robin Hood.

MAID MARIAN by David Porter. From a series of paintings commissioned by *The Granary*, Edwinstowe. *(Reproduced by courtesy of Lada Tvrdik).*

Chapter 7

*"A bonny fine maid of worthy degree, Maid Marian called by name,
Did live in the north, of excellent worth, for she was a gallant dame."*

17th century ballad

AID Marian has no part in the early ballads. The earliest mention of her is in Alexander
Barclay's *Eclogues* published in 1508:

> "Yet would I hear some merry *fit*.   (song)
> Of Maid Marian, or else of Robin Hood."

George Peele (1558-1597), in his play — *Edward I* quotes:

> "Why, so I see, my mates of old,
> All were not tales that *beldames* told,   (Old women)
> Of Robin Hood and Little John,
> Friar Tuck and Maid Marian."

Neither of these writers pair Robin and Marian; the former showing them as characters in separate
conditions and, if we interpret "or else" for *"failing that"*, he shows a preference for a song of Maid
Marian. The latter pairs her with Friar Tuck, a situation which endured for many years.

Marian first became associated with Robin Hood in two plays written in the late 16th century, and
published in 1601, by Arthur Munday and Henry Chettle. The first was *The Downfall of Robert Earl
of Huntingdon,* afterwards called, "Robin Hood of Merry Sherwood: with his love for *chaste* Matilda,
the Lord FitzWalter's daughter, afterwards *his* fair Maid Marian", and the second being *The Death of
Robert, Earl of Huntingdon,* otherwise called "Robin Hood of Merry Sherwood, with the lamentable
tragedy of *chaste* Matilda, *his* fair Maid Marian, poisoned at Dunmow by King John". The accent on
the words *chaste* and *his* are mine, for reasons I aim to exploit and I ask the reader to bear them well
in mind. Also note that the stories are of The Earl of Huntingdon, not a pretended Earl as Stukeley claimed,
or a yeoman raised to the peerage for services rendered as others would have it. The expression "his
Maid Marian" is not without significance, but suggestive of an earlier known Maid Marian. This is
supported by some of the dialogue:

> "Nay, no more honour, I pray thee, Little John
> Henceforth I will be called Robin Hood,
> Matilda shall be *my Maid Marian.*"

That the name was already familiar is, clearly, shown in the lines:

> "First no man must presume to call me master,
> By name of earl, lord, baron, knight or squire,
> But simply by the name of Robin Hood,
> That fair Matilda henceforth change her name
> And by *Maid Marian's name* be only called."

Not only is Marian a well-known historical character, but also famed for her chastity, a theme which
runs through the plays:

> "This youth that leads yon *virgin* by the hand
> Is our Earl Robert, or your Robin Hood."

And even at rehearsals, the ladylike virtues of our maid were not lost sight of. Normally a boy would
play the part but this being a play for the King's court, a girl is used and was quite usual:

> "Faith little Tracey, you are somewhat forward,
> What! *Our* Maid Marian leaping like a lad."

Nor are the titles of the plays the only time the definitive article is used for Maid Marian, giving proof
that she was a character of plays and May Games of some standing, well-known by the early 16th century
and, as we shall see, long before.

Whereas Chettle and Munday name her as Matilda, whose name is changed upon entering the Forest
of Sherwood, in truth the reverse is the case. The "Maid Marian" was originally portrayed as the

81

personification of the Blessed Virgin Mary, who Robin idolised and worshipped. The character then became degraded, evolving over a period of time and eventually embodied in the "Matilda". Thankfully though, in legend, Marian has survived as the sweetheart of Robin Hood, and this author would not wish it otherwise.

Both she and Robin were traditional figures in the Medieval Summer Festivals, in particular in the May Games, and also somewhat loosely associated with the Morris dance, although in this, Marian does not actually dance. The Morris is described by Dr. Samuel Johnson in his 18th century dictionary as "consisting of ten men who danced besides *the* Maid Marian, and one who played upon the pipe and tabor".

Blount, writing on this dance, suggests that the Morris is derived from the word Morisco, a Moor; and also a dance, so called, wherein there were usually five men, and a boy dressed in girl's habit, whom they called *the* Maid Marian. A tract from the time of Queen Elizabeth the First states: "Quintessence beside the fool and *the* Maid Marian, of all picked youth, footing the morris around the maypole".

In the Abbotts Bromley Horn Dance, which is not a Morris, the man-woman is *a* Maid Marian and appears to have been attached in Tudor times together with a boy dressed in green, carrying a bow and arrow which he keeps snapping at the hobby horse. He is called Robin Hood. The Maid Marian does not dance, but carries a curious collecting ladle which is considered a phallic symbol. The last time that I saw the dance performed, the ladle had been replaced with a collecting box.

Joseph Strutt, in his Antiquities (1776), writes: "Besides all this they used to make mock processions, with various pageants etc., amongst which was usually *the* Maid Marian, who was represented by boy, habited like a woman, and he walked with a mincing step to imitate a woman's gait". In his *Sports and Pastimes of the English People* (1800), he says "Robin Hood presided as Lord of May, and a female, or rather perhaps, a boy habited like a female, called *the* Maid Marian, his faithful mistress, was the Lady of May". Later, "the King was disused and *the* Maid Marian was sole sovereign of Queen of the May". It appears that the Lady of May (note the change) was sometimes carried in procession on men's shoulders; for Bernard Bateman, speaking of the Pope and his ceremonies states that He is carried on the backs of four deacons "after the manner of carrying whyte pot queens in western May Games".

Although Strutt describes the whyte pot Queens as a fancy cake, accepting that *the* Maid Marian was played by a servant girl, the term can be deduced from the *Oxford English Dictionary* that Whyte, or white, is Whit, and Pot, meaning liquor, drink; in fact, "Whit(suntide) Ales Queens". The *ales* being the revels where plenty of that beverage was consumed, as well as other merry making. It was the beginning of the degrading of the *chaste* Maid Marian.

The *Oxford English Dictionary* refers to six writers who mention *the* Maid Marian in their works, of similar dates to those given, but not included here. Indeed, to list the number of times reference is made to *the* Maid Marian would be tedious to the reader but the evidence of a personage outside of the Robin Hood story, and of long standing, is overwhelming.

From the various notes made by early historians, it is clear that the Games were not restricted to the month of May; far less May Day; so that either the word May is used loosely or has a *different meaning*. As applied to fifth month of the year it is derived from the Latin Maius, itself coming from the Sanskrist word meaning growth meaning to grow, as being the growing or shooting month. Another translation of the word May is Maia, mother of Mercury (of Roman myth) or Hermes (of Greek myth). These different versions can be found in several Encyclopaedia, but not both in one edition. The association of May (games) with *the* Maid Marian suggests that they were becoming pagan rites.

E.L. Hargreaves, in her book *Festivals, Holidays, and Saints Days,* (1915), states that "The Catholic church has dedicated the month of May to the Blessed Virgin Mary. Of course the Catholic dedication of May to the Virgin mother contains reminder of the Purification and honour due to chastity". In the Catholic hymnary She is honoured in several hymns as "Queen of the May". This is fact, but at some time over the years occurred the substitution of the real meaning of the word May. Of the twelve months in the English (Christian) Calendar, four months are dedicated to Roman Gods Janus, Mars, Maia and Junius; two to Roman Emporers, Julius and Augustus; one to seedtime, Aperire; one to a Roman Festival, Februa; and four by the numerical order in the old calendar. Strange that only one should be re-dedicated to a Christian. The fact is that the term May as applied to festivals comes from the Anglo-Saxon *maeg* — meaning, May, Maiden, Maid, Virgin.

In the pre-Reformation times the peoples feasts, frolics, and plays were associated with, or applied to, religious observances. The progression was Pagan, Christian, Moralities, Peoples' Festivals, with overtones of the earlier forms just as they are today. That is apart from the church festivals or, more accurately, the same festivals as celebrated by the church, For instance there are many who never give a thought to St. Nicholas, Bishop of Myra, patron saint of children and sailors whose Day is December 6th, but now appears as Santa Claus on December 24th. His day is observed by the church on its original date but few people would know very much of him or how the people created a new character over the years which is but a *faint echo* of the original.

This then is the case of *the* Maid Marian, Queen of the May (Virgins). She is a faint echo of *the* Blessed Virgin Mary who was adored in the festivals from which the May Games sprang, and the fact that she is a chaste and pure personality is never lost sight of. It is in this context that Barclay mentions her, although he may not have been aware of it — he preferred songs of her, to those of Robin Hood. It was also in this context and from a similar source that Chettle and Munday introduced *the* and/or *his* Maid Marian into their plays, and they never lost sight of the fact that she was a virgin. In one scene, Robin is asked by the Lord FitzWalter, who has met Robin and Marian in the forest, and who is posing as a blind beggar; why Matilda has changed her name? He is given the answer:

"Because she lives a spotless maiden life
And shall till Robin's outlaw life have end."

The term "spotless maiden" is another way of saying *virgin*. Two antiquarians, Thomas Percy of the 18th century, and Francis Douce in the 19th century, each refer to Maid Marian as Robin's concubine or paramour, for no other reason that, at least in the latter case, he was using the original meaning of the word — paramour, *a sweet innocent love, a great devotion.* (Middle English.)

If Robin has a characteristic which sets him apart from all other outlaw heroes it is his special devotion to the Virgin Mary. He loved Her above all other women, and for Her sake would do no harm — or permit others to so do — to any woman, or a man in a woman's company. She was his protector; his guarantor for a loan made to the gentle Knight. By the might of the mild Mary he would take all manner of risks, and when fighting with Sir Guy of Gisborne to the "utterance" and falling over a root, he faced death. His appeal to Our Lady, "who art both Mother and May" was heard, and he won the day. She was his forest Paramour, and Mother and May — ample evidence that *May* meant VIRGIN! It may seem sacrilege to make such a statement, but in the early Christian plays and pageants enacted at the great festivals, men appeared in the roles of Bible personages — even God.

J. Charles Fox in his edition of Strutt's *Sports and Pastimes* writes: "At Candle Mass (The feast of the Purification of the Blessed Virgin Mary) a man in woman's dress represented the Virgin Mary and carried what might seem to be a baby in his arms". The remark all but mirrors that of Blount. According to Lewis Spence in *Myth and Ritual in Dance, Game and Rhyme:* "In the procession of Corpus Christi, instituted by Pope Urban IV in 1263, the Children of May (young maidens) carried a figure representing the Vigo Immaculata, and others. Maid Marian, I take it, is merely a later and more elaborated form of the Maid May — that is the Maiden of May — the spirit of the burgeoning season; nor can I see any reason why the simple and natural explanation should be set aside". If we were to accept the belief that May means the month then this statement could be accepted but it clearly does not! When Robin appealed to Our Lady she is described as "Mother and May". In no way can we take this as a reference to Maia, mother of Hermes; mother and Maia would not make sense. *Mother and Virgin does.* May, Maiden and maid all have the same meaning: *virgin* and *maiden,* being specific to the Virgin Mary.

"In spite of the claims that the name Marian did not appear in England until the 16th century, it appears to have passed unnoticed that the first recorded use of the name Marian was in the Yorkshire Poll Tax of 1379." In spite of this find by Valentine-Harris, he, along with others, does not seem to have had knowledge of an earlier and more important record of the name.

In the Mercian (Nottingham was part of Old Mercia) and Northumberland version of the Gospel according to St. Luke, edited by W.W. Skeat (1835-1912), appears the following, which is reproduced in both its original form, and the transcipt: "And hie efstende comon, and gemetton Marian and Ioseph and thaet cild on binne alegd." ("And they came hastening and found Mary and Joseph and the child laid in a manger.")

In the Apostles' Creeds, of King Stephen (1135-1154), we have ''born of the maid Mary'', and of Richard II (1377-1399), it was ''and of the Maiden Marie, man was born, without sinful seed''. And the creed of Edward III (1327-1377), ''That begotten was of the Holy Ghost, Born of the virgine Marie, without lust''.

The Anglo-Saxon version may exist that shows man was born of the maeg, or Maegden Marian, without lust, for *the* Maid Marian was a representation of the Virgin Mary who, in post-Reformation times under the puritans, was degraded as Popish, and even further. Only in the peoples' festivals was there no deliberate lowering of her; it was the fact that in their merry-making the people lost sight of both the Christian and pagan roots of their delights. In fact, if we were told we are pagans because we trim the house at Christmas or give fancy eggs at Easter, we would take umbrage, as society accepts both festivals as those of Our Saviour, with some exceptions. The spirit of these pursuits is seen in William Simpson's *Vow Breaker* (1636), where one character, who wants to play the hobby horse in the games, or dance, says: ''Am I not going to buy ribbons and toys (nick nacks, trinkets, gee gaws) of Saint Usurla for *the* Maid Marian''. He has already practised his capers, pirouettes, and prances and well able to perform, and the gift seems to be an added reason of equal substance.

Usurla was a British Virgin Saint and Martyr, said to be an English princess who, with 11,000 virgins, set out on a pilgrimage, but she was compelled by a fierce storm to take refuge in Cologne and was there put to death, along with her following, by an army of Huns. Surely such presents would not be for a lesser person than the sweet Usurla, and the great company that died with her. Nor would it seem that the presents were for a person: we have no note of the boys playing the part of the Virgin Mary or Maid Marian being adorned. It seems in this case an image (or a maypole) is the subject. As the games became more paganised and the religious significance lost, they became more bawdy, rough, and heathen, and eventually were condemned by churchmen and corporation of town and city, but lived on in another form.

Pastor Hall of King's Norton, in a pamphlet of 1660, writes: ''Flora, hold up thy hands! Thou art here indicted by the name of Flora, of the City of Rome, in the County of Babylon, for that thou art contrary to the peace of our sovereign lord, his crown and dignity — has brought a pack of practical fanatics; viz, ignorants, atheists, papists, drunkards, swearers, swash bucklers, *maid marians,* morris dancers, mummers, maypole stealers etc.''. Tough speaking, but *the* Maid Marian has yet to suffer even more degradation.

''Later the maypole was not from a tree which was cut down annually, but became a permanent fixture of the ceremony; in certain areas too, the spirit which was anciently believed to be ensouled in it or immanent in it, was conceived as separate or detached from the tree. In some cases it was represented as a doll or puppet; at others as a living person. Thus English children were in the habit of decorating their May Day hoops of flowers with a doll, which was called ''The Lady of May'' (Lewis Spence). Philip Stubbs, in his *Anatomy of Abuses* (1595), condemns the maypole as ''stinking idol around which they fall to banqueting and feasting, to leaping and dancing about it, as the heathen people did at the dedication of their gods''.

The maypole and the flowered hoops live on, and the spirit which ''was anciently believed to be ensouled in it'' forgotten, but it is still there! The history can be traced. Flora, the pagan Goddess of the Romans, the Blessed Virgin Mary (Madonna) in Christian processions and miracle plays. *the* Maid Marian in semi-christian revels, and today, the May Queen and her maidens are young girls; Mary, according to tradition, was only fourteen years of age when she gave birth to Jesus.

Chambers', *Book of Days: Vol 1 — A miscellany of antiquaries* (1864), gives considerable reference to the May Games worthy of note — ''A woman recalling her trip to France with her mother where she saw under a Gothic arch of an old church porch a narrow step raised and covered with palms. A living being, or a statue, dressed in a white robe, crowned with flowers, was seated upon it, in her right hand she held a leafy branch, a canopy above her head was formed of a garland of box, and ample draperies which fell each side encircled her in their snowy folds. The mother said 'She is the May'. The Virgin of May, the Virgin of lovely days, flowers and green branches. See her beg of the passers by, by asking 'For the May', later to be spent on the activities''. The same book contains several other references: ''The children carried a doll dressed in white which beyond all doubt represented the Virgin Mary, and went back to an earlier period''. ''They were dressed in white with veils, and no doubt a little bewildered at all that was happening and why they should be called *Mays*. Thus we have mirrored in France our own custom minus the May Day hoop.''

Nor did our May Queen join in the revelry of her subjects. She was placed in a sort of bower, or arbour, near to the maypole, there to sit in pretty state, an object of admiration for all the village. In the French revels I find no mention of Robin Hood or one who could be taken for him, but in England he definitely took his part and was accompanied by Little John and other outlaws, followed by *the* Maid Marian and her two bridesmaids, in one instance reported.

The author has experiences of attending several Mayings, some with side-shows, skittles, archery, and other games; the village band playing; and the procession led from the village hall by a young fellow who can just blow a tune on the bugle, the crowning with the new queen sitting on a raised dias with her attendants and their hoops of flowers; and last year's queen doing the honours; then the Maypole dancing, but the Queen does not dance.

Thus was the Virgin Mary . . . later *the* Maid Marian and, along with the girls who are chosen to be the May Queen, adored by the people. In the former case until during the reign of Queen Elizabeth the first, the puritans made considerable havoc among the May Games with their preaching and invectives. Poor Maid Marian was assimilated to the *great whore of Babylon,* and Friar Tuck was deemed a remnant of Popery; the hobby horse an impious and pagan superstition, and they were at length most completely put to rout as the bitterest enemies of religion.

In 1847, Gutch wrote in his book, *The Robin Hood Garlands and Ballads* — "King James *Book of Sports* restored the lady and the hobby horse; but during the Commonwealth they were again attacked by a set of new fanatics; and together with the May Festivities, Whitsuntide Ales etc., they were degraded in many parts of England''. In fact *the* Maid Marian was not only changed in character but also in name, the full meaning of which is given above — whore! *Horne's Year Book* tells us, "After the decline of *the* Maid Marian, the Morris degenerated into a piece of coarse buffoonery and in this she was personated by a clown. This once elegant Queen of the May obtained the name of Malkin!''

To illustrate the process in more detail, I here pause to offer the reader further examples, and ask myself why they have been ignored by other researchers:
* In the *Oxford English Dictionary* the words Malkin, Mawkin, or Maut, are described as *Maid Marian* (obsolete), and Malkin, Mawking 1275-1362 *c.*1440 Prompt Parv 232/2. Proper name Matilda.
* From *The Horace Walpole Letters* (1740): "The first thing I beheld was a mawkin in a chair with three footmen, and a label on the breast inscribed Lady Mary''.
* M. Thomas Fletcher, quoted by *Oxford English Dictionary:* "You must turn tippet, put on the shape of order and humanity or you must marry Malkin, the May Lady.''
* In *Henry IV, Part One,* Shakespeare has Falstaff say: "There is no more faith in thee than in a stewed prune; nor more truth in thee than in a drawn fox, and for womanhood, Maid Marian may be the deputy's wife of the ward to thee. Go you thing''.
* Again, another Dictionary describes the degraded Maid Marian as the Malkin, the lady of May, is also described as, "a dirty, lewd woman, (malkin) a diminutive of Matilda or Maud; a vulgar drudge or scullion in name and condition''.
* In a modern English Dictionary Malkin is given as, "Mawkin — a slovenly woman, a cat, a hare M.E. diminutive of Maalde, Matilda. The name, Mathilda, Latin form of the Germanic name; O.E. Maethilde; second element of which means battle maiden; first element is obscure''.

The development of the name is also explained in *On the origins of Waltzing Matilda,* by Harry Hastings Pearce (1971), printed in Australia and available in England. It can be seen here that their Matilda can be related to our Maid Marian, although by 1770 and after Cook and Flinders had made their explorations and New World settlement began, Maid Marian was the chaste young lady we know today — Robin Hood's sweetheart.

So looking at it through Australian eyes — *Waltz* is a slang word formed to describe the roving of tramps around the country; hence "Uaf der Walz'' — "on the tramp''. I have no knowledge of familiar useage in England. *Mathilda,* as in the Old English, means "mighty battle maid'' and has several forms, Mathilde, Mechtild, Matilde and breaks down to *Mat* with the meaning carpet, blanket, cover, waterproof sheet as foil or protection against the ground; and Hilde (Old German), Amazon. In fact, the blanket-roll carried by swagmen in Australia. In English dictionary — Matilda, a bushman's swag or bundle. The term bag is used in English slang for an unattractive woman — or a loose woman.

Pearce, who interviewed tramps as well as German settlers and authorities on the German language in Australia and Germany, states the *Kundenshickse* in vagabond slang is *Mathilda* or *Matilda,* and is derived from *"Kund"* — *vagabond* and *schickse* — a woman on the waltz — in fact a tramp's baggage! A camp follower! A prostitute!

Pearce also goes on to show the development of this meaning. Mechtild, as already seen, was used at one time for Matilda, and in medieval times gave rise to a shortened form *metze* or *mezze,* a pet form of the proper female name:
1. Derived from Mahtilt, Mahthilt, Mathilda, earliest known use of a pet name in the 11th century.
2. Peasant girl or hand maiden.
3. Then used for a married woman.
4. Girl who is wooed.
5. Then dishonourable, meaning concubine or mercenary of soldier or priest.
6. Frivolous woman, or prostitute.
7. Prostitute, whore!

Nicholas Manuel, Swiss painter and poet, is also quoted by Pearce:

> "You will be just the girl for me,
> I should have metze too,
> Because I cannot cook myself,
> Especially in a foreign country."

In the 18th century, the first ballad of *Robin Hood and Maid Marian* appeared in print in Ritson's *Robin Hood* (1795), from Anthony-a'-Wood's copy (1632-95). It is no more than a foolish ditty, but she is restored from then on to the chaste young lady we know today.

Dr. Joseph Hunter in his *Robin Hood* states "Her name was Matilda, and the ballad testimony is (not the *Little geste,* but other ballads of uncertain antiquity) that the outlaw's wife was named Matilda which name she exchanged for Marian when she joined Robin in the greenwood". In this manner he claims Robin Hood to be one of the men of that name entered in Wakefield Manor Court Rolls who had a wife name Matilda.

There is no such ballad of antiquity that I have found and Hunter may well have been misled by an excerpt from the plays of Chettle and Munday. The only ballad, of little merit, is quoted by J.W. Walker in his *True History of Robin Hood* (1952). This is compounded from *Robin Hood and Maid Marian,* and *Robin Hood's Birth, Breeding, Valour, and Marriage,* in which the name Maid Marian is changed to Matilda in the first stanza of the former, and her dress is described from that of Clorinda . . . and Robin Hood's mother in the latter! The verses are taken literally from these two ballads with the addition of some of the writers own doing and although he is relating the adventures of Robin and Matilda he ends up with the last two lines of the final stanza of *Robin Hood and Maid Marian.*

> "For the people that live in the north can tell,
> Of MARIAN and brave Robin Hood."

The writer should have used more care, and Walker himself should have checked the source before using this as evidence that Maid Marian bore the name Matilda *before* she joined Robin Hood and his merry men in Sherwood Forest. He might also have thought more carefully about Hunter's claim to Robin and Marian being Yorkshire folk. There is little doubt that this ballad which appears only in Walker's book is concocted to fit the theory.

There are her three good examples to illustrate that the Maid Marian was no such simple Yorkshire lass. In on 14th century Flemish woodcut, Maid Marian is portrayed in the dress of a lady of the period and she is standing within a tree, holding a ball, or something similar, in her right hand. This is reproduced in *The Robin Hood Garland and Ballads,* by John Matthew Gutch, F.S.A. (1847 edition, reprint). The picture is entitled — "Ancient Morris Dance". She is surrounded with dancers, musician, fool, and a dog!

Tollet's painted window (which is assigned by Douce to be of about 1460-1470 and if rightly dated, furnishes the oldest representation of a *May Game* with the morris) has besides the fool, a piper and six dancers, a maypole, a friar, and a lady, and the lady being crowned is assumed as the Lady of May. The Lady is dressed in blue — the Madonna's colour. One pane of glass, containing the picture of the may pole, has the words "A Merry May".

Finally, in a circular woodcut preserved on the title page of a penny history (*Adam Bell* etc. and printed at Newcastle in 1772) is the representation of a morris dance consisting of the following personages — (1) A Bishop. (2) Robin Hood (3) The Potter (or beggar) (4) Little John (5) Friar Tuck (6) Maid Marian. Figures 2 and 4 are distinguished by their bows and different size. The Friar holds a cross; and Marian has flowing hair, and wears a sort of coronet. Ritson describes this in his *Robin Hood* but errs in assigning it to the morris, as none of the characters belong to that dance. It is a portrayal of the characters from the May Games.

To repeat then, the Maid Marian was no simple Yorkshire lass. She is a lady in each period and this is also portrayed by Daniel Maclise in his painting of *Robin Hood and his Merry Men entertaining Richard Couer de Lion in Sherwood Forest* (1839). In this, the Maid Marian is placed in a bower with an attendant who appears to be placing a crown of flowers on her head; her dress is of satin and she is a lady of some quality.

Maid Marian was clearly then, a faint echo of the Blessed Virgin Mary, and later degraded to the Matilda, Malkin, or Mawkin. This has been completely missed by previous writers on Maid Marian, although there are some who suggest that the Madonna took the place of Flora, Roman Goddess, in Christian festivals. The evidence here is only a small portion of that which is easy to hand, and confirms that suggested by the early ballads.

In the *Little Geste*, Robin's devotion to the cult of the Virgin Mary is shown and this is nothing to be amazed at for from the 11th to the 14th century she was the central figure of the peoples devotions; in the 12th century the doctrine of the Immaculate Conception was first propounded and a festival was introduced in celebration of it (Virgo Immaculata, 1263). It became a matter of dispute in the 14th century and it was not until 1854 that it became an article of Roman Catholic faith.

We have Longland's word for it that rhymes of Robin Hood were sung before 1377, for these Sloth knew better than his paternoster. Nowhere is he associated with the Blessed Virgin Mary except the ballads, so it can be assumed that his utter devotion to Her is factual for, although we had known outlaws living in the period not one is credited with such faith, and any man who supported the people in their distress and was so close to their adored saint, would be favoured, almost canonised, as was Robin Hood.

Although Robin is claimed to be Lord of the May by one antiquarian, Strutt, there is no evidence that he was ever so represented, nor was the Madonna the Lady of May; both were characterised by other people, hence we have the claims that there was more than one Robin Hood. In fact there was only one, but he was one who was copied, enacted, and characterised by others over the years — and still is. That these figures should be partnered with *the* Maid Marian stems from the fact that they were personifying one who:

> S.8 "A good manner then had Robin Hood,
> In land where that he were
> Every day ere he would dine,
> Three masses would he hear."

> S.9 "The one in worship of the Father,
> And another of the Holy Ghost,
> The third for Our Dear Lady,
> That he loved the most."

> S.10 "Robin loved Our Dear Lady,
> For doubt of deadly sin,
> Would he never do company harm,
> That any woman was in."

In asking the gentle Knight for a guarantor for a loan of £400 he is to make him, he will not accept either Peter, Paul, or John, but when the Knight says :

> S.65 "I have none other," said the Knight,
> "The sooth for thee I say,
> But if it be Our Dear Lady;
> She failed me never on this day."

This is sufficient enough for Robin Hood:

> S.66 "By dear worthy God," said Robin,
> "To seek all England through,
> You find I never to my *pay*   (satisfaction)
> A much better *borrower.*"   (Guarantor)

In *Robin Hood and the Potter* (1500) the report is given:

> *S.3* "Robin Hood was the yeoman's name,
> That was both courteous and free,
> For the love of Our Lady,
> All women *worshipped* he."   *(respected)*

Michael Drayton (1563-1631) in his *Poly Olbion* gives us:

> "The widow in distress, he graciously relieved,
> And remedied the wrongs of many a virgin grieved."

In *Robin Hood's Golden Prize* from the Anthony-a'-Wood collection first printed in the Garland of 1663, Robin warns two monks of their sins and makes them swear to never again tell lies, never tempt maids to sin, or sleep with other mens' wives, and to be charitable to the poor. It was fitting that he should be portrayed as the champion of the distressed, the poor, and protector of the widow and virgin. He was the peoples hero and that is why he has so obscure a place in the written history. And it is fitting he should be coupled with *the* Maid Marian long after his death.

Today we cannot separate him from the Maid Marian, who remains the chaste young lady. She is no trollop, no camp follower, she remains in the background — usually in a castle under house-arrest by the Sheriff, and warns Robin of danger. "She is still his protector". We conclude then that the popular modern-day character of Maid Marian never existed as a real person. That this is not an easily accepted theory, was evident when the author first reported the finding through the media. For a time I was unpopular and many, many people have since said to me: "Please do not rob us of our Maid Marian."

Other attempts have been made to couple Robin, first with Jack Cade's daughter in a ballad of that name, and also with Clorinda, Queen of the shepherds, in the Staffordshire ballad. Although the lady sculptured on the Duke's Folly near Edwinstowe is Maid Marian by popular belief, she is, in fact, Clorinda!

There is one more delightful ballad (undated), and in the true spirit of Robin Hood and Maid Marian; a Derbyshire story, and one I am very fond of — *Robin Hood's Leap*. This is where Kitty Ray, who lived at Edensor, protects Robin Hood in a most charming love story, but there is no wedding. They go their separate ways. It is to be found in *The Life and Exploits of Robin Hood*, Milner and Sowerby, Halifax, 1859.

ANCIENT MORRIS DANCE as depicted in the 14th century. Maid Marian is the central figure, but during this period, this character was normally a boy.

TOMB OF MAID MARIAN. In one legend she was Lady Matilda FitzWalter, who is buried at Little Dunmow Parish Church, Essex.

ST. CUTHBERT'S CHURCH, Doveridge, Derbyshire. The yew tree is the one under which, one legend states, Maid Marian married Robin Hood.

FRIAR TUCK by David Porter. From a series of paintings commissioned by *The Granary*, Edwinstowe. *(Reproduced by courtesy of Lada Tvrdik).*

Chapter 8

"There was he aware of a curtal Friar,
Walking by the waterside."
— *Ballad of* Robin Hood and the Curtal Friar.

LTHOUGH Friar Tuck has now long been a favourite character of the legends, it is some considerable time before he enters the Robin Hood saga, for the elusive Friar has no place in the early ballads, and mention by name only in two of the later ones: *Robin Hood and Queen Catherine* (Percy ms. 1768-1808).

> S.9 "Commend me to Robin Hood," *(says Queen Catherine)*
> "And alsoe Litle John,
> And specially to Will Scarlett,
> Ffryar Tucke and Maid Maryan."

The spelling suggests the ballad is older than one of the same title and content as in the Garland of 1663. *Robin Hood's Golden Prize* (*c.*1620), Garland of 1663.

> S.1 "I have heard talk of Robin Hood,
> And of brave Little John,
> Of Fryer Tuck and Wil Scarlet,
> Loxley, and Maid Marian."

A "Frere Tucke" appeared in a commission dated 1429, when he was pardoned for all crimes, both new and the old ones committed in the time of Henry V, 1413-1422. The name of *Frere Tucke* became a regular alias amongst the criminal fraternity, but there is no difficulty in identifying this law-breaker for Stow informs us that his name was Richard Stafford, a Sussex Chaplain. Although the Friar is not named in the ballad *Robin Hood and the Curtal Friar,* the copy in the Percy ms. (see above), is entitled *Robine Hood and Frryer Tucke* and is maybe, the older of the two. The action here is at Fountains Abbey but in the 1663 edition the locality is Fountain Dale, Nottinghamshire.

The next mention of Friar Tuck is in a fragment of a play from the Paston papers, of the date 1475 or earlier, which has no title, but by popular consent is called *Robin Hood and the sheriff of Nottingham*. In this play is to be found the first clue to his true identity. The commentator here mentions Frere Tucke on two occasions:

> "Beholde Wele Ffrer Tucke,
> How he dothe his bow pluke,
> Yeld yow, syrs to the sheriff,
> Or elles shall your bows clyffe,
> Nowe we be bownden alle in same,
> Frere Tucke this in no game."

A bow is not plucked — it is bent; nor is a bow string plucked — it is drawn. The old ballads use the term *i-bente* and *i-drawne;* never *plucked;* nor is there any note of the term applied to the bow elsewhere. The arrow is nocked and bow is drawn. *The player was taking the part of the fool.* The commentator draws attention to him — "this is no game" (jest, trifle, mimicry). In fact, *this is not a comedy.* It may well have been a mummers story.

The next notice we have is in the play of Robin Hood first printed by Copland in his edition of the *Little Geste* (*c.*1548). In this the Friar is far from the lovable, friendly priest of popular legend and, as far as we know, except for the criminal Richard Stafford alias Frere Tucke, and also the play of 1475, there is no earlier mention. Here, the Friar has fought with Robin Hood and returns later to continue the fray and Robin tells his men:

> Line 10. "There were stypes two or three,
> But I cannot tell who had the worse,
> But well I wote the horeson lept within me
> And fro me toke my purse."

The remains of Friar Tuck's Well at Fountaindale, Blidworth.

Detail from *Robin Hood's Merry Jest* in the *Thriller Comics Library* series, in which the Sheriff is again outwitted by the merry men, aided by Friar Tuck's stew.

He robbed Robin Hood! Some Friar! The action then runs along the lines of the well known story, except that Robin shows no love of Tucke, nor of Friars in general.

> "Thou lousy frere, what wouldest though with *hym*,   *(Robin Hood)*
> He never loved fryer nor none of freirers kyn."

and again:

> "Therefor I *had* lever mete with the devil of hell,   (Rather)
> (Fryer I tell thee as I thinke)
> Then mete with a fryer or a fox,
> In a morning, *or* I drink."   *(ere)*

He calls Tucke a *dote* (stupid or foolish) *Malapert* (saucy, impudent) and a whore's son. Nevertheless he invites him to join the band once honour is satisfied.

Tuck, although seemingly paired with Maid Marian does not share a part with her in the May Games, nor, though others would have it differently, was he part of the morris. Tollet's painted window is a portrayal of the Games — not the morris, and the evidence stands in the pane, just over the hobby horse — a maypole with a banner on which are the words 'A MERRY MAY' — not morris dance. Nor either is the woodcut referred to by Joseph Ritson, it is the May games illustrated. In the first instance the friar holds a garland in his right hand; in the second he holds a cross. Only *the* Maid Marian and a boy (Robin Hood so called), can be related to the dance, neither of which have any likeness to the people of the saga. The woodcut shows people who were characters in the old May Games.

In the Chettle and Munday play, *The downfall of Robert, earl of Huntingdon etc,* the Friar is characterised as Robin's chaplain. The Sloane manuscript states that one of the band was a Friar named Muchel, but as the Order of Friars was not at that time established in the country he may have been another kind of religious man. Child refers to the friar as a loose and jovial fellow in the play of *Robin Hood* and one who presents Robin Hood with a "lady free" not named, but who may be meant for a degraded Maid Marian.

John Skelton, poet laureate, in the *Goodley Interlude of Magnificence,* written about the year 1500 with an evident allusion to some game now forgotten and inexplicable, mentions a Friar Tuck:

> 'Another bade shave halfe my berde,
> And boyes to the pylery gan me plucke,
> And would have me Freer Tucke,
> To preach out of the pylery hole."

In the legend he takes the part of the jovial hard drinking gourmand more akin to a monk than a friar, for the friars were of a hard order vowed to poverty, who held nothing but contempt for monks with the profits from their vast estates and the comfort of the cloisters. The creator of the *Little Geste* was aware of this for he has the Sheriff tell Robin Hood after an enforced overnight stay in Sherwood Forest:

> "This is an harder order than any achorite *(hermit)* or friar."

In the ballad *Robin Hood and the Curtal Friar* we have the same situation as the play but Robin is the antagonist, not the Friar. The carrying of each other across the moat occurs in both play and ballad but neither conclude as to whether or no the Friar joins the band. Everything written of Friar Tuck points, not a holy man, but a burlesque, and preaching out of a pillory hole even though only an impersonation, ridiculing the supposed character of Friar Tuck. Tuck is not compatable with Robin Hood's mood, for Robin was devout and one who was his Chaplain would have been given a dignified and pious nature by the ballad writers.

The name Tuck is derived from the Old English *Tucian* — to afflict, disturb, or torment, and adequately fits the figure of the plays, for in the first he is misbehaving, and in the second, not only does Robin show his detest of the Friar, but tells his men he was robbed his purse by him. No wonder the name became an alias for the criminal fraternity.

I well recall a term used frequently in my schooldays and good enough to start a fight, was "Brother Smut", but it is doubtful if we lads thought any more than that it was not a nice thing to call someone. I have not heard it used for many years and believe that it implied that the person so named had a sordid mind (smutty!). So it was with Frere Tucke — "Brother Tucke" — a trouble maker, for the truth is that Friar Tuck was never a holy man, nor was he just one person, but a character often assumed by minstrels, and professional entertainers, who ofttimes shaved the crown of their heads, and assumed ecclesiastical habit. There is one particular instance which provides sufficient evidence of this, although

THE MOAT, Fountain Dale, where Robin Hood fought with Friar Tuck.

Left: Robin Hood and Friar Tuck meeting at Fountain Dale. A wood-cut from an early edition of *Robin Hood's Garland* (1670-1744).

94

I dare say there may be many more related elsewhere: ''Two itinerant Priests coming toward nightfall to a cell of Benedictines near Oxford, they there upon the assumption of their being mimics or minstrels, gained admittance; but the cellerar, the sacrist, and others of the brethren, disappointed in the expectation they had formed of being entertained with mirthful performances, and finding them to be no more than ecclesiastics, beat them and turned them out of the monastry.'' *(History & Antiquities of Oxford)*. Such was our ''Friar'', but he would have ''sung for his supper''.

By the late 15th century and early 16th century we find the character in another role, which accounts for him being paired with Maid Marian, she sometimes taking the part of the Lady of May. The Lord of the May gave place to the Lord of Misrule, and that to the ''Abbot of Misrule'', a person appointed at court, nobleman's house, or in college or inn or court, to superintend the Christmas revels, and sometimes act as president of the Summer sports. Who better than Friar Tuck.

It is in this role that he became associated with Maid Marian, and also the popular characters of Robin Hood and Little John. Hence in modern times apart from the habit and tonsure, we have nothing of a Friar; nothing of piety, and nothing of poverty. We have a hard-drinking gourmand who is more at home with the quarterstaff, sword and buckler, than spiritual and pastoral matters.

The *Nottingham Robin Hood Society* has a Friar Tuck who is neither a criminal nor holy man by profession, but a regular churchgoer. He loves playing the part and his costume is authentic and he is registered as a friar. As well as being a very popular character he is often addressed as 'Father'. There are some who honestly believe he is Friar Tuck, and, being somewhat mischevious, I have my suspicions.

FRIAR TUCK was not apparently one of the original characters in the history of Robin Hood, but he became a popular figure in the 19th century stories and is now part of the legend today.

LITTLE JOHN by David Porter. From a series of paintings commissioned by *The Granary*, Edwinstowe. *(Reproduced by courtesy of Lada Tvrdik).*

Chapter 9

"The words we'll transpose, so where ever he goes,
His name shall be called Little John."
— Ballad of Little John.

F the thirty eight ballads in James Francis Child's *The English and Scottish Popular Ballads* (1889) Little John appears in all but ten. He is the first named outlaw of the *Little Geste:*

S.3 "And Robin Hood in Bernesdale stood,
And leaned him to a tree,
And by him stood Little John,
A good yeoman was he."

In the third fytte (part) of the *Little Geste* he has a story to himself which stems, probably, from an older, and lost ballad — *Little John and the Sheriff.* Two ballads are devoted to him, *Robin Hood and Little John* (c.1723) and *Little John goes a'begging* (c.1640), and the major part of *Robin Hood and the Monk* concerns Little John, along with Much, the Miller's son. In many instances the names Robin Hood and Little John are inseparable.

John was a man of whom the ballad writer has made scarcely less prominence than Robin Hood. The line from above, "and by him stood Little John", would be John's ideal epitaph. He was loyal. The first at Robin's side when he was in trouble; mindful of Robin's welfare: "To dine would do you much good", he tells his master, when Robin wishes to wait for a guest before he sits to his meal. He turned down the offer of leadership of the band after Robin had shown anger and impatience against him, and in the same story, although seething with anger under the apparent scorn by Robin, it is John who leads the rescue of their leader in *Robin Hood and the Monk.* He was shrewd, giving Robin Hood "good advice" on several occasions.

He was generous. In the story of the impoverished Knight it is John who suggests that they give the Knight clothing, weapons, and a horse befitting a Knight, to which he adds a pair of golden spurs as his own personal gift.

His kindness of heart and forgiving nature are shown in the ballad *The Birth, Breeding, Valour, and Marriage of Robin Hood etc.,* in which he entreats Robin Hood to spare the lives of the yeomen who have attacked them on the way to Tutbury feast, after felling five of them in combat. "And pitiful John begged their lives", and when his request was granted "sent them home safe to their wives" — with good counsel from John. When the impoverished Knight is late in returning to Robin with his repayment of the loan, Robin is impatient. It is John who assures him that the Knight is true and will keep his word.

S.207 "Have no doubt, master," said Little John;
"Yet is the sun not at rest;
For I dare say, surely swear,
The knight is true and trusty."

His swordsmanship is first class and he beat the cook in the story of the *Little Geste* after a long fight. It seems that Little John was a better swordsman than his master. From the first meeting between Robin Hood and Little John (from the ballad of that name) we know who was the better at quarterstaff — and the wiliest — John! At archery, Little John is always chosen to shoot with Robin Hood, and hits the mark each time, but never gains first place. In the ballad *Robin Hood and Guy of Gisborne,* he shoots the Sheriff, a moving target, at some distance. History records a famous shot by Robin, a distance of a mile, off the tower of Whitby Abbey to Whitby Laithes (in fact closer to two miles), but less is made of John, who shoots the same distance. The two places where the arrows landed were marked on Ordnance Survey Maps as Little John's field and Robin Hood's field. Charlton, the historian of Whitby, tells of this event — "It must have been on the occasion of one of his visits to Robin Hood's Bay, that, attended

97

by Little John, he (Robin) was invited by the Abbot Richard of Whitby, to dine with him at the Abbey. After dinner the Abbot alluded to his guests' fame for their dexterity in shooting with the long bow, and begged that they might be treated to an illustration. To this Robin and his trusty henchman assented, and, accompanied by Richard and many of the brethren of the house, went up on the leads of the roof of the Abbey. Then, turning the face towards Hawkser, they each of them, first Robin, and then Little John, drew his bow with his full strength and shot an arrow in the direction of the village. They fell, one on each side of the lane, not far from Whitby-Laths, fully a mile from the Abbey. The astonished Abbot, as a memorial of so outstanding a feat, set up a pillar where each of the arrows fell, which are yet standing in these days; the field where Robin Hood's pillar stands being still called Robin Hood's field and the other where Little John's arrow landed still preserving the name of John's field''. In the author's possession is a photograph of a large garden roller made from Robin Hood's pillar, which alas is now mere rubble under a path.

In *Robin Hood and the Potter* (1500) Little John has fought with the potter at Wentbridge and received three good strikes from him; the conclusion is lacking, but we are told that the potter would have killed Robin in a fair fight had not Little John intervened. Fearless! Nothing that was too much for Robin proved beyond John's prowess; he was ready to jump in with both feet and defend Robin from harm. There is little to choose between them, except that John was a good *servant*. The impact of Little John is as great as that of Robin Hood, both in ballad and story, and the saga would never be the same without him. John was the last outlaw mentioned, the only one to go with Robin Hood to Kirklees; the one who was with his master even "to the death", for he would have given his life for Robin. His is the only story to continue after the death of Robin. It is unfortunate that no historical records exist from which he can be positively identified but it is obvious, true or not, that the ballads old and new have one person in mind. One person around whom a legend has been born as great as that of any outlaw — even Robin.

"This famous companion of Robin Hood had been a native of Hathersage (Derbyshire) and was brought up to the local industry of nail-making, till his wonderful strength and prowess made him try his fortunes elsewhere" (*Annals of a Yorkshire House* — A.M.W. Stirland). Hence his true name would have been Naylor after his profession. The Nuttall cottage which stood close to the church up to the 19th century, was the place where he returned after the death of Robin, heartbroken, and by this manner he died. His body stretched the full length of the kitchen floor. Walker, in *The True History of Robin Hood*, states: "the second son of George Little, farm labourer of Mansfield, and was brought up as a nail-maker by trade which he followed for some time, until his wonderful strength determined him to try his fortune elsewhere. An ancient cottage on the road leading from Edwinstowe to Mansfield has long been pointed out as the one in which he was born". The similarity of the wording to that of the first account prompts one to believe that the former is the source for the latter.

Stirland goes on to add that, "little is known of his career, however, till the Battle of Evesham in 1265 when he fought with the rebels under Simon de Montfort, who was defeated. Little John with Robin Hood and many others of the Earl's followers were outlawed. They forthwith retired to the woods, and escaping the arms of justice, lived a jolly free life till old age took them". "Ebenezer Elliott, the poet, during his rambles around Locksley Chase, Yorkshire, and close to Sheffield, related to Cornelius Brown how Robin met John le Tall at the Battle of Evesham, and after the defeat of Earl Simon's forces returned to their native wilds, (John by trade being a nail-maker, being from the north side of Staffordshire) and finding shelter and abundance of deer in Sherwood Forest, made that their chief haunt" (*Worthies of Nottinghamshire*, Brown 1882).

In the *Little Geste*, Little John tells the Sheriff his name is Reynold Greeleaf and he is from Holderness. He is a servant at Gamwell Hall in the ballad of *Robin Hood's birth etc.*, and by intimation he is a Nottingham man in the ballad *Robin Hood and Little John*. The least worthy claim, not without some amusement, was made by Molly Jackson, Harland County, Kentucky, folk singer and story teller. She claims that her forefathers wrote the ballads of Robin Hood and that her grandfather, William, was a Northumberlander descending from Little John, whom she referred to as "Little John Garland".

P. Valentine Harris, supporting the Yorkshire claim, found a John le Nailor entered in the Rolls under the date 1329 which he terms "a coincidence, but he might have been put into the saga later". Part of the Hathersage claim is that many of the name Nailor, descendants of Little John, are living in Hathersage to this day, but as nail-making was the local trade, this would be commonplace through generations. There is yet another school of thought abroad in Hathersage. The author has correspondence from a lady of that area. ''I happen to be a member of the Littlewood clan of Hathersage, and firmly believe that Little John was *John of the Little wood* — nothing to do with height''.

Whereas these references to his birthplaces are provided with only the unsubstantiated stories that John reputedly lived there, the many claims to his burial sites are often accompanied with more detail.

First, to Ireland: ''There Standeth in Osmantowne Green a hillock named Little John, his shot''. The *Irish Chronicles Vol. II,* Holinshed (1586) relates this story, and continues: ''The occasion proceeded of this. In the Yeere one thousand one hundred four score and nine (1189) there ranged three robbers and outlaws in England, among which Robert (sic) Hood and Little John were cheefeteins, of all theeves doubtless thee most courteous. Robert Hood was betraide at a nunnerie in Scotland called Bricklies, the remnant of the crue scattered, and everie man forced to shift for himself. Whereupon Little John was faine to flee the Realme by sailing in to Ireland where he sojourned for a few days in Dublin. The citizens being to understand the wandering outcast to be an excellent archer, requested him hartilie to trie how far he could shoot at random; who yielding to the behest stood on a bridge at Dublin and shot to the mole hill, leaving behind him a monument, rather by his posteritie to be wondered, than possible by any man living to be counter scored. But as the repaire of so notorious a champion to any countrie would soon be published, so his abode could ne be long concealed; and therefor to eschew the lawes he fled to Scotland, where he died at a town or village called Moravie''.

Again from Ireland, from *Historical Memories of the Irish Bards* (Walker), ''In the neigbourhood of St. Micham's church there is an incident in connection with it worthy of recall. Many Dubliners have read from time to time of the daring feats in Sherwood Forest of bold Robin Hood and his trusty lieutenant little John, but few of them know that after their exploits across the water, the latter was hanged near St. Micham's church Street''. And from *Life in Old Dublin,* by Collins (1913), ''According to tradition little John shot an arrow from the site of the old bridge (now Church Street Bridge) to the present site of St. Micham's church, a distance of eleven score and seven yards, but poor little John's great practical skill in archery could not save him from an ignominious fate; as it appears from the record's of the Southwell family he was publicly executed for robbery on Arbour Hill''.

It is interesting that the two latter historians use the lower case *l* — *l*ittle John, which supports my own theory as to his identity.

The Southwells were an English landowning family settled in Ireland during the 16th century. The most important branch had their English seat at Kings Weston and provided two secretaries of state for Ireland between 1690 and 1740. The papers related to the domestic matters of the family and are in various depositories, but a careful search has failed to produce any evidence of little John's execution. The information on the Southwell family was supplied by the Keeper of Manuscripts at the University of Dublin, but I am unable to establish the location of Kings Weston. Some report that John was buried against St. Mitcham's church, or close by, but no records exist to show it as fact. The grave, if it did exist, is no longer there, and enquiries at the Dublin Archives Office, National Library of Ireland, University of Dublin, and other places, have failed to offer any evidence whatsoever.

The Irish enjoyed some of the Robin Hood ballads and one, *Robin Hood and the Scotchman* according to Gutch's *Robin Hood,* his copy was from an Irish Garland printed in Monoghan, 1796, but the feat of archery and his execution must be put down to legend. The actual culprit of this story was Scaldbrother, a notorious Irish robber, who was hung on the spot where little John's arrow is reputed to have landed. Only one Irish historian makes any reference to John's great stature, he is the Reverend Cosgrove in, *North Dublin City Environs* (1908): ''To the west of this very old road lies Arbour Hill famous for its memories of Robin Hood's gigantic lieutenant, humourously called *little* John''.

The Scottish historians neither relate, nor claim, any exploits of Little John in Moravie (Murrayland), but they do show that a very big man was buried at Kirke of Pettye. ''Moravie, the bones of a huge man are kept, which was called little John'' (*Cosmographic.* Garardus Mercator, 1512-94). The term ''which'', may refer to the skeleton (bones), and not to the man when he was living. This can be seen in the words of John Lesley, the Scottish historian, writing between 1527-1596, when it states: ''In Moray is a church in a village known as Petyn where are preserved the bones of a certain John, whom paradoxically they call small, who ended his life *scarcely thirty years ago* which no one is among us who is not able

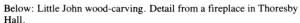

Left: Mr. H.C. Haldane holding Little John's bow. From a photograph taken outside Cannon Hall, Yorkshire, between the wars.

Below: Little John wood-carving. Detail from a fireplace in Thoresby Hall.

Left: Little John's alleged gravestone, which is actually a graveslab, now in Hathersage churchyard.

100

to put his hand and arm into the hip bone at the same time''. He makes no reference to Little John or Robin Hood, and the period between 1527 and 1596 is too late for the legend.

In *The new statistical account of Scotland* (1845), under the heading of Parish of Pettie, it is written — ''That the histories of Robin Hood make his friend Little John to retire like a smitten deer from his gay greenwood and companions, in order to rest his weary bones in the dry sands of Petyn''. This report goes on to say: ''There are places, which it is said, have derived their names from Fingalean heroes who were buried there. Among these Pipan and Ian Beng; nam Fion may be mentioned. We must not omit what seems to be a notice of the latter, a pygmy of fourteen feet, given us by Lesley''. Little John was reported to be just half that height — *Robin Hood and Little John, Stanza 2* relates that:

''Tho he was called Little, his limbs they were large,
And his stature was seven foot high''.

''In Murray land'', writes Hector Boece, the 16th century chronicler (c. 1540) ''is the Kirke of Pette, quare the banis of Lutill Johne remains in grat admiration of pepill. He has bene fourtene fut of hyght with square membris effering thairto. VI years afore the comyng of the work to lyucht we saw the hanche bane, als mekill as the ahill bane of ane man for we schot our arme into the mouth thairoff. Be quhilk apperis how strang and square pepyll grew in our region afore the were made effeminat with lust and intemperance of mouth''.

What evidence there is in Scotland, is that of a fourteen-foot tall giant, a ludicrous exaggeration and one which has no part of the legend in England. The term ''hanche bane'', in which there was a hole big enough for one to put in the whole of his arm, suggests the pelvis. If the object was a broken thigh-bone it would be closed at each end, with a ball-joint at one end and knuckle at the other, and no one could put an arm into it. Only one modern Scottish historian makes any reference to Robin Hood and Little John, that being Bill Burton in his *History of Scotland:* ''Hence there is a very picturesque chapter in British History of which Scotland holds no part — the story of the Outlaw Robin Hood and his merry independent band''.

The main references to Little John and his great height all start in the 16th century writings; prior to this we have no mention of him being a giant. A fourteen-feet long specimen does not suit the matter, so the probability is that he was buried in Hathersage, Derbyshire. ''Little John lies buried in Hathersage churchyard within three miles of Castleton in High Peak; with one stone at his head and another at his feet. A great distance lies between them. Thay say that part of his bow hangs in the said church'', wrote Elias Ashmole. In the church porch against the right hand wall on entering there stands the top half of an ancient gravestone. The cross and shaft are hardly discernable; even less the initials L and I either side of the shaft; these are more recent than the stone. The present gravestones are set thirteen feet four inches apart, and were placed by the Ancient Order of Foresters. The headstone bears the inscription ''Here lies Little John. the friend and lieutenant of Robin Hood.'' By the railings surrounding the grave stands a large scrolled stone at the head of which an antlered deer's head is carved, issuing from a crown, and written beneath — ''The care of this grave was undertaken by the Ancient Order of Foresters, June 14 1929''.

In 1784, at the instruction of Captain James Shuttleworth, the grave was opened by the Sexton and at a depth of six feet below the surface was found a gigantic thigh-bone of from twenty eight inches to thirty two inches according to the several eye-witnesses who saw it being measured on a tailor's board. Eventually it was carried off to Cannon Hall near Barnsley but following a series of unexplained local accidents, the bone was returned to Hathersage for re-interment, upon which the accidents stopped. Subsequently James Shuttleworth found that the Sexton had not re-buried the bone but was displaying it for payment; therefore, on the pretext of taking it to show a friend he returned it to Cannon Hall and buried it under a tree in the park and it was lost forever.

The tradition that people could thrust hand and arm into the bone persisted at Hathersage, as in Murrayland. A claim was also made that the sexton broke a spade on the bone as it was so hard — and another that it was in two pieces, but owning to the preservative qualities of the soil the break was so perfect that the ends matched! What is inconceivable is that these stories could ever have been taken seriously. Such a thigh-bone would indicate the owner's height to have been over ten feet. An impossibility! As already shown, the given height of Little John in the only ballad which states it, is seven feet. It is just not feasible that the Hathersage bone was that of a seven-foot tall man and therefore was not that

Little John's cottage, Hathersage, Derbyshire, as it stood some 100 years ago.

WHITBY ABBEY, North Yorkshire. Little John and Robin Hood are said to have shot arrows from the tower, to Whitby Laithes, a distance of over a mile.

of Little John. The tallest man ever recorded in England was William Bradley (1787-1820), born at Market Weighton in the East Riding of Yorkshire. He stood seven feet nine inches. The tallest man in the world was an American who must have reached eight feet before he stopped growing. Neither of these men would have had a thigh-bone of between twenty-eight and thirty inches. No more feasible is the claim made by another that the body of a tall young man from Offerton occupied the grave in the churchyard.

Let us pause here in Hathersage to examine the statement by Elias Ashmole (1617-1692) that — "part of his bow hangs in the said church". and consider what manner did *part of a bow* become the six-foot, seven inch long weapon as exists today.

It could not be that the horn tips were then missing as they are present, for in 1715 Colonel Naylor strung the bow and shot an arrow from it. His initials and also the date of his exploit are marked on the bow grip, and the legend is that he shot a deer through from side to side at Cannon Hall, and that the bow has never been strung since. At that time the horn tips must have been there as it would have been impossible to string the bow, unless ends were notched, and they are not. When I last handled the bow the ends were pointed to fit into the horn tips. In his booklet *Little John and Hathersage Church,* M. Andrews writes: "The famous antiquarian Ashmole, living over three hundred years ago, said the bow was suspended in Hathersage church in 1625 and there seems no doubt that it was, also it was hanging near the Eyre monument. If so it might have some connection with former Eyres who held official rank of Gentlemen Foresters? The *Victoria County History of Derbyshire* states in the chapter on Forestry that Edward I made a new rank of itinerant foresters known as Bow Bearers who carried a long bow as their insignia of office, or else had the bow borne by an attendant. It was a Crown appointment, carrying the very high remuneration for those days of a shilling a day, and went to men of knightly rank. This is the only explanation, and I have no personal wish to detract from the glories of Little John". To hang the bow and armour of a known outlaw as a perpetual monument in the church does not identify with custom, but to display the armour and insignia of office of a well known family, close to their memorial, as Andrews implies above, does appear more realistic.

Returning to the main theme, that of Little John the man, it is remarkable that no mention is made of John's physique until after the reports of the Scottish historians. The early Irish historians do not refer to his height, only the fact that he was an outlaw, and his feat of archery is considerably more modest than the reputed English legend. Over one hundred years after the first Scottish reference, and sixty four years after the Ashmole claim we receive the first story of a seven-feet tall giant in Robin's band.

The *Little Geste* is the first printed story of the saga and is followed by others over a period years, and in this, none of the characters are described as short, fat, or otherwise. Much, the miller's son, is shown as "There was not an inch of his body that was not worth that of a whole man", which seems to suggest that he was the most powerful member of the band, if not the biggest, although sometimes mentioned as "little Much". That he was a very strong man is suggested by his carrying of Little John upon his back for a mile or more. In the older writings capital-letters are not always used where required; nevertheless it may have some bearing on this case. *The Scotinchronicon,* the work of two authors, John Fordun and Walter Bower, Abbott of Inchcom, who apparently worked on them between 1440 and 1447, refer to him as *l*ittle John. This is also true of the *Little Geste,* in its original form at the Cambridge University Library — *l*ittle John. The title page of William Copland's edition of the *Little Geste* (*c.*1548) illustrates two men, the smaller figure wears armour and has the words "little John", in brackets, above his head. Against this we have on the title page of Wynken de Worde's edition of the *Little Geste,* a lady and gentleman, either side of a smaller figure with the words "My Lord" over his head. Neither of the characters are so dressed as to distinguish rank and it could be a woodcut for the May Games. The taller man carries a staff and the small man carries a sword. The lady and gentleman being of equal height it may be that they are the Lord and Lady of May, the former being Robin Hood as the Lord, as some writers claim he so characterised, and the smaller his lieutenant, little John. There is always a clear possibility of the woodcuts having nothing to do with the characters in the book, merely conveniently suitable enough for purpose of illustration. In the black letter copies of the ballads and books the woodcuts do not portray a big man, the characters are all of equal size, and in the period dress of the Restoration.

To summarise, the various graves offer no useful evidence of John's stature. The Scottish claim is undeniably of a fourteen-feet *mythical* giant; the Irish have no proof whatsoever, either of his grave, or of little John being executed in Dublin, and the Hathersage grave has stones thirteen feet, four inches

LITTLE JOHN'S GRAVE, Hathersage, Derbyshire.

apart, "exactly the old English rod, pole, or perch", according to one writer. I do not dispute that it could have been a land measure peculiar to churchyards, but I have no knowledge of a rod ever being more or less than five metres, or fifteen and half feet. A thigh-bone of any of the lengths suggested could not be that of a seven-feet tall man. We have only the word of those who claim to have seen it, with dubious varying reports on it being whole or broken into two parts. Although it coincided with unexplained accidents at Cannon Hall, the sexton seems to have made good use of it without any harm to himself. Surely, such a relic would have been carefully preserved or, at least its burial place accurately recorded somewhere. Tradition is also answerable to making so great a difference between Robin Hood and Little John in point of stature. There is a tune to which some of the ballads are to be sung and may be from the title of a lost ballad, "Robin Hood was a tall young man".

Not every writer believed little John was a giant, W.J. Thoms, writing in 1827-8: "He who he most affected by reason of his low stature was called little John but not inferior in strength of body and stoutness of spiritis". An earlier writer says the same thing: "but nevertheless he was valiant and brave as any other member of the band". There is no substance to show that Little John was a giant; there is more supportive evidence to show the opposite.

From folklore and word of mouth, Little John is also identified with graves in the churchyards at Thorpe Salvin near Worksop, Nottinghamshire, and Wincle in Cheshire. Visits and enquiries to local village residents have provided the author with no evidence, except perhaps in the case of Thorpe Salvin where the person buried there *may* be The Clerk of Copmanhurst, of Scott's *Ivanhoe* — his portrayal of Friar Tuck.

To trace John's identity from the observations and remarks already given, or additionally from the large amount of available literature not quoted here is, until fresh evidence is uncovered, impossible. If we accept Robin Hood as factual and give him an identity acceptable to the majority then, beyond doubt, we must also accept John. His surname is not known in the ballads; that of *little* is given to him in the ballad telling of his first meeting with Robin Hood and is merely a play on the word *lytel* (old English), *little, small;* or as some would have, mean or deceitful. What has escaped the notice of most, in fact all, who write of John is the fact that the term *little* is used as an endearment! "Bless your little heart", "Oh, you little beauty". Of grown people, no matter what their size or shape how often has one heard the words "You should have seen his/her little face", when a person was facing troubles or disappointment. In this context John was, possibly, termed Little — nothing to do with size; an idiom which expresses something intangible — or both! He was a great favourite with the merry men, and ranks next to Robin and Marian in people's estimation today.

That the "le Tall", quoted Cornelius Brown, is a mishearing of Little, sometimes spoken and written *littul,* is indisputable. The story was told to him by Elliott when roaming the countryside; Brown says it was ironically changed, as John was a tall man, but we can discount this as no other source gives "le Tall".

To give John a family identity, the name of Naylor does have an irresistable ring of credibility, as surnames are, in the majority, derived from either the place or the trade of its original possessor. We have three illustrations of him being a nail-maker, and these could be added to from other sources.

There is no new evidence to go against the established traditions connected with Little John. My own belief is that he was John Naylor, a nail-maker either from Hathersage or Mansfield, who might well have practised his skill in the north of the county of Staffordshire, and where he first made the acquaintance of the man later to be known as Robin Hood.

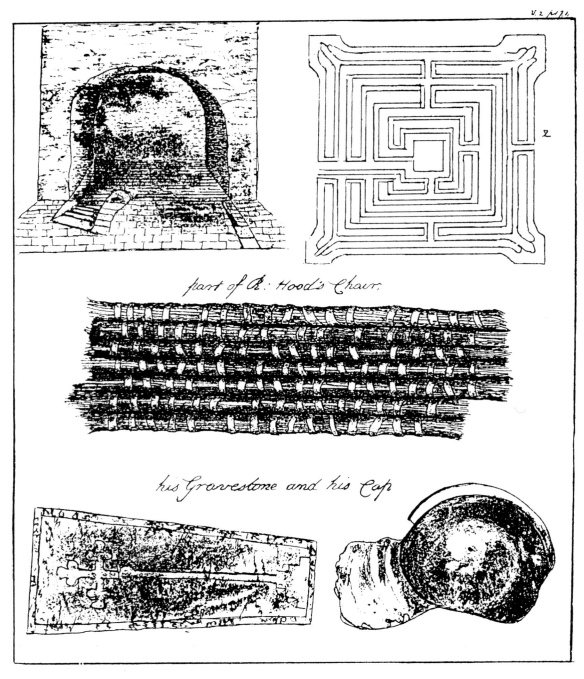

part of R: Hood's Chair.

his Gravestone and his Cap

Robin Hood obiit xxiv kal Decembris mccxxxxvii

Relics reputed to be connected with the Robin Hood legend, once to be seen at St. Anne's Well. From Thoroton's *Nottingham-shire,* Throsby's edition.

Chapter 10

T is not surprising that some of the "Robin Hood Relics", or the memory of them, are still preserved, nor should it be any more surprising if more were to be discovered. Bow staves from the warship *Mary Rose,* of the 16th century, can be seen in fair condition at the White Tower in the Tower of London, and a medieval arrow is on display in the undercroft in the cloisters at Westminster Abbey, denying those who claim that being of wood, Robin's bow could not exist today. Of the cloth-yard arrow at Westminster, the shaft and fletching are original, the tip a replica. That fabrics can be preserved is proved by The Shroud of Turin, which can be traced back to 1204, and for paper we have to look no further than the Public Records Offices.

There is a long period between the death of Robin Hood and the "discovery" of the relics, but in spite of this, they should not be readily condemned as fakes. We find no mention of King Henry VIII's armour being seen by people in their travels, but who would question the authority of the historians who placed it in the Tower? It is with an open mind that one should look at the subject, even if at this point one considered Robin Hood a myth.

"We omitted", says Ray, "the sight of Fountains Abbey where Robin Hood's bow is kept", and in *Travels Over England* by Brome (1700): "Having pleased ourselves with the antiquities of Nottingham, we took horse and went to visit the well, and ancient chair of Robin Hood, which is not far from thence, within the Forest of Sherwood. Being in the chair we had a cap, which they say was his, very formally put on our heads, and having performed the usual ceremonies befitting so great a solemnity, we received the freedom of the chair, and were incorporated into the society of the renowned brotherhood." "On one side of the forest (Sherwood) towards Nottingham", says the author of the *Travels of Tom Thumb over England and Wales,* Robert Dodsley (1703-1764), "I was shown a chair, a bow and arrow, all said to be his, Robin Hood's, property." And W. Hutton, in 1745, writes: "I was pleased with the slipper belonging to the famous Robin Hood, fifty years ago, at Saint Annes Well near Nottingham, a place upon the borders of Sherwood Forest, to which we resorted". A Nottingham Historian, Doug Silkstone, in correspondence states: "Our Robin Hood Close of 1484 and Robin Hood's Well were within what was then, that part of Sherwood Forest known as the King's Wood, or Coppice. The Robin Hood names would exist long before 1484 not suddenly start then. Traditions of the outlaw, in our coppice, which had a variant appelation, Robin's Wood, are strong in history and poetry". I have not observed this, but Mr. Silkstone continues: "Robin Hood's Well is first mentioned 20th July 1500 but the name is older than the time of King Richard II (1377-1399)". And, from *Chamberlains Accounts* we find: "The earliest reference to Robin Hood's Well occurs in a boundary dispute, near Robynhode Well' recorded in the quarter sessions on 20th July 1500". These reports of the 18th century show that some relics were then in existence, and believed to have been Robin Hood's, his chair, cap, bow and arrow, and slipper of which there is no more information, than that given above. The exception is the Well, known as St. Annes Well and also Robin Hood's Well, for which we have proof in the City Archives.

In Thoresby's *Nottinghamshire,* is portrayed a helmet, which may be the cap; this is said to have been loaned to a person for use in a pageant many years ago, and reputed to have ended up at the British Museum. They have no trace of it! The relics which do exist are, mostly, in the possession of private collectors so it is quite understandable that they should be missed by those not making an intensive search into the legend. Relics are notoriously prone to falsification of origin, as the author can vouch, from personal experiences of two old English bows which came into his possession some years ago. Though not of great antiquity, they were of a style similar to ancient bows.

Above: Stone roller made from the stone which marked the spot where Robin Hood's arrow landed at Whitby Staithes. He shot, along with Little John, from the Tower of Whitby Abbey.

Left: ROBIN HOOD'S DRINKING FLASK, at Southwell Minster.

Below: ROBIN HOOD'S HORN. Once to be seen at Loxley Hall, Staffordshire.

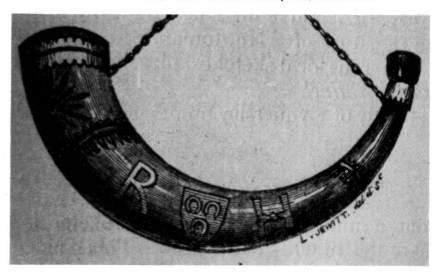

SCHOLAR'S PATH WELLS,
Near Haworth.

ROBIN HOOD'S WELL.

LITTLE JOHN'S WELL.

WILL SCARLET'S WELL.

SCHOLAR'S PATH WELLS. Named after Thomas O'Buckley, scholar, the path is on moorland near Haworth, home of the Brontes, in North Yorkshire. Half-hidden underground, and fringed with fern and bog-weed, lie these three wells which go by the names of Robin Hood, Little John and Will Scarlet.

Above: Part of the Alter tomb of Elizabeth Staynton's Grave.

Right: ROBIN HOOD'S GRAVE. Author Jim Lees examines the reputed original gravestone at Kirklees.

Below: ELIZABETH STAYNTON'S GRAVE, Kirklees Hall, Yorkshire.

The gentleman's bow, together with a print of the black letter copy of the ballad *Robin Hood and the Curtal Friar* was indefinately loaned to the owner of Fountain Dale House, which stands close to the traditional location of Friar Tuck's moat, well and cell, and the place where he first met Robin. Within a very short time the bow was being called *Friar Tuck's Bow* and a new tradition in the making.

The other was a lady's bow and this was also loaned; to Thoresby Hall, Nottinghamshire, where it was first displayed with photographs of relics, manuscripts, places etc., associated with the saga. Two of the exhibits were the traditional bows of Robin Hood and Little John. Although the lady's bow was described only as such, the report was soon abroad that *Maid Marian's Bow* was on exhibition, and another legend in the making.

Robin Hood's bow was the star attraction, loaned by courtesy of Mr. Reresby Sitwell of Renishaw Hall, who states it was at Kirklees at the time of the reformation. It was purchased by his uncle, Osbert Sitwell, who was aware of the bow's tradition when Barlborough Hall and its contents were sold, the bow having come there from Kirklees. Mr. Sitwell has graciously allowed the author the privilege and pleasure of visiting Renishaw on several occasions. The bow is displayed in this beautiful old hall, and is accompanied by a notice which hangs against it: "Robin Hood's bow was given to (by) Mr. Bartlett, by the family at Kirklees Hall in Yorkshire, which was formerly a nunnery, a relation of his being lady Abbess and to which Robin flew for safety, and tradition says that he was taken ill there and ordered to be bled. His relation procured a hole to be cut in the bottom of the porringer by which he bled to death. He was buried in the park where his gravestone is said to be seen." The note has signs of some antiquity in its abbreviations but Mr. Sitwell does not think it of any great age. The notice concludes: "His bow was given to Mr. Bartlett upwards of fourty years ago and has been in the house beyond memory of man and was always considered Robin Hood's."

It would be interesting to know who Mr. Bartlett was, and when he lived — the reference to a porringer with a hole in it is all but unique; I have only seen one other mention; and affords good reason for Robin not noting how much blood he was losing until too weak to do anything about it. There appears to be a ring of truth about it, although the porringer in question might not have been the double vessel we have today but more like a bowl used for broth. It is to be noted that this introduces a unique element to the story, as the porringer is not referred to elsewhere and is not related in any of the ballads. The bow is spliced, or laminated yew, mahogany in colour, either through age or varnish and rounded except for the grip, which is flattened. It would appear to have a pull of 40-44 pounds, but this could only be checked by stringing and tillering, an operation which would break the bow. It is approximately five feet in length and there are no horn tips, or evidence that there ever was, but it is most doubtful that it has ever been strung for many years. In a radio broadcast on the bow, the B.B.C. rejected it as being too modern: "as laminated wood was not known in Robin's time". In fact, splicing was most certainly known to arrow makers. The B.B.C. should have researched with far more care. On information from the British Museum it can be established that lamination was known in the middle-east even before the time of Christ, and there is every reason to believe that it was known and used in England in very early days. This however does not help much as the reverse is now to be found; modern long bows being made from one piece of wood without lamination. A carbon test would show when the tree was growing within fifty years; and possibly the age of the bow within a similar period, but it would not show the original owner. We can choose to either accept or reject the tradition.

Until the Second World War a bow, "belonging to Robin Hood" hung in the great hall at Loxley Hall in Staffordshire, and is believed to have been taken away by American troops quartered there. Furthermore, a *Robin Hood's Horn* was there until fairly recently; and was moved to Sweet Meadow in Mayfield, Sussex, after the purchase of Loxley Hall by the Staffordshire County Council. On the death of the late Mrs. Alice Sneyd Kinnersley, the horn went to her daughter Mrs. Seconde, who is the present owner. Writing in 1886, Redfern tells us in *History of Uttoxeter*, "There is in existence in the family of Kinnersly by the marriage of the heiress of Robert Ferrers to John de Kinnardsley an ancient horn said to Robin Hood's. It has the initials R.H. and three horse shoes two and one in a shield, that being the way in which the arms were borne by the first Thomas de Ferrers of Loxley and probably by Robert, who preceded him apparently towards the close of the 12th century, and as they were on the coloured glass of which I have spoken the traditionary connection of the horn with the name of Robin Hood is interesting. The

NOTTINGHAM CASTLE I

1. The Gatehouse (1252-55)
2. The Black Tower (1181 and 1243)
3. The Middle Bridge (c.1170)
4. The Middle Gate (1185)
5. Edward's Tower (c.1300)
6. The South West or Crusader's T
7. The Chaplain's Tower (1244)
8. The White Tower (1068)

Inner Bailey

Outer Bailey

ROGER HEATON

THE LATE 13th CENTURY

9. The Queen's Chamber
10. The King's Hall
11. St. Catherine's Chapel
12. Postern Gate of Richard I (1194)

13. Armory of Henry II
14. Brewhouse Stairs
15. King John's Tower (1204)
16. Great Hall of Edward I

Above: ROBIN HOOD'S WELL *(Stone)* off the A1, north of Doncaster.
Right: Robin Hood's Stone is first mentioned in the Monkbreton Priory Chartulary, 1322.

Below: ST. ANNE'S WELL (ROBIN HOOD'S WELL). Excavations in 1987 unearthed the remains of the famous Well that was frequented by visitors and travellers, who sat in a wicker chair and held the outlaw's cap and arrows. Historian David Greenwood has revived the *Brotherhood of Robyn Hode* ceremony that was held for several centuries, at least up to 1824.

City well link to Robin Hood

Historic site 'could help tap tourism' — dig leader

A MEDIEVAL well — believed to be Robin Hood's "healing well" — has been unearthed underneath a Nottingham pub car park.

And archeologists say the city must tap the well to boost tourism.

Dig-team leader Mr David Greenwood said the well — at The Gardener's on the Wells Road — could become a major historical site.

Businessman Mr Green-

●Project director David Greenwood at the mouth of the well

horn is mounted with silver ferrules, and has a silver chain attatched to it for suspension. As will be perceived by the engraving, ornamentation is also carved upon it, including a star, which may be emblematic, having long and short radiations alternating and all cut in notches.'' Mr. Redfern fails to have observed a local tradition that Robin Hood won the horn at an Archery match. He also makes the claim that Robert de Ferrers was Robin Hood; others state he was of the Ferrers family; a similar belief is held by the Kinnersley family and their claim is examined in a later Chapter.

In Southwell Minster Library, Nottinghamshire, among a collection of memorabilia bequeathed to the Minister by the Noble family of Southwell, is a leather pocket pistol drinking flask claimed to be Robin Hood's. It is made of leather and has the appearance of a ghurka knife scabbard, and is of a type popular in the 16th century. A similar one was auctioned before the Second World War and fetched a price of £2000, but being decorated with silver would therefore be of greater value. The late Mrs. Noble was certain that it had been a family heirloom always ascribed to Robin Hood, and her sincerity was unquestioned. As far as I am aware the Dean and Chapter of the Minster do not subscribe to the legend, they in fact were unaware of it until I called to see the flask.

On Offerton Moor, Derbyshire, stands Robin Hood's Stoop from which he is reputed to have shot an arrow into Hathersage churchyard, a distance of over a mile. Two Robin Hood Stones stood at Whitby Laithes, and in some correspondence the Borough Engineer and Surveyor of Whitby confirmed the fact, and also related to me that Robin Hood's Houses were marked on an old map he had seen. Although landmarks such as these cannot be termed personal relics, they do have a tradition, whereas crosses, stones, wells, etc. merely bear the name of either Robin Hood, or Little John. Of the relics attributed to the latter, I have already made some mention in Chapter Nine, but to those I would add that in the village of Hathersage, at a local inn there is a large chair that by popular consent is known as ''Little John's Chair''. The cottage at Hathersage was still standing in 1841 and occupied by Jenny Shird. According to Jenny she could trace the tradition of it being John's home back almost 200 years. Her father was born in 1729, and he had received the story from the previous owner of the cottage, who had lived their for sixty years, and he in turn had received the story from his predecessor. The memory, then, would go back to the time of Elias Ashmole, who in 1652 mentions only the grave and part of a bow. Most of the stories are of a mythological origin and not treated seriously, but nevertheless are sometimes appealing, or amusing enough to relate.

Also in that part of Derbyshire is Robin Hood's Stride, two large pillars rising from a group of high rocks. It is situated near Birchover, on the border of the Parishes of Elton and Harthill Moor. Sometimes known as Mock Beggars Hall, local mythical legend has it that Robin Hood in the form of a giant, stood astride the rocks with one foot on each of the pillars. The story goes that Robin passed water onto the meadows below, where seven maidens, upon witnessing this, were all transformed into stone. Only three of these stones remain, but the ''stride'' dominates the landscape.

There can be no doubt that some of the personal relics may have originated, and been used, in the May Games, but when holding such a relic in one's hand, or standing on a particular spot or landmark, and with many years of research behind one, it is not always easy to reject the tradition.

ROBIN HOOD'S STRIDE, near Elton, Derbyshire.

CHAMBER ACCOUNTS OF EDWARD II FOR JUNE 1323. (Public Records Office Document, Reference E101/379/6). This page from the accounts shows that a Robin Hood was in the employ of the King, and that he received wages on 27 June for the period 5 to 18 June. This document disproves Hunter's claim as Chapter 11 will show.

Chapter 11

*"That no scripture think they so true and good
As is the foolish Geste of Robin Hood"*

AS Robin Hood a real man, or was he a figment of collective fertile imagination? "The creation of the ballad muse" as Child, the American collector of *The Popular English and Scottish Ballads.* suggests.

Most certainly, that he was a Will-o'-the-wisp, elf, sprite, fairy, witch, or the echo of some pagan god, is not worthy of consideration, for there is nothing magical or supernatural about Robin Hood. From the numerous references to our outlaw, his reality is rarely in doubt; the only real question is that of identity if we assume that the name of "Robin Hood" was an alias. The existing claims to Robin's identity, though often lacking in their convincing argument, are worth examining if only to see how people have dealt with the problem.

Some of the theories are unpublished; the first I quote is from this category, from a correspondent, J.L. Watson, of Louth in Lincolnshire: "Eudo together with is sworn brother, Pinco, were given lands after the Conquest in the Kyme area. Eudo seated himself at Tattershall and had a son by the name of Hugh Fitz-Eudo. Allowing for dialect and the many mistakes in writing names at the time, could this man have been Robert Fitzooth; later known as Robin Hood." Eudo is a name that was fairly common in medieval times and could be corrupted to Ode, Odo, Hod and Hood, but to arrive at the name Robert is impossible. Now if Hugh had a son Robert then we would have a Robert Fitz Hugh or one of the similar names, but that is not stated. In 1243 a Robert, son of Eudo was in fact pardoned of a crime but this does not improve the claim.

An entry in the *Pipe Roll* of 1230 (Temp. Henry III) is more tempting. Here a man by the name of Robin Hood is described as a fugitive from justice and that the Sheriff of Yorkshire was accountable for his forfeited goods worth 32 shillings and sixpence — "Iden vicecomes debèt. xxxij. s. et. vj. d. de catallis Roberti Hood fugitive." The late Professor Owens of Nottingham University seemed to think that here was the genuine article and relates to the fact that a fugitive is called "Hobbe-hod" in 1226. As Robin Hood is now accepted to have lived in the reigns of Henry III and Edward I this man could well fit the bill were he referred to as outlaw and not fugitive, two descriptions which are not compatible. A fugitive is not an outlaw, although an outlaw *can* be a fugitive. Furthermore it would be difficult to switch Sheriffs at such a late time — the Sheriff of Yorkshire having no part in the Robin Hood saga. Also, from the wealth the outlaw is said to have had, 32s. 6d. would be an understatement. *Little Geste, Stanza 7:* "There is no merchant in Merry England so rich I dare well say." says Little John. So to fit this "fugitive" into the character of Robin Hood requires too much speculation by those making the claim. That he was one of the supporters of Sir Robert Thwing, a Yorkshire knight who rebelled against Henry III is only conjectural, and evidence that Hobbe-hod was the same person as Robin Hood is wishful thinking. Why two alias's for the same man?

The Victorian County History of Warwickshire has the following note: "The tradition that Loxley (Warwickshire) was the birthplace of Robin Hood appears to have originated with J.R. Planche, who, in a paper read in 1864, followed Stukeley's derivation of his name from Fitzooth and connected the outlaw with Robert FitzOdo, Lord of the manor in the later 12th century". FitzOdo was dead in 1196 and left three daughters as *his heirs.* No mention is made, other than the name why this man should be Robin Hood, although the tradition is still to be found in Warwickshire. Another writer says "In the reign of King John there dwelt in the household, or *mainpest* of a Gloucestershire Abbot, a certain Robin Hood . . . One day, most probably not later than 1213 he killed Ralph of Cirencester". To me, it proves no more than it states but the claim is made that he is another candidate for the famous outlaw.

From time to time the theory is put forward by Yorkshire historians that Robin Hood's birthplace was Loxley, in the parish of Bradfield, Yorkshire, the place where his supposed cottage once stood. This is supported by John Harrison in his *Survey of the Manor of Sheffield* (1637), "Great Haggas Croft . . . lying near Robin Hood's Bower and little Haggas Croft . . . wherein is ye foundation of a house or cottage where Robin Hood was borne". Both crofts being in Loxley Firth. The late Willis Crookes, of Loxley, stated in 1931 that the ruins remained until 1834 but "the old Loxley tradition is that Robin Hood and his step-father were working on some land now enclosed in Loxley Chase Farm, when they had a violent quarrel, and Robin Hood cut down his step-father with his scythe and killed him." Another traditional Yorkshire story that emerges at various times is that it was his father's steward that Robin Hood slew, and he then entered Sherwood Forest as an outlaw. Roger Dodsworth (1585-1654), a reputable antiquarian, in a note in 1620 states that "Robert Locksley born in Bradfield parish in Hallamshire, wounded his father to death at plough, fled into the woods, and was relieved by his mother till he was discovered. Then he came to Clifton upon Calder and became acquainted with Little John." In *The Truth about Robin Hood* (1951) P. Valentine Harris quotes: "S.O. Addy, denying the historicity of Robin Hood considered Robin Hood's Bower indicative of May Games being held in Loxley Wood". It has already been seen how several Robin Hood's, and some Robin Hood place-names stem from the May Games, as well as how the games are the base of several ballads. From the mention of "Robin Hood's Bower" in the vicinity of little Haggas Croft it seems apparent that this was once the place of May Games and over the years the name Robert de Locksley and Robin Hood have become one story.

Thomas Harwood, in his *Antiquities of Staffordshire* (1884), being his revised edition of Erdeswick's *Survey of Staffordshire and its Antiquities* of 1593, makes the following note: "Loxley was the birthplace of Robin Hood, whom Camden calls the gentlest thief that ever was". This legend says that his mother was niece to the famous Guy, Earl of Warwick. A rambling life led him to Tutbury, not far from his birthplace where he married a shepherdess under the poetical name of Clorinda, according to Vide Drayton's *Polyolbion*. In 1896 Dent and Hill wrote: "Loxley has attained a degree of celebrity as being, if not the birthplace of Robin Hood, at least the scene of many of his exploits. It is traditionally said that Robin Hood found asylum at Chartley Castle; and its founder, Randolph of Chester, is thus named in connection with the famous Robin by the author of Piers Plowman. For his aid in securing the reversion of the English throne to the Plantaganet claimant Randolph, Earl of Chester, was rewarded the wholesale grant of Staffordshire lordships, a grant which seems never to have took full effect, although in some instances it may have enabled the earl to obtain possession. Among the estates given to Earl Randolph by this abortive grant from the Norman Duke were the whole fee (all the estates) of Radulphis filius Odonis, the latinized form of Od or Hod — wherever the same can be found. That the Odo's lived during Robin Hood's time within three miles of Loxley is clearly shown by a deed relating to the mill of Wolsley, a few miles from Loxley, to which Robert filius Odonis is a witness; although not dated, it is clearly of the early part of the third of Henry III's reign. His signature is Robert fils Odonis of Huytcestri (Uttoxeter). Further evidence of the Hod's living in the neighbourhood is shown — for in 1271 William Hod and two others were presented before the Justices of the Forest of Cannock, having conveyed a dead doe in covered cart from the Hay of Teddesle to the house of William Hod, who was then dead". This is from *Historic Staffordshire*. Throsby, in his 1790-96 edition of *Thoroton's Nottinghamshire,* suggests that Robert, son of William, because of his father's support for the barons against Henry II, lost his lands and entered Sherwood Forest as an outlaw. Obviously he has not the same man in mind and may be referring to a claim made by William Stukeley.

Among some miscellaneous manuscripts in the British Library, I had the good fortune to find a letter from a Thomas Sneyd Kinnersley, dated 2nd February 1825 with the address Loxley Park. I state good fortune as it does not appear to have been seen by any other researcher into the Robin Hood identity. In the letter, Thomas Sneyd Kinnersley is writing to an unknown gentleman inviting him to see a pedigree and other old deeds, relating to the family. He adds: "I understand there is a document in the library of the College of Manchester which shows Robin Hood to have sprung from Loxley under Needwood, that his name was Robert Fitzooth or FitzHugh, thence corrupted to Robin Hood by reason of the "genteel" company he kept; that he was the Earl of Huntingdon and that this estate came into the family of Ferrers by marriage. It came into the Kinnersley family by marriage with a female of Ferrers." It may interest the reader to know that besides the offer to view the pedigree, the unknown gentleman was invited to "partake of what ever the pot may hold". The document referred to cannot be traced at Manchester University, nor at the Oxford Manchester College. A pedigree in the British Library which may possibly be the document to which Kinnersley refers gives Alan de Ferrers, Lord of Loxley, second husband of Letitia (daughter and co-heiress of Robert de Avely, lord of Lee) as having two sons, Thomas de Ferrers and Robert Fitzooth, the celebrated outlaw who died without issue. Redfern, in his *History of Uttoxeter* (1885) writes — "By the second William it (Loxley) was granted to his younger son, Wakelin, and it was held by a Robert, an Alan, a Thomas and a Henry (Ferrers)". Apart from the reference to an Alan in the pedigree mentioned, I have found no such person. In a later edition of Redfern's book, he makes the claim that Robin Hood was a member of the Ferrers' family but gives no source.

Some suggest that the Staffordshire claims exist because no Loxley has been found in Nottinghamshire, and that no substantial evidence has been produced to establish Robin Hood being of Loxley, Yorkshire, whereas in Staffordshire there is considerable evidence of a family with the name of Od or Ode living at or close to Loxley manor of that County. And legend does associate the outlaw with Loxley long before Sir Walter Scott made the name synonymous with Robin Hood.

The claim made by Dent and Hill in *Historic Staffordshire* is based on the ballad *The Birth, Breeding, Valour and Marriage of Robin Hood* (1621), together with a claim made by William Stukeley that our outlaw was one Robert Fitzooth. The ballad states that Robin was born in Loxley, Nottinghamshire, but puts Sherwood Forest close to Tutbury, and is sung by the King of the fiddlers. It is a poor source of history, being based on a May Game: "I am King of the fiddlers, and sware't is a truth" (*Stanza 44*) "And then I'll make ballads in Robin Hood's bower, and sing em in merry Sherwood" (*Stanza 55*). However, we cannot disregard the legend that Robin Hood had some exploits in Staffordshire.

Towards the end of the 17th century, Dr. William Stukeley, of Holbeach in Lincolnshire produced a pedigree showing that Robin Hood was a descendant of a Ralph Fitzooth, who came over with William Rufus from Normandy. He shows how Robin became the *pretended* Earl of Huntingdon by his descent from Judith, wife of Watheof, last Saxon Earl of Northumberland and Huntingdon, and niece of William the Conqueror. This much copied pedigree of Robin Hood Earl of Huntingdon first appeared in Stukeley's *Palaeographia Britanicca, Origines Roystoniae* — Part 2 (Stamford, 1746). He was in fact, defending his claim that Royston was an Anglo-Saxon settlement and not a Roman one. His remarks on Robin Hood are in showing the family of Roisa de Vere and are, more or less, asides. In a contemporary report, Stukeley is described as "One of the most painstaking of antiquitaries, but alas, one of the least trustworthy in any case in which a Roman camp be suggested". Perhaps so, but although he made several mistakes in his pedigree of Robin Hood, he nevertheless came very close to the truth.

In his *Robin Hood* (1795), Joseph Ritson coupled Stukeley's pedigree with the ballad *The Birth, Breeding, Valour and marriage of Robin Hood* and gives considerable notes. It ran into several additions and still remains the classic guide to the Robin Hood legend in the early modern times but, alas, he failed to correctly identify the outlaw.

Of those researchers who advocate that Robin of Yorkshire, perhaps the most forceful argument comes from Dr. Joseph Hunter's *Robin Hood* (1852), the fourth, and last, of his series of *Critical and Historial Tracts*. His theory was accepted and enlarged upon by J.W. Walker in *The Yorkshire Archeological Journal*, and also his work *True History of Robin Hood* (Wakefield 1952). Other writers soon followed their line of reasoning, and Robin Hood had become a Yorkshireman; to some apparently beyond doubt! Seemingly undisputed evidence included *The Wakefield Manor Court Rolls* of the late 13th and 14th century, and the *Household accounts of Edward II* for 25 April to 25 November 1324, together with the *Little Geste*. Their argument located our hero in Barnsdale, Yorkshire, which was never a forest in the true sense of the word, and most certainly never under the jurisdiction of Nottingham's Sheriff.

Both Hunter and Walker made their errors in placing faith and great emphasis on an entry in the *Wakefield Manor Court Rolls*. The record in question was of the marriage of a Robin Hood and a girl named Matilda, both of Wakefield. Then, from my research, completely without foundation, they claimed that this Matilda changed her name to the Maid Marian on entering the greenwood with Robin Hood, basing their findings on ballads of uncertain antiquity. Hunter states in *Robin Hood:* "Her name was Matilda, and the ballad testimony is she exchanged her name for Maid Marian". I have found no such ballad, but both Hunter and Walker seem content with a concoction derived from two ballads of no consequence, and which

Walker relates in *True History of Robin Hood*. These claims cannot go unchallenged, and it will help the reader to have the arguments explained.

Robin Hood's Stone, also known as his well, is mentioned in a charter that, according to Walker, is dated 1422, but he forced the evidence, as can be seen in my exchange of letters with the British Library after I inspected the charter. "The date of the charter you mention is given 6 June 1322. I do not know why Walker rejects this date." And again, "I regret I am unable to comment on J.W. Walker's reasons for suggesting that the date 1322 for the Robin Hood charter (this date is unquestionably what is written) is a copyist error for 1422." And another, "The date in Latin is die dominica in fest sancte trinitatis and anno domini millesimo ccc^{mo} vicesimo secundo. The misdating of the 1422 doubtless arose from the misreading of ccc^{mo} as cccc^{mo}." One more: 'The charter mentioning Robin Hood is dated 6 June 1322; the dating clause is at the end of the charter of F.185''. Four reports from different people. As Hunter suggests that Robin Hood was outlawed in 1322 after the Battle of Boroughbridge then that would be too early to have a stone or a well named after him.

A Robin Hood's Well in Nottingham was known before the Yorkshire one but proves no more than that it was dedicated to a man who was so named. If we accept it as proof of the outlaw being in that locality how do we explain Robin Hood's Walk near Boston, Lincolnshire, or Robin Hood's Tower in Richmond Castle, and many other such places? The best answer is given in Miller's *Doncaster* (1831) "I add that we collect from the name itself that this place (Robin Hood's Well), which seemed formed by nature for the purpose, was one of the seats of the disports of the Middle Ages, in which both princes and peasantry joined, particularly at the returns of May Day, Whitsuntide and Midsummer."

The *Little Geste* is used to supposedly prove most points, but conveniently ignored where it is not in harmony with the theory. For instance, we are told that Robin Hood and *all* his men are invited to serve the King at his court:

> S.416 "I will come to thy court,
> Your service for to see.
> And bring with me of my men
> Seven score and three."

The figure is exaggerated but we are told that Little John and Will Scarlet are with him:

> S.435 "By then the year was all gone,
> He had no men but twain,
> Little John and good Scathelocke,
> With him all for to go."

No reason is given for these two outlaws being unmentioned in the *Household Accounts of Edward II* in spite of the *Little Geste* stating that they remained with him to end of his service at court, and in one instance twenty eight others are named with Robin Hood *(Journal de la Chambre — 25th April, 1324)*. The King's journey from Nottingham round the Lancaster lands is shown as a tour Edward II made in 1323 through Lancashire and Yorkshire, ending back in Nottingham on 9th November, where he stayed until the 23rd of the same month, 1323, when he pardoned Robin Hood and all his band.

This in no way supports the *Little Geste,* nor is there any record of the said pardon. No reason is given for the King not going into Barnsdale of Yorkshire to find our outlaw; in fact Yorkshire receives no mention. Hunter's *Matilda* is accepted without any further search even though the source is there, "chaste Matilda, the lord FitzWalter's daughter." This was in two plays and not a ballad as Hunter says. That these gentlemen have been careless in their search is graphically shown in Chapter Fourteen by examining *their* record of the inscription on Elizabeth Stainton's gravestone — and the *true* one recorded by me. The same is to be said of Robin Hood's epitaph, which varies in spelling by the different writers; it is apparent that they never actually saw either the gravestone or the epitaph. This author has seen both!

Furthermore, Hunter states that prior to the entry in the Household accounts of the King, under the date 25th April 1324, a similar account shows the period 8th July 1323 to the 15th April 1324, where the payments are shown in gross without specifying the name of any person receiving weekly wages etc. In my early days of research I had read that an earlier reference to Simon Hood, Robin Hood and others of the later accounts existed, but failure to obtain a copy from the Public Records Office, along with their assertion that there was no such item, made me think it was either wishful thinking on my part, or a misreading. Recently the document has come to light, and my belief vindicated. This consists of fragments of two folios of an account book in very bad condition, which in order to be read had to be washed in gall and then subjected to ultra-violet light. It is from a day book of the Chamber for the period 14 April to 7 July 1323; and reveals that on 27th June of that year Robin Hood received his wages along with Simon Hood and other porters of the King's chamber for the fourteen days from 5-18 June: "I can confirm that E101/379/6 contains a reference to Robyn Hod in the context you state. A legible copy could only be obtained by means of an ultra-violet photograph" (Public Records Office letter of 28/7/82, Search Dept.). No wonder it was not available when I first wrote, as the transcribing and treatment of documents is improving all the time, and I had no source reference in my early days. This discovery puts an end to the Yorkshire case unless they change their story more than somewhat.

Another theory, and far from authentic, was that Robin Hood was born to a poor Saxon lass and later adopted by King Henry II, being brought up as a companion of Prince Richard. Because Robin would not accept a title, nor join the Crusade, Richard outlawed him on his return to England. In Richard's absence Robin was Regent of England. The story reads like that of King John and Fulk fitz Warenne and is certainly not an isolated claim, there being several along these lines.

An even less plausible version was put forward by a Staffordshire Headmaster who aimed to publish that "Robin Hood was Alfred de Hunterton, a nobleman thrown out of the manor near Penkridge, Staffs. for revolting against Henry II. He took to the woods around Cannock Chase, from where he robbed the rich and kept the loot for himself. The King's officer was the Bishop of Lichfield, Sheriff of Staffordshire. Needless to say the book has not appeared to date.

I do not scorn any of these people in their claims, or their theories, as I believe them to be as sincere in their own belief's as I am in mine. There will be no shortage of future plausible attempts to challenge my own conclusions, and I for one welcome this. I ask the readers to consider the following. The *Staffordshire Rolls* have an entry: "Robert, outlaw, listed with John and William, outlaws whose goods worth 8s. 3d. are siezed." The date, 1189, puts them into the period of King Richard I reign, and we have Robert — Robin Hood? John — Little? and William — Scathelock? By making "Much" of this we could conveniently identify them all as the original outlaws. What is surprising is that no one has jumped on this particular bandwagon. Perhaps now someone will — who knows.

Not one of the above claims are acceptable; in the remaining chapters you, the reader, can decide whether my claim is to be put in the same category, or accepted.

CHARTLEY CASTLE, where Robin Hood received asylum from his uncle.

ROBIN HOOD'S CHAPEL at Loxley Hall.

Loxley Bank 2d Feby 1825

Sir

My good Friend Mr Carlisle of Belmont has written to me, a wish of yours to see the Pedigree of the Family of Kynnersley. I beg leave to assure you that it will give Mrs Sneyd Kynnersley and me much pleasure if you will come to this place, & partake of such fare as the spot will afford and any information either as to Pedigree or Old Deeds &c that may be in possession of I shall gladly communicate to you. I am no Herald but my 2d Son is beginning to take up the Study as his amusement & I think would be glad to see the old Deeds you mention relative to the Manor of Lea. I understand there is a Drawing in the Library of the College at Manchester which shews Robin Hood to have sprung from Loxley under Needwood — that his name was Robert FitzHugh or Fitz Hooth & thence corrupted to Robin Hood by reason of the genteel Company he kept — that he was Earl of Huntingdon & that this Estate came into the Family of Ferrers by Marriage — It came into the Kynnersley Family by Marriage with a female of the House of Ferre The earliest date I have of the Kinnersleys is The Commissioners of William the Conqueror find an old Gentleman (blind) with 12 Sons living at Kinnersley Castle in Herefordshire from whom it appears this Family is descended. I am the youngest Son of four, the Issue of my late Uncle's eldest Sister Penelope, she died, I believe at Matlock after giving birth to her thirteenth Child. My eldest

LETTER FROM THOMAS SNEYD KINNERSLEY of Loxley Bank, referring to family-lore on the descendancy from Robin Hood. *(See page 118). British Library Ms. 6696.*

ROBIN HOOD by David Porter. From a series of paintings commissioned by *The Granary*, Edwinstowe. *(Reproduced by courtesy of Lada Tvrdik).*

124

Chapter 12

"This Robin so much talked on was once a man of fame,
Instyled Earl of Huntingdon, Lord Robert Hood by name."
A True Tale of Robin Hood. Martin Parker, 1632.

CHIVALRY, the pursuit of the knightly ideal, was predominently in vogue in the 13th and 14th centuries, and traversed all national frontiers, even if it did tend to apply *exclusively* to those of the *nobility.* One of the earliest descriptions of Robin Hood's character is:

"Robin was a proud outlaw, whilst he walked on ground,
So courteous an outlaw as he was never none found."

The word "proud" as used in the epic poem, the *Little Geste*, quoted here, is a poetic or rhetorical epithet of persons, their names etc., of exalted station, of high degree, of lofty dignity; lordly! The word "courteous" was descriptive of knighthood. Ritson, in 1823, said of Robin Hood: "He obtained the principal distinction of sainthood, in having a festival allotted to him, and solemn games instituted in honour of his memory, which we celebrated till the latter end of the sixteenth century; not by the populace only, but by kings and princes, and grave magistrates, and that in Scotland as in England."

Although Camden (1551-1623) referred to Robin as the "gentlest of thieves", as do others, they are all in error with their choice of noun — the adjective is correct. The manner of his *robbery,* so styled, is clearly shown in the *Little Geste.* Close examination will prove that his faith in the Blessed Virgin Mary was the motivating power — his dislike of a liar — and belief in the miraculous intervention of Our Lady which was far from uncommon until the Reformation, but lives on in the Roman Catholic Church to this day. Against this must be considered the fact that Robin Hood supported the cult of the Virgin, and it shows most in the character presented by the early ballad writers. In all things he is pious, courteous and a gentleman.

He killed twice. In the play of *Robin Hood and the Sheriff,* it is not clear whether it is Sir Guy or Robin who makes the challenge: "Let us fight at outtraunce, (to the utterance) he that fleeth, God give him mischance." The fight is retold in the ballad *Robin Hood and Guy of Gisborne* (1765), but the challenge of a fight to the death is not included. In the *Little Geste* the scene is re-enacted with the Sheriff as the antagonist. In all three versions Robin cuts off his victim's head. He does not kill for money, nor does he threaten any foe in the manner of the highwayman: "Stand and Deliver."

In the *Little Geste* he recognises the monks his men have brought to the camp to dine with him, as from St Mary's Abbey, i.e, the Abbey of his patroness; he thanks them in the belief that they are returning the loan made to the gentle Knight, Sir Richard at the Lee, on her surety:-

S.242 "And thou art made her messengers,
My money for to pay,
Therefore I can thee more thank,
Thou art come at thy day."

On asked by Robin what is in their coffers they tell him, "Syr twenty marks, as I may thrive." Most courteously, our outlaw replies:

S.244 "If there be no more," said Robin
I will not one penny,
If thou hast need of any more,
Sir, more shall I lend thee."

Little John, on Robin's instructions, inspects the monks baggage and "tells forth" £800:

S.245 "Sir," he said, "the monk is true enough,
Our Lady hath doubled the cast."

By a miracle, Robin is repaid plus interest!

MEETING OF ROBIN HOOD AND LITTLE JOHN. Plaque on Nottingham Castle Wall (Photograph by Dan Hyndman).

Later, the Knight returns to pay his debt, having been delayed on the way, but Robin will not accept it from him as "Our Lady's messengers have delivered the money." He, further, gives the Knight the four hundred pounds which Our Lady "overpaid to him."

A similar situation is encountered in the ballad of *Robin Hood's Golden Prize* (c.1620) where, in the disguise of a friar, Robin stops two priests in the greenwood and begs of their charity. They swear by the Holy Dame that they have no money on their person as that morning they have been robbed. Robin invites them to pray with him to Heaven for help, and after praying for an hour asks them to see how much they have. They profess to have nothing. Robin suggests they pray again, with the same result. He then suggests that as prayer would not fail him, they search each other, upon which it is found that whereas he has nothing, they have £500, so he rewards them with £50 each because "They prayed so heartily", and keeps the rest. The ballad writer does not make Robin a thief or con-man; it is the churchmen who are put in the wrong! Both of them lie under oath, and the taking of the money is merely accepting, and sharing with them, a gift from Our Lady. Such thinking was not remarkable for a period when many miracles were done in the Virgin's name, relics of saints worked wonders, when even the sea was set on fire, and life was cheap. The several references in the ballads to washing and wiping before a meal reveals that Robin was a man of manners and quality, not a filthy, flea-bitten rustic as many state. Soap making was known in the 13th century and in Biblical times: "For though thou washe thee with lye and take thee soap," (Jeremiah, Chapter 22). The word lye is derived from the Old English leah, leag, to wash.

Two instances from the *Little Geste are:*

    S.32 "They washed and wiped both, and sat down to their dinner."
    S.231 "They made the monks to wash and wipe."

And in *Robin Hood and the Potter:*

    S.41 "He is full welcome" said the sheriff, "let us wash and go to meat."

He is termed as a yeoman which, according to Chaucer, is one step lower than a squire. Although Chaucer was Comptroller of Customs and Subsidies on wools, skins, and hides at the Port of London in 1374; Comptroller of Petty Customs in 1382; Justice of the Peace for the County of Kent in 1385, and also Knight of the Shire in 1386, he described himself as a yeoman. His grandfather, Robert, and his father, John, had associations with the wine trade and were reasonably well to do.

In my judgement the term yeoman, as used in the ballads, does not imply any rank but is the equivalent to a *good fellow.* The Oxford English Dictionary defines the term as *servant of the crown,* and this is to be seen in the ballad of *Robin Hood and the Monk*

    S.58 "The King gave Much and Little John
        Twenty pounds in certain,
        And made them yeoman of the crown,
        And bade them come again."

It was also used for landowners with the accent on the smaller holdings. The gentle Knight is asked "I trow thou were a Knight of force, or else of Yeomanry." By service to the Crown? It would seem that a yeoman could be a Knight.

In 1445 the Scottish chronicler, Walter Bower, wrote under the year 1266 that: "Then from among the dispossessed and banished arose the famous freebooter Robin Hood and Little John with their accomplices, who the foolish multitude are so extravagantly fond of celebrating in *tragedy* and comedy." Geoffrey Chaucer gives the following lines in his *Canterbury Tales* with the words of the host to the monk — *The Monk's Tale*, prologue:

    "*Tragedy* means a certain kind of story,
      As old books tell, of those who fell from glory,
      People that stood in great prosperity
      And were cast down out of their high degree.
      Into calamity and so they died."

As the former states, Robin was celebrated in *tragedy*, and the latter gives the substance of the early tragedies (and who better to do so that the *Father of English Poetry),* then surely it is right to accept that songs were sung of a nobleman who fell into outlawry. None of these have come down to us in written form but the tradition persists that Robin Hood was of noble birth. The plays (tragedies) of Chettle and Munday are about an Earl of Huntingdon who was otherwise called Robin Hood and, incidentally, a lady of noble birth who joined him and was cruelly murdered — the Lady Fitzwalter.

William Stukeley set the matter right in making Robin Hood "the *pretended* Earl of Huntingdon"; there is a difference, but later writers dropped the word "pretended", and made him into a full-blown Earl. Ritson settles the matter in the following manner; he is quoting from the plays of Chettle and Munday: "The quotation may be of service to Dr. Percy who has been pleased to question our hero's nobility, because, the most ancient poems make no reference to his earldom and the old legend expressly asserts him to have been a yeoman. It is true; and we shall not only find his title established, but also discover the secret of his not being usually distinguished or designed by it."

Enter Robin Hood

King	"How now Earl Robert."
Friar	"A forfeit, a forfeit, my liege lord,
	My masters laws are on record.
	The court roll here your grace may see."
King	"I pray thee friar read them me."
Friar	"One shall suffice, and this is he,
	No man that cometh in this wood,
	To feast or dwell with Robin Hood,
	Shall call him earl, lord, knight, or squire"

Ritson continues: "Now the reason that most ancient poems make no mention of this earldom and the old legend expressly asserts him to have been a yeoman appears plainly enough to be that as pursuant to his own injunction he was never called by his followers or in the vicinity, by any other name than Robin Hood, so particularly the minstrels who were always, no doubt, welcome to Sherwood, and liberally entertained by him and his yeomanry, would take special care never to offend against the above law; which puts an end to the dispute."

The fact is that nowhere are the ballad writers concerned with Robin's earlier life; they relate the story of an outlaw! A loyal outlaw!

Little Geste

> S.386 "I love no man in all the world,
> So well as I do my king,
> Welcome is my lord's seal
> And monk for thy tiding."

Robin was one whose enmity was towards *some* churchmen, but not the church, for he held ministers of the church in great reverence.

> S.15 "These bishops and these archbishops,
> Ye shall them beat and bind
> The high sheriff of Nottingham,
> Him hold ye in your mind."

The chief benefices of the church were given to the Italians, and this was resented by the common people, who rose against them, pillaged their barns, wasted their lands, and insulted them. The benefices of the Italian clergy was 60,000 marks per annum, higher than the revenue of the Crown in Robin Hood's time. Many of them were barons with no knowledge of pastoral and spiritual duties; the first victim of the barons' insurrection was Peter de Aigueblanche, Bishop of Hereford, in the reign of Henry III.

So Robin styled himself as yeoman of the Forest — Keeper of the Wood — an outlaw without lands or title but the ballad writer did not lose sight of his character — a character which implies noble birth! In the full title of the *Little Geste* the Sheriff is referred to as the "proud sheriff", but as Robin is also described as "proud" in the opening lines, this is not compatible with the two men, one a King's Officer and the other an outcast.

In the *Oxford English Dictionary*, the word *proud* is defined as brave, gallant, stately, valuing oneself on account of rank — quality etc. (Middle English). It was not until later that the adjective came to mean haughty or arrogant, so both Robin and the Sheriff originated from equal positions of high birth. In the ballad *Robin Hood and the Potter*, the Potter is a man of some substance with his own business and a member of a trade guild. He is described as proud. Again, in the *Little Geste* the term is used:

> S.367 "Then bespake a proud forester,
> That stood by our King's knee."

The *Little Geste*, it is suggested, was written by a man equal to Chaucer in his command of English at that time, and he is right in giving the forester rank, for it was a position given to men of noble status. The fact he stood by the knee is further evidence of his priviliged status.

A lesser evidence of Robin's status is the word *good*. The Middle English meaning of the word was quantitive not qualitive; thus suggesting that Robin was a man of property: "a *goodly yeoman*" was he! Once he owned lands! The earliest example of *good* in this sense is chronicled in the *Oxford English Dictionary* during the 13th century, in the period of Robin Hood's life. Today, such landowners would be known as landed gentry, but this does not imply they were not of noble birth but, more likely, junior members of a noble family. Robin is shown as courteous and his manner is that of a Knight of old. In the ballad of *Robin Hood and the Tanner (Stanza 14)* our outlaw selects and cuts himself a stave and then measures it against that of the Tanner to ensure that he has no advantage in extra length:

"But let me measure," said Jolly Robin'
"Before we begin our fray,
For I'll not have mine to be longer than thine,
For that will be foul play."

Such courtesy predominates in the *Little Geste* and, at all times, he is gallant. The word *courteous* had the Middle English meaning of either gracious, benign or gentle, or all of them.

The word *meyne*, which I initially mistook for the ancient form of *men*, is shown in the *Oxford English Dictionary* (Middle English) as meaning either retainers, attendants, followers, and dependants. The Knight who owns his own castle and has considerable lands worth £400 per annum is shown in the *Little Geste* as saying:

S97 "Then bespake the gentle Knight unto his *meyne*."
And the King, after granting Robin's pardon.
S.419 "Sell me some of that cloth (Lincoln Green) for me and all
my *meyne*." (He was accompanied by Knights and nobles.)

The abbotts passing through the forests are attended by their meyne, and some of them put on a better show than Royalty. King, churchmen, knights and barons all had their meyne; surely then Robin Hoood is not the odd man out, and the word used in derision. It is worthy of note that we never met up with "Robin Hood and his *gang*", or "Robin Hood and his forty *thieves*" or the like, but always "Robin Hood and his merry *men*" — a corruption of *meyne*.

Little John, a yeoman of the Crown, always called him master and so did the merry men who were "of his cloth and fee." In the ballad of *Little John and the sheriff (Little Geste, third fytte)*, John says to the cook, after a stiff fight, that he should come with him, "to serve my master in fee and cloth." In the same ballad he is invited to serve the sheriff but replies: "I have a master, a courteous Knight." It is Robin Hood who is his master. Consider the preparation for the Knight's journey to York and the lending of £400 to him — in *Stanza 67*: "Go forth Little John and go to *my* treasury and bring me forth £400 and look well told it be," says Robin; not *our* treasury. John suggests they give the Knight fresh clothing: (S.70/71) — "Master his clothing is full thin, *you* (not *we*) must give the knight a livery to lap his body in. For *you* have scarlet and green master, and many a rich array. There is no merchant in merry England so rich, I dare say," Little John says.

At this point in the ballads they have not been in the forest long, and it is unlikely, in view of their question on whom they should rob to which Robin answers that there is no need, that the goods were stolen. This is what the ballad writer is saying and he must have in mind a man of substance — a man of quality, as there is no suggestion from any of the outlaws that the goods are theirs (ours). Later the men are asked to seek another guest to dine with their master, be he Knight or squire, or:

S.210 Little Geste
"If he be a poor man of *my* goods he shall have some."

The word *sir* according to some, is used loosely but should be considered: "Good Sir steward, I pray thee" — Stewards to the nobility were landowners and men of some degree. "Sir Abbott" and "Sir Justice" each refer to men of very high rank. The Knight addresses Robin, "Gramercy Sir," and Little John tells Robin:

"Sir, the knight is true enough"

The outlaw chief is called Sir again, and again. The climax must be, and would be so seen in the Middle ages, when the King meets the outlaw in the forest. He addresses Robin by name only until after the

STATUE OF ROBIN HOOD outside Nottingham Castle.

latter's plea for a pardon for he and his men; caps must have flown in the air when the listeneres heard the words:

> S.415 "And come home Sir, to my court,
> And there to dwell with me."
> "I make my vow to God," said Robin,
> "And right so it shall be."

Here we see, not only freedom for Robin and his men, but his re-instatement to Knighthood.

Here, beyond any doubt, is the message which the ballad singers gave to their listeners, in the true essence of poetry: brevity. Whether fact or fiction, in all of the stories, Robin Hood was of noble birth, and this is what they persisted in saying (singing). He is placed above all other outlaws in the ballads; the others, although in some cases a very close copy of their chief, wore his livery and were paid for their services of his "cloth and fee." He was their master, and always addressed so.

Robin cannot be surrendered to the Sheriff by the gentle Knight until the Knight has the King's will; he cannot be treated by the Sheriff after his capture in St. Mary's church in Nottingham, without the King's writ. It takes the Sheriff with forces strong to attempt to rout him out, without success, and this is recorded in history and ballad even though Robin Hood is not named in the former case; he is associated with the rebels. The evidence given by the minstrels cannot be written off as worthless. Had the balladeers wanted to present either a man of the soil or a common man, they could have so done, but in fact they chose to sing of a rich nobleman; proud, courteous, outlaw, with many loyal members in his retinue. To interpret Robin Hood as a man of lesser stature from the ballad evidence and text would be impossible unless (as some have) one misrepresents the word *yeoman*, which is debatable over its meaning and useage. In the *Little Geste* it means a stout fellow, a good companion, "one of the best," be he Knight, Squire, potter, or Robin Hood! To look for his identity among the common people is to get nowhere, so we must look for him among the nobility, of which the early chroniclers and antiquaries all write when they claim he was of noble birth, and outlawed for debt or "wild living."

Who was he? The answer is forthcoming in the next chapter. He *was* of noble birth; he *did* come from one of England's biggest land owning families; he *was* outlawed for alleged "wild living"; he *was* pardoned — twice! He was the people's history.

He served the King, but died an outlaw.

ST. MARY'S CHURCH, Nottingham. An illustration from Deering's *History of Nottingham*, 1751.

131

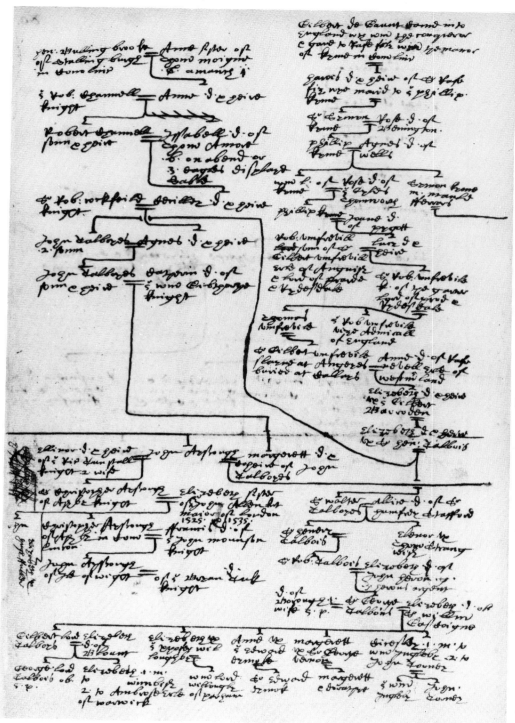

HERALD'S *Visitation, Lincolnshire,* 1562. *Harl. British Library Ms.* 1550.

Chapter 13

"They were outlaws, as't is well known
And men of noble blood."

Anon

LTHOUGH the early ballads establish Robin Hood as both an outlaw and a yeoman, unfortunately for the researcher, they do leave questions unanswered. We are given no specific reason for him having been outlawed. They tell of his pardon by "our comely King Edward", without indicating which King Edward is intended. They describe his subsequent short period of service at the King's court, and his return to the greenwood, then ultimately his death at the hand of a nun, a Prioress, of his own kin.

This is very scant information with which to identify the man, but what evidence there is indicates that he lived in a period in the reigns of Henry III and Edward I. "The former made frequent visits to Nottingham" according to *Letters Patent, Southwell, Newark, Nottingham Calendar of Patent Rolls & Close Rolls,* proving the popularity of the town with the King, and also vice versa; for in the year 1265 there was popular rejoicing when King Henry III was in the town with his son, Prince Edward, and gave to him the custody of the castle. "Edward, when King, showed the same regard for the town and is recorded as being there in the years 1279, 1280 and 1290". (Miss V.M. Walker, late of Nottingham Public Library).

In fact Nottingham was a very popular venue with the monarchs and nobility, and the town fathers made good use of it in procuring grants and charters. The visit of the King and Prince in 1265, following shortly after the battle of Evesham, agrees exactly with Fordun's report of Robin staying in the greenwood to avoid the wrath of the King and the rage of the Prince.

The period of unrest which led, in 1265, to the Battle of Evesham, and its aftermath, has the support of many as being the time of Robin's outlawry, and Gutch, quoting Spencer T. Hall, states "that subsequent to the battle of Evesham he was the acknowledged leader of a regularly organised band of men, astonishingly expert in archery"; and later, quoting Jabez Allies, "it is evident he was at the Battle of Evesham."

Hector Boece, author of *Historia Scotorum* (1527) in his thirteenth book places the outlaw in the late 13th century, after the Battle of Evesham, and although Thierry in his French *Conquest of England* puts him in the reign of Richard I, he in fact blundered badly, as his stated source was that of Fordun's *Scottish Chronicles.* These Chronicles overwhelmingly place him in the 13th century, but they give no reason for his outlawry, except by implication. The early writers who do attempt an explanation are in agreement, and we can examine their credibility here.

In *Grafton's Chronicle* Vol. 1, we find, "The truth is that in his youth he was of a wild and extravagant disposition, insomuch that his inheritance being consumed or forfeited by his excesses, and his person outlawed for debt, either from necessity or choice, he sought an asylum in the woods and forests (of which I find only two; Sherwood in Nottingham, and Needwood in Staffordshire, close to Loxley."

Because of his debts so many actions and suits were commenced against him to which he failed to answer that by order of the court he found himself outlawed. Two old manuscripts in the British Library bear silent witness to this claim; *A Memoir of Robin Hood,* in the Sloane manuscript collection, No. 708, and the *Robin Hood Note,* so called, No. 1233. Both are of the 17th century.

In stating that our outlaw was among the dispossessed and disinherited following the defeat of the Barons at the Battle of Evesham, Fordun implies that the outlaw was without means, but we have no real evidence that Robin was actually at the battle — at least in his rightful name.

Therefore Robin Hood was outlawed because of debt brought about by his wild living. More important is the fact that he is shown as a man of property or, at least, expectations. As he owned, or expected to inherit, property, then his family would have been of some status. Again quoting *Grafton's Chronicle* that "he was descended of noble parentage, or rather being of base stock was for his manhood advanced to the dignity of earl", is considered purely legendary by some, whereas others take the opposing view, among whom I stand four square. The Sloane manuscript says — "He was of . . . birth", the missing word is generally accepted as "noble", the very term used by John Leland in describing the outlaw's grave at Kirklees, during the reign of Henry VIII, "At the monastry of Kirklees is the grave of that nobleman outlaw, Robin Hood".

Another claim that he was of noble extraction is made by Joseph Ritson, in which he is taking a cue from Dr. William Stukeley's claim to Robin Hood being a pretended Earl of Huntingdon. This is further supported by the *Harleian Manuscript* (1233) which confirms "he was of noble birth, no less than earl". Chettle and Munday make good use of his nobility in their two plays, and the legend has never lost sight of it. Neither the plays or legend can be termed as history *but* their sources may well in fact be of historical substance. With such evidence and the fact that the *Little Geste,* whilst using the term "yeoman", puts our outlaw well above that status and shows how he was restored to his title, it is difficult to see why Hunter and others should have failed to look elsewhere. I do not believe, nor accept, that the "yeoman" of the *Little Geste* is intended as a rank, although even if it was so it would not affect the matter too much.

The word *yeoman, yuman,* or *yoman,* in the Middle English is derived from the Anglo Saxon, and kept its several meanings until the 16th and 17th centuries. The origin of the word is *youngmen;* sons of a Thane of which there were three classes; *King's Thane,* equivalent to our Parliamentary peer; *Middle Theine,* of the greater gentry; and *Smaller* or *Less Thegne.* of the smaller gentry. All were landowners of the King or Lord, for military service. That a man of high rank should also be a robber is not the kind of thing we would normally expect, but a look at the facts will help the reader see things as they really were.

John Major, in his *History of Great Britain* (1521) writes: "It is estimated that about the time of Richard the First there flourished those most famous robbers, Robert Hood, an Englishman, and Little John, who lay in wait but spoiled of their goods only those that were wealthy. They took the life of no man unless either he attacked them or offered resistance in the defence of his property. Robert supported by his plundering one hundred bowmen, ready fighters everyone, with whom four hundred of the strongest would not dare engage in combat. The feats of Robert are sung all over Britain. He would allow no woman to suffer injustice, nor would he spoil the poor, but rather enriched them from the plunder taken from abbotts. The robberies of this man I condemn, but of *all the robbers* he was the most humanist and the chief."

Major was professor of philosophy at Glasgow University in 1518, and he appears to have had some knowledge of the *Little Geste,* but had not noticed that the King named in it is "Our comely King Edward". That Major should conceive Richard I as the King (and he was the first to make the assertion) proved most unfortunate for history and the legend. The error originated from the fact that in the reign of Henry III, who came to the throne at the tender age of nine, his brother Richard, King of the Germans, and for some time regent of England, was hostile to the Earl of Leicester, Simon de Montfort. This Richard was known as "King" Richard, as well as, more correctly, Richard D'Allmaine, and at one time came to terms with the rebel Barons for a goodly sum, but realised it would have cost his brother his throne and turned down the offer. A ballad does in fact relate this story, but makes the twist that Richard double crossed the barons. Robin Hood has no part in this ballad. "King" Richard (D'Allmaine) and the Prince Edward were the dominant personalities and Henry III a very weak leader, so both his brother and son appear as the antagonists of the rebels.

In condemning Robert for his robberies, John Major makes him the most humane of robbers. This, in no small measure, redeems our outlaw but what Major fails to mention is that robbery was commonly practised by kings, barons, knights — and clergy! In *The Baron's War* Blauw writes, "even the poor were plundered of their bed straw in order to furnish supplies for the chieftans castles". Article 4, from *The Mise of Lewes* (1264) states: "The King was expected to be moderate in his expenses and grants until his old debts were paid off, and he was enabled to live on his own means, without oppression to merchants and the poor", was a provision insisted upon by the barons after their victory at Lewes. Once matters were reversed at the Battle of Evesham, a treaty was drawn up by King Henry III known as the *Dictum of Kenilworth,* by which rebel barons could redeem such of their lands as the King saw fit. The terms were harsh; "'but *knights and squires who were robbers,* if they had no land etc. had to find cash''. How? By robbery? Hulme tells us: ''In 1429 two merchants of Brabant came to the King at Westminster complaining of being robbed by men whom they knew, as they saw their faces everyday in the King's court.'' This case was heard by a panel of twelve Knights of Hampshire and found in favour of the accused, but so great was the outcry that a second panel was constituted and the verdict reversed. Naturally, the first panel included members of the Court.

Robbery in the middle ages was a form of business from which few were exempt. The Robin Hood story survived for centuries, and lives on, because he restored to the poor the goods taken from them. If that fact had instead been merely a figment of the Minstrels' imagination only, then the legend of Robin Hood would hardly have been received by the common people through the ages with such fervour. There is no act of robbery by Robin Hood in the early ballads!

To summarise, we now have a period — that of Henry III and Edward I. The cause of Robin's outlawry can be stated as debt through wild living, squandering his money, or lending it to others, and thus having to forfeit his estates. Added to this, perhaps also that he was among the rebels who were outlawed following the Battle of Evesham, in 1265.

Dr. William Stukeley, 1746

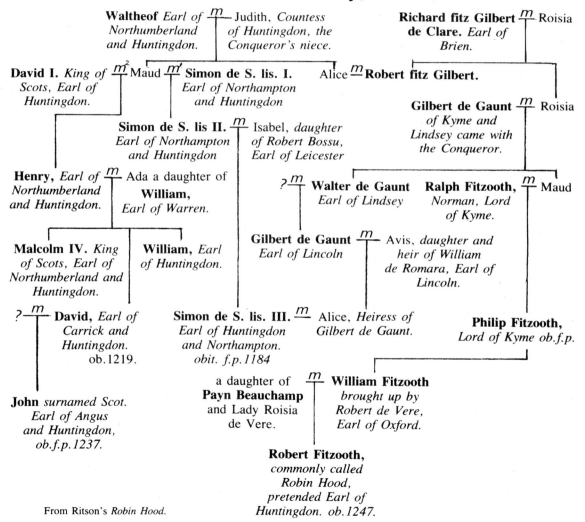

From Ritson's *Robin Hood*.

135

The real Robin Hood

If we are to believe the legend, we also have to accept the fact that Robin Hood was of Saxon blood with some pretence to the Earldom of Huntingdon (or some other). Also, as the Huntingdon's are known from the time of the last Saxon Earl, Waltheof, until the death of John, surnamed the Scot, it would not be difficult to find the outlaw if he actually was of that Earldom. That erudite work *The Complete Peerage* informs us that, ''Robin Hood, otherwise known as Robert Fitzooth, the famous forest outlaw, popularly ennobled in legend as the Earl of Huntingdon never possessed that earldom or any other. Of the writers who claim his noble birth only William Stukeley names him as the *pretended* earl''.

Dr. William Stukeley, in fact, gives the lineage of the Earls of Huntingdon up to 1354 with fair accuracy, but overall, his pedigree of our outlaw is inaccurate, and incomplete. In this he is not alone, for the family has several Simons, Philips, Williams, and Roberts; there is also confusion on the distaff side with Rohese, and although one of the greatest landowning families with knights fees in excess of many barons, little is known of their origins. Nevertheless, Stukeley did at least give us a name on which to work — Robert Fitzooth of Kyme.

To arrive at such a name without good foundation is not the kind of thing which would have given Stukeley the appelation ''painstaking'', and as he gave no source the following may have been his inspiration — ''Hester Stukeley married into the family of Kyme of Boston who lived at Rochford Tower, or by some Richmond, whose ancestors have been famous in that county ever since the Conquest''. Hester was William's great-aunt, and she lived in London; William Stukeley enjoyed visits to his aunt and uncle and on one occasion he was told of the Kyme family lore that Robin Hood was one of them.

Curiously, many years before beginning serious research I was told that the Gregory family of Lenton in Nottingham, were related to Robin Hood; a matter that I gave no further thought until very recently. Whilst browsing through the plates of Heraldic Coats of Arms in Thoroton's *Nottinghamshire,* I noticed the Kyme family crest of red, with ten crosses surrounding a gold chevron (Gules, Crusselle d'Or, un chevron d'Or), but unusually, with three extra crosses on the chevron, Gules. On checking the index, I found that they belonged to the Gregory family of Highurst, Lenton. It read, ''In the year 1662 when William Dugdale, Norroy King at arms, made his visitation, George Gregory esq., son and heir of the said John and Elizabeth, not exhibiting sufficient proof as since he hath, thought fit to take a grant of arms and crest he now useth from the said Norroy, in relation to his descent from the ancient family of Kyme.''

The senior branch of the Gregory family are believed to have emigrated to Australia, nevertheless this author now had knowledge of five living families who claimed descent from the immediate family of the man who I believe to be Robin Hood. None of these families were hitherto known to each other.

Stukeley's claim is that Ralph Fitzooth, a Norman knight, Lord of Kyme, married Maud, the daughter of Gilbert de Gant, earl of Kyme and Lindsey. By her he had issue, Philip, Lord of Kyme, who died *without issue;* and William brought up by the Earl of Oxford, Robert de Vere. The said William married a daughter of Payn Beauchamp and Roiasia de Vere, and by her had issue, Robert Fitzooth, commonly called Robin Hood, the pretended Earl of Huntingdon who died 1274. The truth is, and it has escaped the attention of researchers hitherto, that it was Robert Fitzooth, not his father, who was brought up

---

Opposite: THE PEDIGREE OF ROBIN HOOD

Alias Robert de Kyme, disinherited Lord of Kyme, Lincolnshire.

During the author's early days of research he found a reference, obviously in a charter (source then unknown), to:
''*Robert de Kyme, son of William de Kyme, and his sister, Margaret.*''

   This Margaret was not named in any Kyme family pedigree, although most show a daughter issue of William and Lucy. More recent research has revealed a Margaret, daughter of William de Kyme, and who married Algeri Wilberfos of Yorkshire, and had issue of a son, Henry. The evidence that she is the Margaret that the author sought is provided by her father, ''William by inquisition post mortem 44 Henry III (Obit 1259) was proved to hold Manors in York, including Wilberfos and Manors in Lincolnshire''. Thus, she was the sister of Robert, and ample confirmation of the missing charter.

   The source for this revelation is Heralds' Visitation to Yorkshire *(1584/5 and 1612). Proof that Margaret was not the daughter of William's second wife Lucy, but issue of this first wife, Rohese, is in the fact that had Lucy been her mother, Margaret would have been only seven years of age when she married.*

   My research into this claim when first publicised bought a response from Mrs. Marion Kime of Wainfleet, who advised me of the family-lore surrounding their descendancy from Robin Hood's family. This has been handed down for generations and the family live on land once owned by the Kymes.

Norman

Ralph The Sewer 1086 (Fitz Oswey or FitzWith)

Ralph de Kyme. 1106 Died c.1147. Came with the Conqueror or William Rufus

Saxon

Anschetil Died before 1086

William Fitz Anschetil Died 1115-19 Domesday tenant of Waldon, the Engineer

Beatrice = **Simon** FitzWilliam. Died 1162   A daughter   ROGER 1194 Agnes

hawise = **Philip** Lord of Kyme, Dapifer. Sheriff of Lincolnshire 1167. Died c.1189   William 1162   Simon FitzSimon Knight. Died c.1198   Walter 1162   Ranulf 1180

Rohese c.1205-28 Co-heiress of Robert de Maltby = **Simon** de Kyme, Knight, Lord of Kyme, Sheriff of Lincolnshire 1197. Died 1220   Philip c.1175-84   William de Kyme, Dapifer c.1175-1220 Married Margaret, Co-heiress of Robert de Maltby   Walter 1184   Roger (Canon)

Agnes de Welles = **Philip** de Kyme, Knight, Lord of Kyme Died 1242   Simon 1214   Robert Died 1201

Daughter of William de Roos, Grandson of William, King of Scots, Earl of Huntingdon

Maud de Ferrers. Died 1299 = **Simon** de Kyme, Knight Lord of Kyme Died 1248   Rohese Died before 1251 = 1 **William** de Kyme, Knight, Lord of Kyme Died 1259   2 = Lucy Died 1279

Robert Outlawed 1226 Pardoned 1227 Outlawed 1265 Died c. 1285

Margaret Married to Algeri Wilberfos

Henry Wilberfos

Philip de Kyme, Knight, Lord of Kyme Died 1323

Simon de Kyme Knight. Sheriff of York-shire 1301

by the Earl of Oxford and married Roiasia de Vere. "Alberis, Earl of Oxford, died in the sixteenth year of the reign of King John without issue", says Leland, and *Dugdale's Baronage* adds this, "his brother Robert, succeeded giving 1000 marks to the King for the livery of his lands and inheritance, with the castles of Heningham and Tamenent(?) together with the wardship of the heir of William FitzOates (Stukeley's Fitzooth) to marry his neice". Not only does this set the story on a new course, but as Ralph Fitzooth came over with the Conqueror and Robert is shown as a minor in 1214, the generation gap is too great, and there are several missing generations. A reasonable average is five generations in one century; viz: Since 1902 we have had Kings Edward I, George V, George VI, and then Queen Elizabeth II, the Prince Charles of Wales, and his offspring. Four generations living at one time is common today.

As people in the time with which we are concerned were married at a much earlier age than today, then three generations from 1086 (Ralph Fitzooth) to *c*.1200 (Robert Fitzooth), is clearly just not feasible. There are some missing. And in further evidence I offer my own pedigree (on page 137).

Stukeley made another attempt, based on the ballad *Robin Hood's Birth, Breeding, Valour, and marriage,* but qualifies it with a note on Lady Roisia: "where is Robin Hood's true pedigree".

The *Ross manuscript* in the Lincoln City Reference Library agrees that Ralph Fitzooth and Maud had issue, a daughter, Hawise, who married Philip de Kyme. She had two brothers, Ralph and William in the wardship of Robert, Earl of Oxford etc. It is apparent with this work being between 1801 and 1870, that Ross is taking his source from Stukeley with a reference from Dugdale, who had also failed to see the error, but nevertheless is correct in making Philip de Kyme, Lord of Kyme, the son in law of Ralph, for he assumed the surname Kyme on his marriage to Hawise, daughter of Ralph Fitzooth.

Of Ralph, I find no more in Lincolnshire, but a Randalphus or Raulph appears as a witness to a charter in Staffordshire in 1072. He had a son, Robert Filias Radulphi, later shown as Robert FitRalph owning the manor of Weston and a tenant of Earl Ferrers and later as Ralph Fitz Odo (Ooth?). Also, a descendant is shown as Robin Hood. The reason for the interruption in lineage will be obvious to the reader in due course but for the moment I will merely state that Robert is probably the mysterious Fitzooth put forward by both Stukeley and Ross. Both of them were seeking a Robin Hood of Kyme, and both confused Dugdales's FitzOates with FitzOdo (Ooth).

The Kyme family was of Saxon blood and held tenancy of their lands before the Conquest. The earliest name I find is Anachetil, temp., William I, whose son, William, was tenant of Waldon, the engineer, at the time of the Domesday Survey (1086). He had issue, Simon, known as FitzWilliam, founder of Bollington Priory (*c*.1139), who married Rose of Bennington and by her had issue, Philip. This Philip was Sheriff of Lincoln in 1167 and had brothers, William, Simon, and Ralph, proving that Ross and Stukeley are both in error, the one showing that Philip died without issue, and the other showing William and Ralph as brothers-in-law of Philip. As this William was still living in 1162, he would not have had a son who died in 1274 or later, so we must look elsewhere.

Philip's son, Simon, Sheriff of Lincoln, in 1197, supported the barons against John, married Rohese, co-heiress of Robert de Maltby, and died in 1220. Simon had a son, Philip, who was on the baron's side until 1217. Philip had issue by Agnes de Welles, Simon de Kyme, Lord of Kyme, who died without issue in 1248 (Simon left a widow, Maud, daughter of William de Ferrers, Earl of Derby, Lord of Loxley). On the death of Simon, his brother William inherited and took the name of Kyme. This man is the William de Kyme, Lord of Kyme, of the Stukeley and Ross claims. By his first wife Rohese, William de Kyme had one daughter, Margaret, and a son Robert. Around the period 1240-1250, Rohese died and William took a second wife Lucy. Also in this period, a second son, Philip was born to the family, and Lucy is presumed to be his mother, Rohese being thought to be dead by then. Later, Lucy gave birth to William's third son, Simon. Lucy was the daughter of William de Roos, and the great-grand-daughter of William the Lion of Scotland, Earl of Huntingdon! The eldest son Robert, as a minor held lands in Oxcombe, Lincs, of his uncle Simon, who held them of the Earl of Chester. According to the *Testament of Neville,* (1213) — "Earl of Chester the fee of half a knight, and the eighth part of one knight's fee which Simon de Kyme held in Oxcombe." In (Lincoln) *Notes & Queries*, Vol. VII, we find, "Robert, son of William, who held 1/10th., knight's fee at Oxcombe was the same man who warranted half a bovate of land in 1231". The Oxcombe lands were tenanted by, Matilda de Martin, 1/16th fee; Robert, son of William, 1/10th fee; and William de Swaby 1/12th fee, and as the words heading the list are held *by* and *of* the Kymes there is no doubt that Robert and William were Kymes. Further evidence of this is the fact that only the elder members of the family would be entitled to that surname, or the Lordship of Kyme, and William, being a junior member of the family, did not carry the surname until he succeeded to the Lordship (Barony). It should be emphasised that surnames were in fact rare in those times, a man would be known only as his father's son, i.e. Robert's Son, hence Robertson etc., unless he was heir to a title.

Here we have to dispose of a red herring. In 1242, a Robert, son of William of Tetford held lands of Simon de Crevequer. Robert is mentioned, with his son Gilbert, in the list of those responsible for the Inquisition of 1242 in Hill Wapentake: "In 1203 Simon (de Kyme) paid (pro transfetations) six marks for two knights fees in Lincolnshire in virtue of the guardianship of Walter, son of Robert, son of Simon." *(Records of the Kyme Family, C.D. Wedd).* I know of no records of a Robert de Kyme's son Walter, who may have died young but there are many records of another Robert de Kyme between 1226 and 1278, and it is important to remove him from the picture at this point. Working on the *assumption* that he was the younger son of Robert fitzSimon and that he must have been born about 1200 before or after, he would be 78 or 79 when he died. Wedd later adds, "He (Robert) married Beatrice of Toynton. In 1246 he made an agreement with Simon, Lord of Kyme (*possibly* his cousin) to give up to him in return for an annuity his rents and tenements in Boston."

It is at this point that the Ross manuscript, *Barons of Kyme,* causes confusion aplenty by wrongly identifying this Robert as the younger son of William de Kyme by Matilda or Lucy. Although he lived between 1200 and 1278 he was shown to be married to Beatrice, and could not have been Robert the outlaw.

Before continuing, we now have to remind ouselves of the claims of Robin Hood (FitzOoth, Ode, Odo, etc.) being of Loxley in Staffordshire. Firstly, E. Hargrove in 1791, writes: "The earliest I find is William Fitzooth, father of our hero, to which his dwelling at Loxley (Staffs.) seems to point, might suffer with them (the Barons) in consequence of that rebellion (Henry II) which could not only deprive the family of their estates but also their claim to the Earldom of Huntingdon. Robert's ancestors were Normans and possessed the Lordship of Kyme. There is a market town in the County of Lincolnshire called Stainton." Robin Hood *was* a Kyme!

The Kyme's were a Saxon family, which married Normans, starting with Philip and Hawise. This is repeated by Throsby in his edition of Thoroton's *Nottinghamshire* (1795). Planche, in his *A Ramble with Robin Hood* connects him with Robert FitzOdo, Lord of the manor of Loxley, Warwickshire. In the *History of Uttoxeter,* Redfern claims Loxley in Staffordshire to be the reputed birthplace of Robin Hood and also, in error, that he is believed to have been no other than Robert de Ferrers. Dent and Hill, in their *Historic Staffordshire* (1844), quoting from Thomas Hardwood's edition of *Erdeswick's Survey of Staffordshire* (1593), state unreservedly that Loxley of that County was the birthplace of Robin Hood. In 1825 Thomas Sneyd Kinnersley made the same claim, and I submit that the source is older than that of Stukeley. The family lore lives on to this day, and the author has examined a pedigree of the Kinnersley family which was loaned to Nottingham's Lord Mayor by a lady member of that family, claiming relationship to our outlaw. In fact, both the Kyme family and the Kinnersley family can rightly claim their descent from Robin Hood's kin, just as those who have stated that Robin was a member of the Ferrers family, are also correct. The descent is by marriages: that of Simon de Kyme to Maud, daughter of William Ferrers, and that of John Kinnardsley to Joanna, sister and heir of Thomas de Ferrers, Lord of Loxley. William Ferrers was great-uncle to Robert de Kyme and great-great-grandfather of Joanna. They all relate to the one man — Robert de Kyme, confused by Stukeley with *FitzOoth,* and he in turn with Dugdale's FitzOates, or Odo etc. The outlaw's name, as we have seen throughout, was Robert, diminutive — Robin.

In reality *Robin Hood was the nom-de-plume of Robert de Kyme.* Let us discover more about the man.

Robert de Kyme, born *c.* 1210, the eldest son of William de Kyme (Lord of Kyme after the death of his brother Simon in 1248) by his first wife, Rohese. In 1226 he was accused of crime(s) and outlawed; the following is recorded in a Patent Roll of King Henry III, *"Concerning Robert de Kyme. The King. Greetings to all. Know ye that we have declared in full pardon to our beloved and loyal subject Robert de Kyme and have dropped all anger and indignation (outrage) which we have borne against him because of a certain charge which a lady made before us at Wenlack against him of robbery and disturbing the King's peace. And testified in our court 1226. The pardon is dated 25th., May 1227."* The charges match the claims made of his riotous living, and supports the testimony in the *Little Geste* of Robin's loyalty to the Crown. "I love no man in all the world so well as I do my King." The year in outlawry was

CALENDAR OF PATENT ROLLS: HENRY III: 1225-32, page 125, showing a pardon for Robert de KIMA on 25 May 1227. Document Reference C.66/35. *(Reproduced by courtesy of The Public Records Office).*

reason enough for Robert's father to disown him, his great-grandfather had lost his lands by joining the barons against King John, and his grandfather all but suffered the same fate — a risk his father and uncle Simon understandably did not wish to take.

Being born in or near to, 1210, and outlawed young; being pardoned by the King, returning to his forest haunts as an outlaw until he died of old age, and dying an outlaw agrees with the *Little Geste*. That ballad takes up his story in Nottinghamshire sometime just before Evesham, and from his first outlawry to that point he was in Staffordshire, maintained by the Ferrers. Legend has it that he died at the age of 87, but there is no way of proving this or any definite age, except that he dare not come out of the forest for dread of King Edward. The legend has it that he was in the forest for 22 years after his second pardon of 1271, which would bring his death to 1293. However, I would place his death as before that, but after 1274, bearing in mind the entry in the *Staffordshire Rolls* under 1275 of Sir Richard at the Lee (See Chapter 6), although as I have shown, this event may have been earlier. "Estates of minors were always in the hands of their lords" (Hume), and Simon, Robert's uncle, was his Lord, and not of much wealth. A charter of 1246 shows that Robert sued his uncle for arrears of 23 quarters of wheat, 23 quarters of barley, and 50 quarters of oats. It was agreed that Simon should render every year of his life the above items, plus fourteen marks of silver and 40d. at three terms etc., and moreover Simon has already given 30 marks of silver to Robert. The payments are to be made at Kyme, and Robert quit claims from himself to Simon and his heirs all arrears of corn and pence and all damages which he said he sustained by reason of the witholding of rent.

In 1248, William de Kyme succeeded to the title and the Kyme lands. The Charter No. 1 made at York (in a later hand changed to Lincoln) is dated 25th June 1246, and may have been made whilst Robert was still a minor. Stukeley's claim that Robert Fitzooth, who died 1274, was Robin Hood, and of which no evidence has been found to support it (except Ralph FitzOswey, norman knight), fails in the fact that no Philip Fitzooth has been found as son of Ralph, and there is no evidence of Fitzooth being lords of Kyme. Stukeley endeavours to connect Robin Hood with the elder branch of the Kyme family, but in fact he was wide of the mark in making William Fitzooth a Lord of Kyme.

There is no valid reason to deny that "Robert, son of William, holding lands at Oxcombe", was not a Kyme or that he quit claimed lands gifted to him by Thomas de Multon, to his uncle Simon. Philip, who inherited from William De Kyme, was born *c.*1240-1250, as we have seen, presumably to William's second wife Lucy, and the family's known offspring consisted of Robert, Margaret, Philip, and Simon, but to which the Ross manuscript and other sources add William, John, and Ranalfus. Although they show a daughter by Rohese they fail to name her. I have, Margaret! Only Simon is shown by all as the issue of Lucy. Philip succeeded to the title as a minor so that Robert was either dead, or as I believe, *disowned,* just as the earlier writers claim. That he was claiming arrears and quit claimed all damages seems to point to some kind of trouble from which a regular payment would have saved him — in fact, debt.

The next we hear of him he is at Chartley Castle, Staffordshire, having of his own choice taken the name Robert Hood. According to Redfern, writing in 1864, "It is traditionally said that Robert Hood found asylum in Chartley Castle and its founder, Randolph of Chester, is thus named in connection with the famed Robin Hood by the author of *Piers the Plowman*".

"It is quite a strong tradition that a member of the Ferrers (Robert) was at Loxley under the name of Robin Hood, hence the traditional horn and (lost) bow. Others associate Robert Odo (Hood) of Uttoxeter, and we have a note of Ralph Fitz Odo holding several lordships in Staffordshire, and a Robert Fitz Ralph being a tenant of the Ferrers. From this comes the tradition of Robin Hood being one of the Staffordshire Odo's."

One thing is certain: Robert de Kyme *was* related to the Ferrers, by the marriage of his uncle Simon to Maud Ferrers. The confusion arose from Robert's selection of a new surname after his first outlawry and disinheritance, and he may never have been aware of his pardon.

Following the death of William de Ferrers in 1254, his son Robert de Ferrers succeeded to the estates and Lordship. He supported the Earl of Leicester, Simon de Montfort, against Henry III, and Robert de Kyme being one of his tenants, was again in trouble, for so wicked was de Ferrers that it was not until 1271 that all tenants of Robert were pardoned: "Hethersfield, 19 April 1271. Pardon to all tenants of Robert de Ferrers all trespasses, actions, and injuries against the King, our father". Many did not accept the pardon, including Robin Hood. The final pardon, according to the *Little Geste,* was to the

KYME FAMILY SEALS

Right: SEAL OF WILLIAM DE KYME, Lord of Kyme and father of Robert de Kyme alias Robin Hood. This facsimile is from the *Ross Annals*, volume 2, and copied from one such seal in the *Hollis Collection*.

Left: SEAL OF PHILIP, Lord of Kyme, who inherited the Lordship of Kyme due to the disinheritance of his elder brother, Robert. This seal is also from the *Ross Annals*, volume 2.

(The Kyme Family seals are reproduced by courtesy of the Lincolnshire County Council Library.)

outlaw leader and all his men, well-known archers in Sherwood Forest. J.E. Morris states: "For some special reason Derbyshire and Nottinghamshire for which there was one Sheriff, were called upon, and the reason is obvious for the foresters were notoriously good poachers and good marksmen". A Sherwood Forester was one who lived in the forest, which included outlaws. Rebels returned to the King's cause willy-nilly, taking up their old lives after supporting the King's successes. The Folvilles of Leicestershire are an example of this, and Maurice Keen in his *The Outlaws of Medieval England* (1961) gives account of how one, Eustace, was living in outlawry and then supporting the King at his convenience. A Patent Roll, in the Middleton Manuscript, lists offences of theft, burglary, murders and the harbouring of felons in Nottinghamshire and Derbyshire, and this includes the said Eustace. He, and many of the other offenders were acquitted by the juries, and others were never caught, being unnamed.

Following Robert's disinheritance, and of his life in Staffordshire, none of the exploits of the ballads are ascribed to him there. Whilst in the asylum of his uncle he played the part of a medieval country squire and held lands in Uttoxeter and Loxley of his great-uncle, upon whose death, Robert became tenant of that notorious Robert de Ferrers. It is following the defeat of the Barons at Evesham, that we learn of the first exploits of Robin Hood in Sherwood Forest.

In spite of the claims that Robin fought at Evesham, from the lists available there is no evidence to confirm this. Nor is there any report whether the Kymes were active against the King, supported the King, or remained neutral. The latter appears to be the case, as loss of lands and income would have been fatal to the family. The ambitions of Philip, father of Simon, had left his heir with the inescapable legacy of debt and encumbered estates. Simon joined the rebels in 1214 against King John, but the Kymes appear to have returned to the King's peace when Henry III ascended the throne. Clearly Robin Hood had a background of rebellry, and as Robert de Kyme had taken the name of Robert Hood, he would not be a subject of written history, but of the peoples history (verbal).

Finally on his kinship, there does in fact exist the conclusive proof sought by Hunter, as to the family of Robin Hood, and it does confirm that he was a Kyme. Hunter maintained that if a relationship between Robin and the family of the Prioress, Elizabeth Staynton, could be established, this would settle any dispute as to his family origins. Here, I reveal that connection.

Robert's great-grandfather, Simon, and great-grand-uncle, William, respectively married Rohese and Margaret, daughters and co-heiress of Robert de Maltby, steward to William de Percy, and by these two marriages brought the manor of Staynton in Yorkshire to the Kymes. There we have the "kinship" of Elizabeth Staynton and Robin Hood.

Volume XXIV of *Lincolnshire Notes and Queries* contains the following: "Having thus set out the descent which we find also confirmed by Charters to Bullington Priory, by William de Kyme, we seem unable to doubt that the estates in the county of Yorkshire, of which he died possessed, were a portion of the inheritance which had devolved upon him as descendant of Rohese, his grandmother, and heiress of Robert (de Maltby) Dapifer." Consequently, a Prioress of Staynton would have been "near of his kin" as the *Little Geste* states, if not "of his kin", the term *aunt* and *niece* being used somewhat loosely.

Where Stukeley went wrong was in basing Robert's claims to the Earldom of Huntingdon upon the fact that he descended from Robert FitzGilbert and Alice, daughter of Waltheof (Earl of Northumberland and Huntingdon) and his wife, Judith (Countess of Huntingdon), the Conqueror's niece. That Robert's stepmother was descended from William, the Lion of Scotland and Earl of Huntingdon, he unfortunately failed to notice, but it is a moot question as his claim to this Earldom may stem from the plays of Chettle and Munday. Others merely state he was of noble birth — Kyme also means *prince* or *noble*.

The truth is that the family of Kyme were known as the Earldom of Kyme, and are shown as such in *The Annals of Worcester* and elsewhere. This then is the *pretended* Earldom. Had he succeeded his father, he could in fact have laid claim to this ancient Saxon Earldom, and, if an Englishman held the throne, the Earldom of Huntingdon too. It may well have been the cause of his insurrection and wild ways, as lands once held by them from the King, they now held as underlords, their overlords being Frenchmen. Robert de Kyme fits the spirit of Stukeley's claim, and Stukeley was the first to identify the outlaw's background; he just failed to pick the right name. This Robert also identifies with both legend and the claims by earlier writers. Had Stukeley noticed that Ralph Fitzooth's daughter married Philip, Lord of Kyme, he himself would have discovered the real identity of Robin Hood — Robert de Kyme (born *c*.1210, died not earlier than 1274, and not later than 1293).

Epitaph on the stone of Robin Hood's grave at Kirklees.

144

Chapter 14

"Yet he was begyled, i-wise — through a wicked woman,
The pryoresse of Kirkesley that nye was of hys kynne."
— Little Geste.

HE *Little Geste* tells us that after twenty two years in the greenwood, Robin informed his men:
"Tomorrow I must to Kirkesley, craftely to be leten blode." *(S.454)*. No reason is given
for him taking this step, but it was to end in disaster, for the Prioress of Kirklees and
a cleric, Sir Roger of Doncaster, who was her special favourite, conspired together to kill
Robin.

S.455. "Sir Roger of Doncaster by the Prioress he lay,
And there betrayed good Robin Hood,
Through their false play."

It is left to the reader to assume whether or no our outlaw was bled to death by the Prioress. The Sloane
manuscript reports: "Distempered with cold and age; he had great pains in his limbs; his blood being
corrupted; therefore to be eased of his pain by the letting of blood, he repaired to the Prioress of Kirklees,
which some say was his aunt, a woman very skilful in physic, and surgery, who perceiving him to be
Robin Hood, and knowing how fell an enemy he was of religious persons, took revenge of him for her
own house, and all others, by letting him bleed to death." The story is expanded upon in the Percy
manuscript ballad, *Robin Hood, his death* (1765), where Robin and Little John meet an old lady on the
way who was *banning* (cursing?) Robin Hood, and a little further on he meets some who are weeping
"for his dear body, that this day must be let blood". Red Roger is introduced into the story and he
fights with Robin, who has perceived the treachery, and although he receives a sword thrust through
the side, he kills Roger.

It is somewhat strange that one who never hurt a woman, or man in womans company, should be
portrayed as an enemy of nuns. In fact he refuses Little John's request to burn down the Nunnery because,
"if he did any widow hurt, at my latter end, God would blame me". He instructs his friend, "to bear
him to yonder street and make him a grave of gravel and greet, and bury him with his sword at his
head, his arrows at his feet, and his yew longbow by his side; also his met-yard wi . . ." (the end is
missing). In a ballad of the same name of 1786 neither Red Roger or Roger of Doncaster are mentioned;
nor is treachery suggested; but again Robin refuses Little John's request to burn down the Nunnery.
It is in this version that the story of the last arrow being shot by Robin to mark the place for his grave
makes its appearance; also the epitaph is given for the first time, in a ballad, and the legend, as accepted
today, is completed. Thus, one who defied the might of Kings and Sheriffs died through the treachery
of a woman. It is interesting to note that one who worshipped the Virgin Mary makes no appeal to her
— his trust is in God! The reformation was responsible for this change in the ballads, and evidence of
the church's changed attitude towards Our Lady.

ROBIN HOOD'S GRAVE

The grave at Kirklees Hall has been badly vandalised over the years. It still stands in woodland in the
park of the Hall, near Mirfield, Yorkshire. Only a portion of the original gravestone remains, due to
unfortunate legend that, "a superstition existed that a chip from it was an effectual cure for toothache,
so that when the Lancashire and Yorkshire Railway was being constructed in the second quarter of the
nineteenth century pieces of the stone were chipped off by the navvies on the work, not as mementoes
of Robin Hood, but to place under their pillows as a cure for toothache."

The gravestone is actually more like a boulder, of some size, with a smooth surface and no sign of
chipping; too heavy for me to lift, and does not appear to have been a gravestone — except only in that
it was of great thickness. Several of the writers on the legends have referred to the grave, but it is evident

145

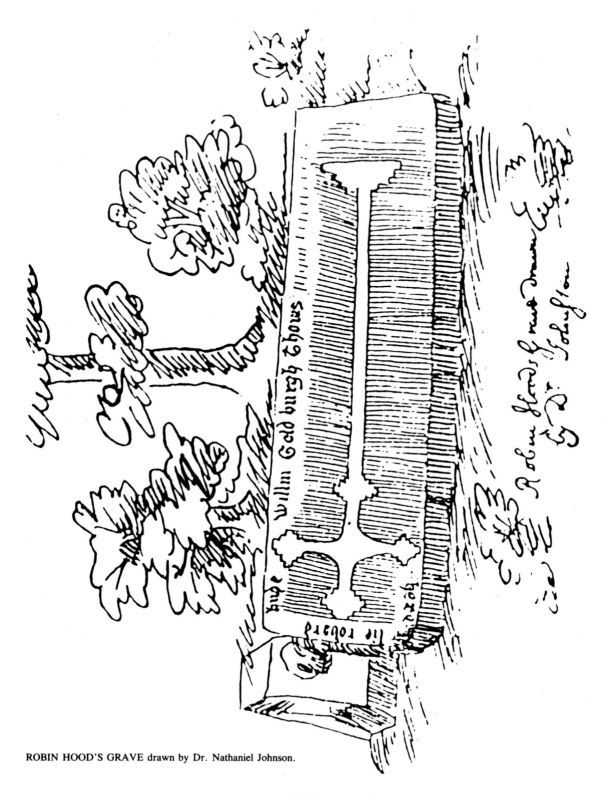

ROBIN HOOD'S GRAVE drawn by Dr. Nathaniel Johnson.

from the following statements that not all of them actually saw the stone, but relied upon the observations of others.

"Kirklees nunnery in the woods whereof Robin Hood's grave is, is between Halifax and Wakefield upon Calder." Ritson, *Robin Hood.*

". . . as Calder comes along, It chanced she in her course on Kirkley set eye, Where merry Robin Hood, that honest thief doth lie." Drayton, *Polyolbion.*

"The first notice I found of it (Robin Hood's Grave) was not earlier than 1677." Hunter, *Robin Hood.*

"Upon his grave the prioress did lay a fair stone, with a raised cross bottony on a calvary of three steps sculptured thereon, and an inscription, 'Here lie Robin Hood, William Goldburgh and Thomas . . . ,' the rest is obliterated. The writer also states that at either end of the tomb was erected a cross of stone, which is not to be seen there at present." Grafton. *Chronicle* (1562).

"At Kirkless nunnery Robin Hood's tomb with a *plain cross on a flat stone* is shown in the cemetery. In the ground at a little distance lie two graves, one of which has an inscription for Elizabeth de Staynton, prioress, there." Camden, *Britannia,* (1607).

In the *True History of Robin Hood,* J.W. Walker gives the following story: "In his *Ancient and Modern History of the Famous City of York,* (1730) Thomas Gent relates that he has been told that Robin Hood's tombstone, with his effigy on it, was ordered by a certain Knight to be placed as a hearth stone in his great hall. Three times it was found to have moved, and fearing the supernatural the Knight had it returned (where, it is not stated). Whereas a pair of oxen and four horses were used to return the stone it took twice that number to bring it to his home. Dr. Nathaniel Johnston, 1665, made a drawing of Robin Hood's grave at Kirklees, on which is the same inscription as recorded by Grafton a 100 years earlier." Walker also includes an illustration in his book which was drawn by Ethel M. Walker, and based upon Dr. Nathaniel Johnston's sketch of 1665. However, whereas Johnston's original drawing is oblong with rounded edges at the head, the Walkers' version is square at the corners, tapers from head to foot, has three steps whereas the former has four, and has a surround which is not on the original.

In Gough's *Sepulchral Monuments* (1786) is "the drawing of the stone on the grave of Robin Hood (in Kirklees Park being a plain stone with a sort of cross fleuree thereon) now broken and much defaced, the inscription illegible."

It will now be appreciated by the reader the confusion that has surrounded the grave, which, according to one writer who failed to divulge his source, was referred to as early as 1450. He could have been correct, the earliest mention known to me is by Leland, in his *Collectania,* published in 1770, but actually written in the reign of King Henry VIII (1509-1546), little less than a century after that earlier recorded observation.

There is no reference to either a burial or a grave in the *Little Geste,* and because in the Percy manuscript of 1765, *Robin Hood his Death, etc.,* the Prioress is reported to have buried Robin Hood by the roadside, and because also the road from Mirfield to Clifton-upon-Calder is some distance away, some have claimed that this discredits the authenticity of the grave. Again, they could never have seen it. What has escaped notice is a track that runs right by the grave which stands on high ground. It is not an animal track. It is most ancient; I followed it and examined it for some distance. It is the ancient Roman Way from Mirfield following the ridgeway, and in evidence a wall close by has some of the stones used by the Romans.

The likelihood is that Robin Hood is buried at Kirklees, at, or close to, the present site and there is always the possibility that his bones may have moved some distance by natural causes. Skeleton remains do have a habit of moving especially when buried on high ground, and reports have been made of them laying against church walls, having moved some distance.

EPITAPH

The original epitaph ascribed to the grave, and found among the papers of the late Dr. Thomas Gale, Dean of York (1697-1702), is given as:

> "Hear undernead dis laitl stean,
> Laiz robert earl of huntington,
> Near arcir ver as hie sa geid
> An pipl kauld im robin heud,
> Sick outlawz as hi an iz men,
> vil england nivr si agen.
> obiit 24 kal. dekembris 1247."

The words are sufficiently close enough to the present epitaph set in the rear wall of the grave, to be accepted. There are several variations of the wording, of which the above is a fair example. It seems that this was set in the wall when, to guard against further damage, Sir George Armytage, Bart. enclosed the grave in an iron cage upon a low wall during the 19th century.

Samuel Armytage, the owner of the hall, caused the ground to be dug a yard deep in the seventeenth century, and as he found it had never been disturbed, so assumed that the stone had probably been brought from another place; and that by vulgar tradition had been ascribed to Robin Hood. The grave, being in woodland for many years, would have a covering of soil and mulch undisturbed — they should have dug deeper. There was no set depth for graves in earlier days; it was controlled by time and the type of ground.

It is to be regretted that the epitaph on the gravestone is considered spurious by some writers. The stone is a tribute by one of little scholarship, trying his hardest to use Old English, as indeed some of the ballads may be, and not of pleasing scholarship. It is doubtful that the layman would notice the mistake in the date; or the mis-spelling of old words. In one work we can see the same word with different spellings, for there was no standard form in early days. It is a stonemason's tribute, and in no way detracts from the authenticity of the grave — despite his lack of scholarship the man who cut the stone was not an illiterate — he could write — he could carve — he was a skilled worker. Later writers, too, offer the epitaph in a variety of spellings: Hear, Here; Underneath, undernead; laiz, laz; hie, he, etc. Does this make *them* illiterate? Does this make their claims spurious? The answer is *no*, it only shows that they never actually saw the grave, and that they failed to copy correctly from what evidence they had, or made unsuccessful attempts to imitate the spelling of an ''uneducated'', but skilled stonemason. Here for the purist is the epitaph as copied by the author direct from the stone whilst on a visit to Kirklees:

> "Hear Underneath this laitl Stean
> Laz robert earl of Huntingtun
> Ne'er arcir ver as hie sa geud
> And pipl kauld im robin heud
> Sick utlawz az hi an iz men
> Vil england nivr si agen.
> Obiit 24 kal; Dekembris 1247.''

In the first line *this*, the *h* and *s* are visible but the *t* and *i* are very faint and do not show up on the photographs that I took. The word appears to be *shs* and may be *dis*, but the first, very faint, letter does not touch the down stroke of the *h*, therefore I am convinced that the original was *this*. The mason did not continue the curve in the *h* to the upright, but a dot appears next to it suggesting *i*. The ballad of *Robin Hood's Death* gives the following lines:

> Robin Earl of Huntingdon,
> Lies under this little stone,
> No archer was like him so good,
> His wildness nam'd him Robin Hood,
> Full thirteen years and something more
> These northern parts he vexed sore
> Such outlaws as he and his men
> May England never see again.

These lines are stated to have been the Epitaph to Robin Hood, as set upon his tombstone by the Prioress of Kirkley Monastry, and at the end of Martin Parker's *A true tale of Robin Hood* (1632), is added, ''The epitaph which the Prioress of the Monastry of Kirkes Lay in Yorkshire set over Robin Hood.'' He adds the date, ''Decembris quarto die, 1198; anno regni Richard I Primi 9.''

The ballad of *Robin Hood and the Valiant Knight* (before 1741) gives the same reading but starts, ''Robin Earl of Huntington.'' The place given is Birkslay Monastry, and is without a date.

There are two or three other epitaphs reported, much along the same lines, with additions, but all of them are the work of playwrights and ballad writers. No one person tells of the wording being on the grave until after it was enclosed by Sir George Armytage, Bart., when the mason made use of the legend perpetuated by the ballads. Grafton states that there were three names on Robin's stone; Camden writes that the name of Elizabeth de Staynton is inscribed on the Prioress of Kirklees's stone, but does not say there is anything but a plain cross on Robin's stone. Thoresby states that the inscription is scarcely legible and makes no attempt to identify any of the words. Richard Gough writes that the words are illegible. The wording on Elizabeth de Staynton's is clearly readable after being buried for several years.

There is no explanation of there being any other name on Robin Hood's stone except that, according to Grafton, it may have been brought from somewhere else and then used for a second person — William Goldburgh, and then again later, used for someone by the name Thomas. No reasons given by Grafton for the three names and the only explanation I have ever heard (without qualification) is that in olden times it was quite normal to take an old gravestone and re-use it. That being so then it looks as though the last burial was that of Thomas.

The only evidence provided by Camden in his *Britannia,* is that Robin Hood was buried at Kirklees under a large stone, Elizabeth de Staynton's gravestone was discovered among the ruins at Kirklees Priory in August 1706; like Robin Hood's it is a flat stone bearing a raised cross upon a calvary of two steps, surrounded by the following epitaph in Lombardic characters — DOVCE : JHV : DE : NAZARETH : FILS : DIEV : AYEZ : MERCI : A : ELIZABETH : STAINTON : PRIORES : DE : CEST : MAISON. (Camden's *Britannia* 1789, Plate II, Page 38). The Prioress's grave is an altar stone raised about four feet from the ground and the above inscription is on a kerb around an empty space! The words are in English!

Near the site there is part of a stone remaining with what appears to be the base of a calvary with the letters AUM. EPD. These are not clear on my photograph but the letters (nazar) ETH : GRANT clearly show; (upon the soul of one, Elizabeth Stainton late Prioress of this house). The small stone, part of a tombstone, is placed where the raised cross should be; no signs of this are to be seen. As the few letters on it cannot be matched with the supposed calvary tombstone, it cannot possibly be the original.

THE PRIORESS

Elizabeth Stainton was a Prioress of Kirklees during the 13th century, and her name is accepted to be that of the Prioress of the legend, and as such, also Robin Hood's aunt. Both Hunter and Walker attempted to place her (along with Robin), in the following century, the 14th, and in doing so served only to discredit their claim beyond question. If my interpretation of the ''evidence'' on which they based the theory is correct, then Elizabeth would have been less than twelve years of age when she conspired to kill Robin. Walker adds that, upon realising the dreadful thing she had done, she committed suicide. Hardly the actions of a minor! Dodsworth and Dugdale, in their *Monasticum*, establish her in the 13th century, and the person mistaken for the Prioress by Hunter and Walker, was, I believe, *an* Elizabeth *of* the Parish of Staynton, who lived at Kirklees during the period which *they* place the saga. This Elizabeth is mentioned in this passage from the *Yorkshire Archaeological Society Journal, Vol. xxxvi:*

''By his wife, Joan, John de Staynton, had four daughters, the eldest of them being under the age of *twelve years* at their father's death. His relict married a Hugh de Toothill, who with the consent of his wife, caused the two eldest, Isabel and Joan, to marry his two sons and placed the younger, Elizabeth and Alice in Kirklees Priory so that his two sons might enjoy the Staynton property which descended to the four daughters equally.''

''William de Notton, Joan Toothill's brother, and uncle of the four children was appointed guardian of the girls by their father took proceedings to insist upon proper provision being made for these nuns, Elizabeth and Alice, and to annul the placing of them in Kirklees Priory alleging that their profession as nuns had not been promoted by Hugh de Toothill, through devotion or charity but to gain their patrimony for his sons; also the girls profession had been made before they were old enough to distinguish between a spiritual and temporal life.''

''Elizabeth and Alice de Staynton however, came to their uncle, William de Staynton, the prior of Monkbreton and in the presence of Hugh de Toothill, besought him that he would not revoke their profession as nuns at Kirklees if Hugh would give them certain rents for their support out of the tenements which had come to them by their father. To this claim Hugh agreed, and in the presence of William de Staynton prior of Monkbreton, Sir Thomas de Staynton, rector of the moiety of the church of Bolton, Robert Clarel, Henry de Staynton and William de Staynton, cousins of Elizabeth and Alice de Staynton agreed to pay an annual sum of fifty shillings to William the Prior and William de Staynton for the life of Elizabeth de Staynton. If Elizabeth cease to be a nun, and claim the fourth part of the lands descended to her from her father this indenture to lose effect. Executed at the Priory of Monkbreton 20 December 1347.''

GATEHOUSE AT KIRKLEES HALL. In legend, Robin Hood died in the upstairs room. In reality the building is Tudor and much too late for the time of the saga.

FLIGHT OF ROBIN HOOD'S LAST ARROW which he is reputed to have shot whilst he lay dying.

At the date stated, Elizabeth would have been under the age of twelve, and it is the same year (1347) that the Yorkshire advocates claim Robin died. This girl hardly seems the person to have done such a deed, and as to her being the aunt of a man who would have been (were these claims correct) 57 years of age, it is not credible — and the Yorkshire claim much less so. The *Monkbreton* indenture makes no mention of Elizabeth de Staynton being the Prioress as a minor in 1347. She must have died quite young if a Margaret de Saville succeeded to the position of Prioress in 1348, as Walker claims. According to Thoresby, Margaret was still the Prioress in 1359.

In *The True History of Robin Hood*, Walker omits the reference to the uncle of the two girls coming to an arrangement with the Prior of Monkbreton and Hugh de Toothill, which was published eight years after his article in the *Yorkshire Archeological Society Journal*. He merely states "If it is true, as according to the *Little Geste*, that Robin Hood spent twenty two years in the greenwood after leaving the King's Court, which would bring him to the year 1346/7 and if Elizabeth de Staynton ceased to be Prioress of Kirklees by committing suicide the day following the murder of Robin Hood in the same year, it would give us the real date of Robin's death as 1346/7 which curiously enough is just one hundred years later than the one inscribed on the 17th century stone inserted in the wall around Robin Hood's grave at Kirklees." Nevertheless, Walker does contradict himself on the subject when, on considering the gravestone at Kirklees, he says, "The cross bottony on a three step calvary as drawn by Richard Gough is as an almost exactly similar gravestone to be seen at Bridgenorth in Shropshire, one at Besthorpe in Norfolk, and another in Willoughby in Lincolnshire. The design was a very common one in the thirteenth century." Hunter is at least consistent when he suggests that no authority is given for, "assigning the era of Elizabeth Staynton to the thirteenth century and if, as I suspect, there is no more authority than the grave stone which covered her remains, still existing and an inference to date, from its style, I must beg to place here after not before." However, it is more probable that the gravestone drawings referred to are of the period stated, 13th century, and based upon the reports of other writers.

If Elizabeth was reponsible for having a stone erected over Robin Hood's grave within less than 24 hours of his death, she would clearly have had to use an existing, older, stone, and then had Robin's name inscribed upon it. Either that, or her successor had it placed there.

That the Prioress was involved in the conspiracy to kill Robin Hood is never in doubt, whether or not it was with Red Roger, Sir Roger of Doncaster, or another of the clergy is conjecture. In the ballad of *Robin Hood and the Valiant Knight*, it is the monk who bleeds Robin to death, and in *A True Story of Robin Hood* it is a friar who does the deed, but in each case it is again the Prioress of Kirklees who sets up the epitaph and the stone.

In the previous chapter we have established the kinship between Robert de Kyme and the Staynton family, and that it is assumed Robin's death was caused by his aunt, though some do state cousin, loosely used. As an Elizabeth de Staynton *was* a Prioress of Kirklees during the 13th century, the next known Prioress being Margaret de Clayton in 1306 and Robin died sometime between 1274 and 1293, then this Elizabeth must be the Prioress of the ballads, and nigh unto his kin.

THE GATEHOUSE OF KIRKLEES PRIORY as it was in the 19th century, based on an etching printed in Ritson's *Robin Hood*, published in 1795.

ROBIN HOOD STATUE at Thoresby Hall. The figure stands to the left of the fireplace, with the figure of Little John on the opposite side.

Chapter 15

"I love no man in all the world, so well as I do my King,
Welcome is my Lord's seal, and Monk, for thy tiding."
Little Geste — Stanza 386

THESE words by Robin Hood are used by those who dispute the belief of John Seldon (Jurist, 1584-1654) that "There is more historic truth in many of the ballads than in many modern histories", to scorn the truth of the Robin Hood saga. The cynics exploit the fact that ballad writers borrowed from common stock and point out that others too disguised as Potters, or tricked clergymen in the manner of Robin, and helped Knights in trouble. That the ballads represent Robin as a loyal man who so opposed his king, is derided, but the written history of the period provides ample comparisons.

The Earl of Leicester and the Earl of Clare, opponents of Henry III, and more actively using force of arms, at the request of others wrote: "May your excellency know, that as we wish to preserve the health and safety of your person, and with the fidelity due to you, proposing only to resist by all means in our powers those persons, who are not only our enemies, but yours, and those of the whole kingdom. 13 May 1264, near Lewes." *(The Baron's War* — Blaauw, 1871). Their insurrection was entirely in compliance with the spirit of Magna Carta (1216) and even when victorious, the law was seen to be kept by them insomuch as no harm was done "to our own person and those of the Queen and our children." (Article 61).

The discontent of both the English nobility and common folk at that time arose from the bitter resentment to foreigners, particularly Frenchmen and Italians, holding office of high rank, i.e, sheriffs, barons and clergy. These men were often mercenaries who, under a strict interpretation of the Magna Carta should have been sent back whence they came. Among such men was Philip Marc, expressly mentioned, and the Sheriff of Nottingham in 1215! He was re-appointed in 1216, in spite of this edict, "All evil customs relating to forest and warrens, Foresters, Warreners, SHERIFFS, and their servants, or river banks and their wardens, are at once to be investigated in every county by twelve sworn knights of the county, and within forty days of their enquiry the evil customs are to be abolished completely and irrevocably" (Magna Carta, Article 48.)

Gerald de Athee was Sheriff of Nottingham in 1208-1209, hence we have two of the foreign favourites serving as sheriffs of the town. "We will remove completely from their offices the kinsmen of Gerard de Athee, and in future they shall hold no office in England." (Magna Carta, Article 50).

In *The History of England*, Hume writes, "Following the expulsion of Hubert de Burgh, the ablest and most virtuous minister that Henry III ever possessed, Peter, Bishop of Winchester, a Poictevin by birth, succeeded him. Once again the nation was under the control of foreigners, men who when the laws were at any time appealed to, in opposition to their oppressions, scrupled not to reply 'What did the English Laws signify to them? They minded them not'. And as words are often more offensive than actions, this open contempt of the English tended much to aggravate the general discontent, and made every act of violence committed by the foreigners appear not only any injury, but an affront to them. Meanwhile all the chief benefices of the Kingdom were conferred on Italians, great numbers of that nation were sent over at that time to be provided for; non-residence and pluralities were carried to an enormous height; Mansel the King's chaplain, is computed to have held at once seven hundred ecclesiastical livings; and the abuses became so evident as to be palpable to the blindness of superstition itself."

During this troubled period of history, Nottinghamshire and Derbyshire were the most turbulent parts of England, so that a man who maintained defiance of these foreigners who were imposed upon them, both religious and secular, would become a hero of the common folk. The fact that Robin Hood was against "*these* archbishops and bishops" does not detract from his piety and veneration of God's ministers. Does not the word *These* imply certain clergymen? As the King's Chaplain had seven hundred ecclesiastical

MEDIEVAL NOTTINGHAM

Above: THE OLDE TRIP TO JERUSALEM, reputed to be the oldest inn in England.

Left: NORMAN ARCHES, on the south side of Broadway, in the Lace Market. Probably stray pieces of the old Norman Church of St. Mary's.

Below: THE ROCK HOLES, Castle Boulevard, which, in Norman times, was the home of an important group of religious hermits.

livings, and he was not alone in this, then many of the bishops would be foreigners, and barons with military tenants. In fact as we have seen, this was the main grievance among the English at the time; the moreso as Henry III was pouring money into Papal funds with the ambition that his younger son, Edmund, would be crowned King of Sicily.

These bishops were the enemies of Robin Hood, and these were the men he robbed:

> S.378 *Little Geste*
> "And ye have churches and rents both,
> And gold full great plenty,
> Give us some of your spending,
> For Saint Charity."

The churchman, an abbott, has but forty pounds and taking it Robin divided it into halves giving his men the one, and the other:

> S.383 *Little Geste*
> "Full courteously Robin did say,
> Sir, have this for your spending."

Granted the above is taken from a ballad which could be suspect as history, but compare the following from Matthew Paris, writing before 1259, "King John once demanded 10,000 marks from a Jew of Bristol; and on his refusal, ordered one of his teeth to be drawn every day till he should comply. The Jew lost seven of his teeth and then paid the sum required of him".

This is from history, but if the incident had been related by a ballad singer then both the amount demanded and the number of teeth extracted might well have been either exaggerated or understated for the sake of rhyme or rhythm, but the report would still be based upon fact. The value of 10,000 marks was £6,616.13s4d, consequently those sums of money quoted in the *Little Geste*, i.e, the gentle Knight's income of £400 per annum, are not exaggerations as some suggest.

History is not always what actually occurred, but that which people saw, or heard, happen. The Venerable Bede reveals that when writing his work on *History of the English Church and People* his principle authority and adviser was the Most Reverend Abbott Albinus, an eminent scholar, "He carefully transmitted to me *verbally* or in writing through Nothelm, a priest of the church of London, anything he considered worthy of mention that had been done by disciples of the blessed Pope Gregory in the Province of Canterbury or the surrounding regions. Such facts he ascertained either from records or from *long-established traditions.*"

The written word is permanent; the spoken word changes either by embellishment, mishearing or uncertain memory. It is undeniable that history can, and does, contain inaccuracies if we are to accept the word of the modern historians, some of whom are even attempting to rewrite events of two recent World Wars. Some medieval battle dates are in question, and it is not certain whether the figure receiving the arrow through the eye in the Bayeux Tapestry is King Harold or another, or even if that was the way in which he was killed. There are numerous further examples, emphasising that written history cannot guarantee the pure truth. Neither should it be accepted to be the exclusive source of past events.

The ballads of the 15th and 16th centuries have authentic mention of several matters that are historically accepted. The giving of cloth and fees was in every day use in the 13th century; a retainer of one Lord could not accept the fee of another, so that Little John has to have the word of his master before he can enter the Sheriff's service. Also, the fact that there was a High Sheriff and a Town Sheriff before the 16th century. The longbow receives no mention in the *early* ballads; it is not until much later we read of it, but in spite of this fact Robin Hood has been discredited by some who point out that the longbow did not exist in the 13th century. *In Robin Hood and the Monk,* the King's writ must be sought before action can be taken against Robin, and simple protection for him to be brought to the King's court is given. This is repeated in the *Little Geste,* where the Sheriff is told to get the King's will before the Knight will release the outlaw into the Sheriff's hands. The placing of Barnsdale adjacent to Nottingham, and other items are equally factual.

It has been established from the ballads, that the character of Robin Hood is not that of a superman, either magical or supernatural. He is a man of moods; pious, courteous, with some humour, and his human weakness is best seen in the two archery contests of the *Little Geste* and *Robin Hood and the Monk.* In the former, where the outlaws show their prowess before the King, and again in the latter, where he shoots for pennies with Little John, he loses! The best archer in the land! It is a fact that anything

MEDIEVAL WEAPONRY

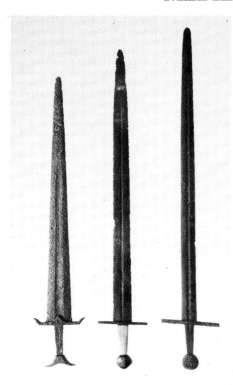

Above: Three broadswords (European).

Right: Mid-14th century mail shirt and aventail. (The helmet is modern and for display purposes.)

Below, left: Large broadhead arrow head with straight barbs.
Below, right: Large broadhead arrow head with inward curving barbs.

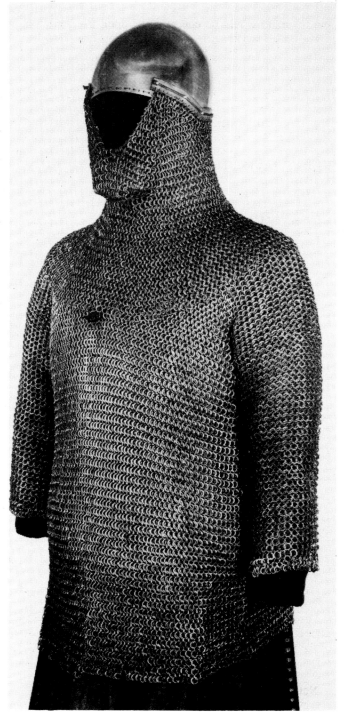

(All the medieval weaponry illustrated on this page are in the Royal Armories Collection in H.M. Tower of London, and are reproduced by courtesy of the Board of Trustees of the Royal Armories.)

which distracts concentration can affect the efforts of even the best. In the first instance Robin is concerned over the Monk, who carries the King's seal and tells Robin that he is to come to Nottingham to meet, and dine with, the King. The outlaw's mind would be a confusion of elation at the possibility of a pardon, and fear of a trap! In the second story he is sick at heart because he has not heard mass for a fortnight, and his mind would be concentrated upon the service he was about to attend.

The ballad writer was a good psychologist, or knew his stories from experience, for minstrels would be received in the greenwood with the same enthusiasm as in village or castle. They were immune from attack, hence we find King Alfred in the Danes camp in the disguise of a Saxon minstrel, and Blondel in Austria in search of King Richard — singing an English love song which he and Richard had composed.

The balladeers and minstrels picked up their news wherever they went, and passed it on in song. The method of rhyme and rhythm assisted memory with uncanny accuracy, in addition to which the ballad singers would inevitably have been men with good powers of observation, retention, and recall. The story of the ballad singers, minstrels, poets, bards, call them what you will, needs a whole volume to tell; theirs is a profession of great antiquity; they were the reporters of everyday happenings *and* the history of the tribe; the news carrier, the entertainer, and they live on today as folk singers. These balladeers were the men who related the activities of Robin Hood and his men in the greenwood, and so excellent and effective was the telling that for hundreds of years those who accept him as a man of history far exceed those who do not.

We are told in the 14th century that songs of Robin Hood and Ranulph, Earl of Chester, were in existence (1377). In the 15th century it is reported that the common people delighted in the ballads and plays beyond all others. During the same century historians made note of Robin Hood, he appeared in literature, he was characterised in the May Games, and the first written play and ballad was put down on paper. In the early 16th century the first printed book was published and this could be for only the learned and the wealthy; more and more references appeared in literature, and the ballad writers reflected the trend. In the following century a ballad writer attempted to write the *Life, Breeding, Valour and Marriage of Robin Hood,* and it was used by Ritson, together with the first ever "true" identity, by William Stukeley.

The ballads had by then laid the foundations of a saga that has endured the succeeding centuries, and which has continued to be embellished and developed even in modern times, and which will be perpetuated by future generations. To list every reference that our outlaws has received would be all but impossible, and since the ballads began it all, books, plays, pantomimes, operas, fiction, TV and big screen films have taken up the story so that Robin Hood has become the most popular and best-known outlaw hero in the world. Every year there is at least one new book published, mainly fiction, but attempts to identify the man and his life and times are increasing. Also there must be a considerable amount of amateur material, for the author receives many requests from students, needing help in preparing a thesis or paper on Robin Hood. Also, from schools, where the children are doing a project on our outlaw hero, and where among the juniors new variations emerge. Robin fighting the Romans (how near the truth), Robin Hood in a space ship, and other imaginations. Remove the obvious fiction, take out the nonsense ballads such as *Robin Hood and Maid Marian, Robin Hood and Jack Cade's daughter* and several of the later ballads, including those already shown as stemming from the May Day games, and we are left with the earliest ballads of *Robin Hood and the Monk,* The *Little Gest* and *Robin Hood and the Potter,* the two plays of *Robin Hood and the Sheriff,* and Copland's play. Take a close look at all of these and we have one character, although Copland makes him less courteous than any other writer; possibly because the play is obviously a comedy. The conclusion is that the central character was a real man. Langland pairs Robin Hood with the Earl of Chester; there were ballads of real historical outlaws, other than Robin in existence at that time, out of which only Robin Hood remains popular. Clearly, Langland saw him as a real man.

Fordun tells us that Robin Hood and Little John were from among the dispossessed and disinherited after the battle of Evesham, in 1265, and of whom plays were enacted and songs were sung to the delight of the people; Wyntoun states Robin hood and Little John were living in 1283, without reference to the plays. The conclusion is that both writers received their information otherwise than from the ballads and plays.

Not one of the historians who make reference to Robin Hood, his death and his grave, state or imply one who was mythical or fictitious — the conclusion being that they were reporting on a real man.

13th CENTURY MONARCHS

Right: KING HENRY III.

Below: HENRY III AND ALIX DE BOURGOGNE. From a wall painting in Notre-Dame-Aux-Dominicans. *(Reproduced by courtesy of H.M. Tower of London Royal Armories and the British Museums.)*

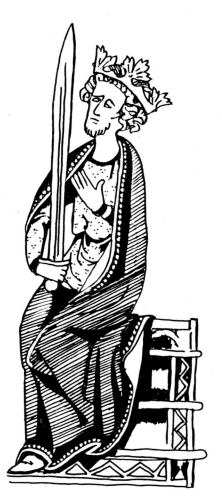

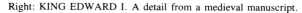

Right: KING EDWARD I. A detail from a medieval manuscript.

In the early ballads there is no action which is supernatural or improbable: his skill with the bow is not much greater than that of the others; a buffet from the King lays him as flat as any of the others; he finds his way through the forest although Little John is implied as the one who best knows the ways through the forest, possibly because he was "local" man, or that he was there some time before Robin (we must not discount the whim of the ballad writer in this). But Robin never receives help from strange lights in the manner of Hereward, nor does he receive a magic sword, or make himself invisible as known outlaws are said to have done. One of the reasons that our outlaw remains so popular is undoubtedly the fact that there is nothing in his make-up with which the average man cannot identify himself, he was courteous, he was brave, he was a good fellow, he was a man of noble birth, who associated with, and lived among, ordinary men. He was English, he was "The Spirit of England".

Ask where you may, and in the main, the general conclusion is that Robin Hood was real, although many stories have been added that are not true, and that is fair enough comment — and conclusive! Robin was a real man! Why it cannot be left at that is understandable. There are many who would like to know more of our hero, and there are those who would wish to make him a man of history by establishing an identity which can be matched with a name, and a family, in public records or private papers. The pity of it is the fact that failure to give him an identity other than his alias of Robin Hood is, to some, an implication that no such person existed except in fantasy; and identities that are suspect do not help.

The only way to establish proof of an identity is to link it together with the early ballads, the early chroniclers and historians, *and* the legend. The latter, stripped of the imaginations of Sir Walter Scott, and the activities at the May Games, is that Robin Hood, an outlaw in Sherwood Forest, took from the rich to help the poor, which could include clergymen, and impoverished noblemen. His relationship with Maid Marian does not come out strong, nor does his pardon and manner of death, but that he was of noble birth does.

The chroniclers link his name with that of Little John and his followers; name him the gentlest and most courteous of thieves and place him in the woodlands and thicket; some giving a specific locality — Barnsdale. That he took only from the rich and aided the poor is evidenced and many of them give a date or period in the reign of King Henry III. They add the circumstances and manner of his death, and place of burial. They give a reason for outlawry. The early ballads stress his piety, love of the Virgin Mary, and name some of the other outlaws. Here too, his noble birth is implied, and that he did take from the rich to assist the poor is shown in his aid to the gentle Knight; also his regular statement that if the sum stated by his "victims" is all they have, and they have need of more for their spending he will give it to them. Furthermore, he orders three of the outlaws to bring back guests to dine with him — and "Of my goods he shall have some, if he be a poor man", *(Little Geste)*. The King of the ballads is named as "Edward, Our comely king", and Robin's death at the hands of the Prioress, "near to his kin", at Kirklees Nunnery, is related.

For over 400 years there is no suggestion that he was any other than Robin Hood. Nothing will ever change this. Those who would deny the fact that he was a real man of history can only do so by denying a whole mass of evidence based on word of mouth, ballads which were for generations the way of telling history, and numerous remarks by all kinds of people from the historian to the common folk; folk who passed on the story as they heard it.

In summary, we have seen why Robin Hood was so opposed to certain bishops, archbishops — and also the High Sheriffs of Nottingham. At no time is any sheriff of any other county named. He is not associated with the sheriffs of Cumberland, Lancashire, or Yorkshire in any ballad in spite of the various claims to him being in Barnsdale, Yorkshire; Inglewood, Cumberland; and Lancashire. That no ballad names any other sheriff than Nottingham's must be sufficient evidence, beyond any doubt, that he was a Nottinghamshire outlaw. It is conceivable that a Sheriff of Yorkshire might have appeared in some obscure, long lost ballad, but if so, any local traditions stemming from it have faded into the mists of time. Field work in Yorkshire produced no stories of Robin Hood in the localities named by Yorkshire claimants, whereas people of that County interviewed, without fail believed that our hero was of Sherwood Forest! When their attention was drawn to the claims of Robin being of Yorkshire they attached little credibility to it, although this was in the early 1970's, since when the claim has been cleverly exploited in the media by some who also claim even Lady Godiva and Mary, Queen of Scots for Sheffield, and so the Yorkshire theory is therefore better known today. However, its acceptance cannot be supported

ROBIN HOOD'S NOTTINGHAM

Robin Hood surveys the town of Nottingham. Adapted from the title page illustration in *The Legendary Exploits of Robin Hood* by Jim Lees.

162

when there is no Matilda to be found in the Robin Hood ballads; the Barnsdale of the baliads is clearly shown as adjacent to Nottingham town; and in spite of the King staying for five days at Rothwell, Yorkshire, it was to Nottingham that he came to seek Robin Hood. Rothwell is closer to Barnsdale, Yorkshire than to Nottingham.

Finally, to reaffirm Robin Hood's real identity, Robert de Kyme. There is no reason to describe Stukeley's claim as jocular, or a forgery as some have done, or plain guesswork. His great-aunt married into the Kyme family and received the family lore that Robin Hood was of their kin from her husband John Kyme; and no doubt hearing of the name Robert.

That Stukeley's pedigree had some substance is shown in the fact that later scholars made use of it, and for many years a printed copy was issued by Nottingham authorities to enquirers after Robin Hood. It makes no pretence that Robin was an Earl of Huntingdon, but shows how he might have had, albeit a very poor, claim to it. It looks very much as though Stukeley knew that a Robert, a member of the Kyme family, was the famous Robin Hood living in the time of King Henry III (and there is little to dispute the fact that our outlaw was of that period), and worked back with disastrous results. He missed several generations, one of which would have shown the connection between the Kymes and a Prioress of Staynton — he failed to find that Philip, whom he names as Fitzooth, was a Kyme, and far from dying without issue, had issue of five sons and three daughters; one of the sons being a Philip, who did die without issue (c. 1175-84). In this he is far from alone, as a pedigree of the Kyme family in the papers of Queen Elizabeth I, and also others, will show.

There is no evidence that the Kyme family supported the barons, or the King in the insurrection of the 13th century — or if they remained neutral, but they certainly supported the barons against King John.

The fact that Robert was a junior member of the dynasty who lost or sold his patrimony because of debt, he would therefore not appear in his own name in the *Book of Fees* and any Inquisition. Unless some evidence can be produced to show that Robert, son of William, holding lands in Oxcombe in 1242 was not a Kyme, and also that Robert de Kyme who claimed arrears of rent was not the son of William, Lord of Kyme, then my conclusion is that this Robert de Kyme, stepson of a direct descendant of an Earl of Huntingdon, and heir to the Earldom of Kyme, living in the 13th century, was Robin Hood. Though heir to the Earldom as the eldest son — his younger brother Philip inherited at an early age under the wardship of Hugh de Bigod, a favourite of the King, due to Robert's disinheritance through his "wild living" and debt.

Prince Edward was active against the rebels, although for a while he supported their demands against his father, King Henry III. During his father's lifetime he would be Prince Edward — but once King he would be so termed, and clearly the period of the saga was during his time as Prince.

Coat-of-Arms of the Kyme Family.

Bibliography

The Little Geste of Robin Hood (1500) — Wynken de Worde

Robin Hood and the Sheriff of Nottingham — Malone Society's collections

Downfall of the Earl of Huntingdon afterwards called Robin Hood etc. / Death of Robert, Earl of Huntingdon etc. (1601) — Plays by Chettle & Munday

Robin Hood. A collection of all the ancient poems and songs and ballads now extant (1823) — J. Ritson

Collection of Early English Prose Romances (1827) — W.J. Thomas

Lytell Geste of Robin Hood etc. (1847) — J.M. Gutch

Great hero of the ancient ministreley of England, Robin Hood (1852) — J. Hunter

English & Scottish Popular Ballads (1889) — F.J. Child

Life and Exploits of Robin Hood (Garland) (1859) — Milner & Sowerby

Robin Hood, Garland (19th century) — Bell and Dalby

Reliques of English Poetry (1705) — T. Percy

Merry Adventures of Robin Hood (No date) — Howard Pyle

The True History of Robin Hood (1944) — J.W. Walker

The Truth about Robin Hood (1950) — P. Valentine-Harris

The Life of Robin Hood — E.W. Fithian

The Haunts of Robin Hood (1970) — W.R. Mitchell

The Outlaws of Medieval England (1961) — M. Keen

Sherwood Forest. A guide (No date) — Ward, Lock & Co.

Robin Hood (No date) — Martin Daniels

A Forester's Offering (1857) — Spencer T. Hall

Early Yorkshire Charters — W. Farrars

Final Concords of the County of Lincoln — C.W. Foster

Scottichronicon (15th century) — Harl. MS.54764, p139-408L

Canterbury Tales (1968) — G. Chaucer

Baronage (1675) — Dugdale

Victoria County Histories: Nottinghamshire, Lincolnshire, Warwickshire, Staffordshire, Yorkshire, Rutland

A Brief collection of the laws of the forest (1562) — J. Manwood

Magna Carta (transcript and original) — H.M. Tower of London

Monkbretton Chartulary. — Ms.50755. f 185. BM.

Robin Hood's Epitaph — Ms.33938. Fol.1.

Kinnersley *Letter & Pedigree of Robin Hood* (1825) — Ms.6696. p33 etc.

Ashmole Ms. *(Little John's grave)* (1625) — Ms.1651. Bod.Lib.Oxon

Wakefield Manor Court Rolls (13th/14th century) — Yorks. Arch. Soc.

Household accounts of Edward II — PRO E101/380/4

Pedigree (Kyme) Domestic Papers Elizabeth I — BM.Vol Cl. p38

Sloane MS *Life of Robin Hood* (17th century) — BM780. ff46-48b

Nottinghamshire (1797) — Throsby

Toxophilus (1544) — Roger Ascham

King Henry III and the Lord Edward — Powicke

The Welsh Wars of Edward I (1927) — Morris

English Wayfaring life in the 14th Century — Jusserand

History of Whitby (1779) — Charlton

English Archery (No date) — F.L. Bilson

Nottinghamshire, a gazeteer & directory — Francis J. White

Anecdotes of Archery (1846) — Hargroves

Conquete de'lAngleterre — Thierry

History of England (1824)	Hume
English Forests & Forest Trees	Ingham Cooke & Co.
Monasticum (17th century)	Dugdale
History of Doncaster (1831)	Miller
Deanery of Doncaster (1850)	Hunter
Honours and Knights Fees	W. Farrars
Lincs. Cathedral Charters	
Sherwood Forest maps . . . various	Notts Archives
Records of the Kyme family of Friskney	Wedd Ms. City of Lincoln
Kyme Barony	Ross.Ms. Reference Library
Midwest Folk lore. Indiana University (undated)	Vol. VII 198-201
Southern Folk lore. Quarterly. Tennessee University (1940)	Vol. IV P 15-21
Journal of American Folk Lore. Denver University	No date p.23-38
Sleaford, the Wapentakes of Maxwell etc.	Trollope
Lincs. Notes and Queries	Vol. XXIV p10-14
Lincs. Notes and Queries	Vol. XXIII p60-62
Lincs. Notes and Queries	Vol. XXIII p115-119
History of Sleaford (undated)	Verberg p274-275
Registrum Premonstretense	Sloane MS.4934 p103
Architects Reports and Papers (Lincs.)	Vol. XXXII
History of Uttoxeter etc. (1886)	F. Redfern
Historic Staffordshire (1896)	Dent & Hill p101-5
Paloeagraphic Britannica	Stukeley No.1 *1743*
The Gentlemans Magazine	*1793* p.-26
Records of the Borough of Nottingham	Vol.1 p47 etc.
History of Sleaford & District	Creasey
Sherwood Forest	J. Rogers
North Dublin City and Environs (1908)	Rev. Cosgrave
The Dictionary of Dublin (No date)	Cosgrave and Strangeways
A History of the City of Dublin (1861)	Sir J.T. Gilbert
Life in Old Dublin (1913)	J. Collins
Irish Chronicles 1586 (1586)	Vol.II. Holinshed
Historical Memoirs of the Irish Bards (No date)	Walker
Robin Hood, Myth or History	C.A. Federer
A Story of Dublin (1932)	D.A. Chart
Worthies of Nottinghamshire	Fuller
Sherwood Forest Place names	Leman, Ms. Notts. Archives
Robin Hood's bow and death Loose paper	Renishaw Hall
Antiquities (1776)	J. Strutt
Sports & Pastimes of the English People (1800)	J.C. Cox edition
Myth, Ritual in Dance, Game & Rhyme (1947)	L. Spence
Festivals, Holidays and Saints Days	E.L. Hargreave
The Middleton Forest Book	Ms. Nottingham University
On the Origins of Waltzing Matilda (1971)	H.H. Pearce
Staffordshire Rolls Series	Staffs archives
Aunt Molly Jackson & Robin Hood (undated)	Journal of American Folk Lore
Rimes of Robin Hood (1976)	Dobson & Taylor
Some Historical Mansions of Yorkshire and their associations (1887)	W. Wheater
Roman Roads in Britain	Ivan D. Margary
By Moor & Fell in West Yorkshire	Haliwell Sutcliffe
Robin & Marian	James Goldman
Robin Hood (1982)	J.C. Holt
Anatomy of Abuses (1595)	Philip Stubbs
OXFORD ENGLISH DICTIONARY (Large Edition)	

SUBSCRIBERS
LIMITED
EDITION

1 British Library
2 Nottingham City Council
3 Nottinghamshire County Council
4 Nottingham Local Studies Library
5 Nottingham Castle Museum
6 Newark & Sherwood Council
7 University of Nottingham Library
8 Nottingham Evening Post Library
9 H.M. Tower of London — Royal Armouries
10 Bodleian Library, Oxford University
11 University Library, Cambridge
12 National Library of Scotland
13 Library of Trinity College, Dublin
14 National Library of Wales
15 Robin Hood Society

16 Jim Lees
17 Keith Mellor
18 Emrys Bryson
19 Roy Smith
20 Barrie Smith
21 Roger Heaton
22 Dan Hyndman
23 Gemini Typesetting
24 Mike Bush
25 Tom Foy
26 David Greenwood
27 John Lomas
28 Robert Hardy
29 Lada Tvrdik
30-50 Temple Nostalgia
      Press
51 Graham Russell
52 Donald Winfield Hanby
53 Digby & Linda Atkin
54 John Shoemaker
55 Dick Smolen
56 Mrs Biddy Walker
57 Dr P.J. Toghill
58 Dr Sheila Hart
59 Patricia Watts
60 R.N. Cooke
61 Dorothy Huckerby
62 Elaine Carnell
63 Wendy Whitley
64 Bernadette Mellor
65 Tony Mellor
66 Ian Mellor
67 Ian Sparrow
68 John Kirby Lees
69 Ann Gee
70 Michael Kay
71 Nottingham Evening
   Post Library
72 Vina Cooke
   Doll Museum
73 John Pope de Locksley
74 Yoshiko Ueno
75 L.F. & M.R. Tvrdik

76 Ernest Padley
77 Jennifer May
78 Clare May
79 Patrick May
80 Bill & Carol Donaldson
81 Alec Casterton
82 A.J. Webb
83 Isobel Morgan
84 Clifford Deane
85 Eric T. Cawkwell
86 S.M. Cumberworth
87 Kate Readman
88 Mrs. M.J. Parker
89 Phyllis Summers
90 Robert E. Butler
91 M.W. Spick
92 Ian Paul Overton
93 Ian Paul Overton
94 E.M. Bradley
95 E.M. Bradley
96 Frank Lawrence
   Starbuck
97 David Glynne Fox
98 Diane Sandra Willis
99 Barbara Rogers
100 A.O.Y. Associates
101-122 Notts. Local
        Studies Library
123 P.A. Nix
124 Dr R.W. Morrell
125 S.W. Henley
126 Irene Mary Mellor
127 Mavis Green
128 Joy Weatherall
129 Martin & Josie Kilkie
130 Trent Jetfloor Ltd.
131 K.F. Marshall
132 S.J. Marshall
133 P.A. Saul
134 D. Peeks
135 R.V. Hardman
136 C.D. Tracey
137 I. Dingwall

138 J. Powlesland
139 R. Smith
140 S. Putman
141 D. Gough
142 N. Galleymore
143 J.P. Duffy
144 D. Wood
145 M. Warner
146 G. Carter
147 K. Broadfoot
148 A. Trust
149 W. King
150 R. Parker
151 B. Newton
152 S. Richardson
153 B. Howe
154 B. Snowden
155 R. Jarvis
156 R. Wilson
157 M. Lowe
158 S. Henderson
159 A.J. White
160 D.D. Bell
161 Newark & Sherwood
    District Council
162 Jane E. Jackman
163 Alexander W. Currie
164 Beatrice Peat
165 Grahame C. Smith
166 Christopher Taylor
167 David Dempster
168 James Kyle
169 Tony Squires
170 Jim McCready
171 R. Schwetz
172 D. & S. Wightman
173 P. Flello
174-176 Trent Jetfloor Ltd.
177-180 The Granary
181 John Hobbs
182 John Hobbs
183 Sarah & Julian Shaw
184 Diane & Philip Shaw

185 Jo & Jeremy Shaw
186 Gwen & John Shaw
187 Elizabeth Tower
188 Catherine Seconde
189 John Whawell
190 Arthur A. Gibbons
191 William T. Murray
192 William T. Murray
193 Anthony M. Lawrence
194 Florence Coley
195 Edward A. Hart
196 Ann Reynolds
197 Janet Beeston
198 Gillian Rogers
199 Norman E. Hatton
200 Jack M. Joiner
201 Thomas W. Mathers
202 E.M. Shipley
203 David C.T. Edwards
204 Mark John Abdey
205 Keith D.J. Manning
206 Martin Lindley
207 Ted Bradford
208 Pamela M.A. Elliott
209 Frank J. Buttle (Fox)
210 Mrs Laura Horobin
211 K.R. Screen
212 Kenneth R. Hunter
213 Thomas J. Miller
214 Jon Jayes
215 William J. Kinsman
216 Rev. Dr Yvonne
    Cawcutt
217 Frederick Hedley
218 P.H.L. Sands
219 Clive Charles Baker
220 Julian Mark Baker
221 Brian P. MacGregor
222 Miss D. Pickard
223 David Woodruff
224 Stephen Bloomfield
225 Mark Owen Easton
226 Victor R.J. Nicholas

227 P.R. Badderly
228 Graham Jukes
229 Michael John Friend
230 William R. Billam
231 Keith Corbyn
232 John Waterfield
233 Alan J. Wiggington
234 Keith Gadsden
235 Howard Thelemann
236 Howard Thelemann
237 R.L. Marshall
238 Robert Graham
239 Sheffield City Libraries
240 Sheffield City Libraries
241 David Yemm
242 T. Stubbs
243 Robert J. Ellis
244 William H. Taylor
245 Mr & Mrs D.W. Potts
246 Andrew Woolliams
247 Miss A. Rochford
248 Donald Raybould
249 Douglas & Mary
    Chamberlain
250 Timothy Chamberlain
251 Angela M. Middleton
252 Angela M. Middleton
253 N.J. Barton
254 Albert H. Kirkham
255 Geoff Kelly
256 W.W. Felstead
257 Andy C.A. Andrews
258 Margaret Taylor
259 Yasuhiko Kageyama
260 Marion Kime
261 John Kime
262 Jeremy Kime
263 George Kime
264 Fred B. Bear
265 Pandle Andre
266 Dave Hill
267 E.R. Coddington
268 David Warrender
269 Jayson Forrest
270 Dr Tom Venables
271 Dr Tom Venables
272 Dr Tom Venables
273 F.S. Mosley
274 H.I. Robinson
275 Ian C. Gray
276 Eric L. Carlin
277 Mrs B.E. Olisa

278 Mrs A. Morris
279 Peter Marsden
280 David Porter
281 B.H. Holland
282 B.E.T Kember
283 David J. Burd
284 Albert de Dominicis
285 Albert de Dominicis
286 C.E. Wells
287 Mrs I.A. Johnson
288 H.B. Hall
289 Denise J. Marriott
290 Phyllis Felose-Summers
291 Phyllis Felose-Summers
292 Keith Reynolds
293 Joe Frobisher Alltoft
294 Timothy A. Edwards
295 Alan Beattie
296-299 Derby &
        Chesterfield
        Local Studies
300 Alexandra L. Pearson
301-332 Nofotec Group
        of Master
        Craftsmen
333 Dennis Reed
334 Kenneth R.B. Reed
335 Don Church
336 Joy Pinkney
337 Bob Marsland
338 Brenda Carter
339 William Bellaby
340 Lisa Ann Wilson
341 Marjorie & Anthony
    Wilson
342 Elizabeth Russell
343 B. Whitehall
344 R.C. Maddocks
345 A.E. Jackson
346 P.R. Townsend
347 Brian Odell
348 M.J. Crocker
349 A.W. Raybould
350 Ken Smales
351 Mick Hurst
352 David Brealey
353 Michael John Bond
354 Alan Walter Harding
355 Henry A. Harrison
356 Ken G. Bearman
357 Graham Bennett
358 Kevin Mason

359 Mr & Mrs A. Allwood
360 Ian William Bettinson
361 Christopher A. Hole
362 D. Shannon
363 John Taylor
364 Buck Lewis
365 J.R. Cave
366 Roger Sinclair Allen
367 Anthony Robinson
368 David McCarthy
369 Greg Cullingham
370 J.W. Ruston
371 Chris Hassell
372 Stephen Gill
373 Mrs Mary Thompson
374 James Cork
375 Richard Head
376-477 Trent Jetfloor Ltd.
478 Ronald Stanley
    (Jack) Richards
479 Peter Greaves
480-482 Lincolnshire
        Library Service
483 John Anthony Smith
484 W.F. Webster
485 Christopher Tomlinson
486 Dennis F. Smith
487 Rodney Gill
488 Michael Foster
489 P.L. Foulsham
490 Robin M. Morris
491 Tateo Kimura
492 Stephen Lester
493 Mrs Daphne White
494 Graham N. Stockhill
495 Maurice Chittenden
496 Mrs Valerie Olifent
497 Alison Orchard
498 Ronald S. Cooper
499 D.J. & A.S. Harper
500 University of
    Nottingham
501 Robert J. Hallam
502 Richard H. Grundy
503 Laura Thomas
504 C.A. Barton
505 John Underwood
506-520 Trent Jetfloor Ltd.
521 Avalon Entertainments
522 John P. Evans
523 Mr R. Rust
524 Philip O. Gardiner

525 Bernard A. Stevenson
526 Bob Burgoyne
527 Helen Edensor
528-530 Jean Nicholson
531 D.L. Rhodes
532 Joy Wilson
533 Mrs A.M. Cooper
534 Mae MacDougall
535 Mr M. Challans
536 Mr M. Challans
537 Cristian Cook
538 David Marsh
539 John Kiddy
540 Mrs Dorothy Morris
541 James Brian Ward
542 Frank & Peggy
    Vickerstaff
543 Barry Hayward
544 Jon Morley Wozencroft
545 John Wilfred Turner
546 Matthew Oliver Cutler
547 Peter Booth
548 John Peck
549 Stanley Maltby
550 Mrs Edna Robinson
551 Mr V.T. Bridgeman
552 David & Leona Wilson
553 Carl Henderson
554 David John Kelly
555 Oliver Dyson
556 Michael Adamson
557 Alexander Platts
558 Tineke Arthur
559 Richard Bailey
560 Toru Supino
561 Michael John Brown
562 Dr D.A.B. Ashcroft
563 M.L. Hyde
564 R.E. Fox
565 David Green
566 Michael George
567 Mr & Mrs E.G. Price
568 Mr & Mrs E.G. Price
*Remaining Subscribers
unlisted*

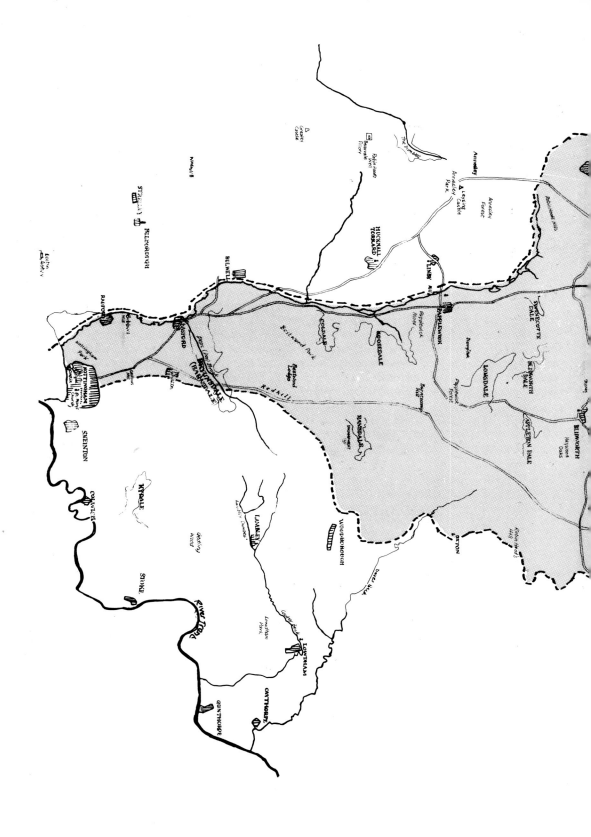

ACKNOWLEDGEMENTS

In the preparation of this volume I have received the goodwill and assistance of so many people and I should like to thank the following for their own various contributions.

Firstly, the Editor Keith Mellor whose enthusiasm and efforts made this book possible beyond the bounds I ever conceived. The publishers, Temple Nostalgia Press, for perseverance of such a complex project and the outstanding volume they have produced. Emrys Bryson, *Nottingham Evening Post,* for the Foreword. The present Sheriff of Nottingham, Royce Young, and all of those former Sheriff's including Councillor Barrie Parker who have expressed their kind wishes for the book. Stephen Best and his staff at the Local Studies Library, Nottingham for assistance and contributions to the illustrations. Robert Hardy and Guy Wilson, H.M. Tower of London, Royal Armouries. Dr. Alan Rogers, late of Nottingham University. Prof. J.C. Holt, Cambridge University. Prof. Barrie Dobson, York University. Dan Hyndman, R.P.S. and Kingsford Mayers for their photographic services. David Taylor, Nottingham City Council. Ian Hill, Nottinghamshire County Council. Lada Tvrdik and David Porter for the dust cover paintings. Roger Heaton for artwork. Gemini Typesetting. The Duke of Rutland. Mike Bush, Nofotec Group Ltd. Peter Saul and fellow directors of Trent Jetfloor Ltd. Ian Sparrow. David Greenwood. Vina Cooke. Malcolm Perkyns. John Pope de Locksley. Graham Greenfield, Newark and Sherwood Council. Marion Kime. Alice Sneyd Kinnersley. Gen. & Mrs. P.T. Tower. Finally, to the many librarians and archivists in England, Scotland, Ireland, U.S.A., and Australia. University Libraries, the Public Records Office and the British Museum.

As my research was so wide there are some I may have missed and I take this opportunity to thank them here. Also, among the photographs donated are some where despite considerable efforts it has not been possible to establish if they are subject to copyright. Should any such rights have been unintentionally infringed an apology is made herewith.

Jim Lees
1987

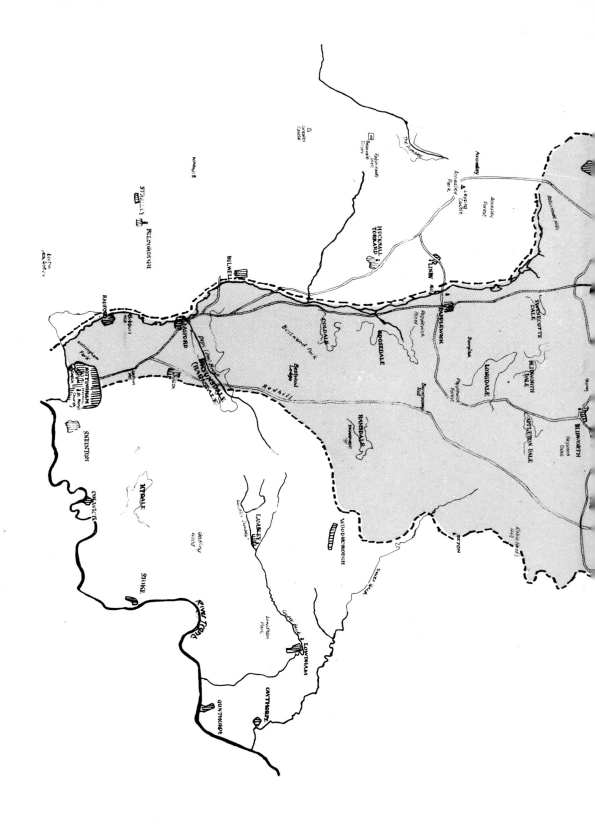